The Radio Office

Ships, Storms & Submarines

By Harry Scott

An exciting first-hand account of the dangers faced by the sailors of the British Merchant Navy, seen through the eyes of Ian Robert Hendry Waddell, a Seagoing Radio Officer during World War II, taken from his journals, letters and photographs.

Radio Officer Ian Robert Hendry Waddell

All rights reserved © Harry Scott 2013

Republished July, 2015

Harry Scott asserts his right to be identified as the researcher and author of this work.

No part of this book may be produced in any manner whatsoever without written permission from the author except in the case of brief quotations embodied in critical articles or reviews.

The photographs reproduced in this book are by permission of Ian Briggs except where credited otherwise.

Contents	Page
Acknowledgements.	5
Foreword by James T. Walker.	6
Introduction.	7
Chapter 1 – Schooldays, Battlefields Trip & Premonitions of War.	13
Chapter 2 – Leith Nautical College & Ian's first posting – the Oil Tanker 'Oleander'.	39
Chapter 3 – Ian's first taste of war. Bombing of 'Oleander', and loss of HMS 'Courageous'.	51
Chapter 4 – The 'Battle of the Atlantic' and the 'U-boat peril' – Jedburgh man's ship attacked by U-boat.	71
Chapter 5 – Ian's appointment to 'Fylingdale' and first Atlantic crossing to Canada.	79
Chapter 6 - Sinking of HMS 'Penzance' and rescue of survivors.	85
Chapter 7 - Second crossing of Atlantic to Sorel, Canada – near hit from German bomber.	101
Chapter 8 – Christmas on board 'Fylingdale' – Ian meets Monica.	112
Chapter 9 – Ashore in Boston – The sinking of S.S. 'Carlton'.	125
Chapter 10 – Voyage to Canada – rough weather & reports of many ships sunk.	133
Chapter 11 – Ian's dream of being bombed, and sunk by U-boat – 3rd Radio Officer goes mad.	153
Chapter 12 – Ian's posting to 'Treminnard' - Cardiff to Argentina, Halifax Nova Scotia & Boston – Chief Radio Officer goes mad.	162
Chapter 13 – Ian signs on to 'Narragansett' – Cardiff to Galveston, Texas.	174
Chapter 14 - 'Narragansett' attacked and sunk by 'U-105'.	182
Epilogue	194
References	195

Acknowledgements

The first acknowledgement goes to Ian Robert Hendry Waddell for writing such wonderfully descriptive and amusing journals and letters about his life and work at sea, and to his sister Nancy who kept them safe for so many years.

Next, my sincere thanks to Ian Briggs, Nancy and Ian Waddell's nephew, and named after Ian Waddell, who allowed me to sift through his letters, journals and photographs, which enabled me to write this book.

Sincere thanks are also due to the following, without whose help this book would not have been published:-

Jim and Connie Walker for providing their support and for proof reading the book. Jim, Ian's cousin, knew Ian and his family well when they were both young men, and he has provided some vital insight into Ian's family background as well as writing a moving foreword to this book.

The U-Boot Museum and Archive in Altenbruch, Germany, for their assistance in sending me copies of the log books of 'U-37' and 'U-105', and allowing me to use photographs from their archives and information from their web site.

The Editor and staff of the 'Border Telegraph' for agreeing to reports from the newspaper being used in the book.

Gudmundur Helgason, (www.uboat.net), and Mike Holdaway, (www.convoyweb.org.uk), for providing much valuable assistance and allowing me to use information and quotes from their web sites in the book.

My good friends, Evelyn Watson and Bruce Ormiston for being kind enough to proof read the book and providing me with such positive and corrective feedback.

Mr. Owen Rowlands and Dr. Simone Wood for assisting me by translating German documentation into English, and Jacqueline King in Swansea, and Chris Hussy in Dublin, who both undertook enquiries on my behalf to try and trace the friends of Ian who figured greatly in his life.

The staff at Heriot-Watt University for allowing me access to archive material, and Mr. Timothy K. Nenninger, Textual Archives Services Division, National Archives, College Park, Maryland, U.S.A., for tracing and providing details of the U.S. Navy aircraft which went to the assistance of 'Narragansett'.

Jennifer Borthwick and Alan Baird for their kindness in purchasing the commemorative poppy planted at the family home by Ian Waddell's nephew, Ian Briggs.

Last, but by no means last, my wife Sheila, daughter Karen, son Steven, and his partner Stephanie, for their support and encouragement.

Foreword by James T. Walker

I think my cousin, Ian Waddell, would have approved of his diaries, letters and jottings being published. As a boy at Galashiels Academy, art and literature were Ian's strongest subjects. He loved producing miniature newspapers, which had his cartoons, spoof news stories, and jokes in their small pages, the spines of which were bound with cotton thread stitching. These were eagerly sought after by his fellow scholars.

My first memory of Ian (he was 9 and I was 4½), was of him drawing cartoons of Mickey Mouse to keep me amused, when on a visit to his home in Dean Street, Galashiels. Later, when we lived in adjoining houses in Abbotsford Road, I was always keen to be in his company, and he was very tolerant and kind to his younger cousin.

Ian was a keen and accomplished amateur photographer, and he taught me how to develop and print black and white films. We would exchange books and magazines (usually detective stories and American comics). Ian absorbed the slang in the comics (as evidenced in his diaries) and this would undoubtedly annoy his mother, who was a stickler for being correct.

The war came and the gap in our ages disappeared, for during wartime, young boys and girls were enrolled in cadet corps, and also served (sometimes underage) in the emergency services of the Air Raid Precautions, Home Guard and fire watching. Thus it was that my education in life was sharply accelerated, and so before I went into the Forces, Ian would seek me out for company when he came home on leave. I would skip my night school lessons so Ian and I would have evenings together, for I was working through the day.

Ian would send me postcards from different ports, and I would write letters giving him the local news and gossip. My last letter to him was returned, 'could not be delivered'.

This book captures the essence of Ian Waddell's short, but eventful life. Ian's talent for writing descriptive prose, and capturing graphic scenes in his diaries, have produced a fascinating account of one young man's war. All credit to his biographer, Harry Scott, for presenting us with this absorbing account, with such a wealth of researched background information. It is a worthy tribute to Ian, whose death, as the result of a German submarine's torpedo, affected me considerably, for I had dreams of Ian coming home (having been rescued from a desert island!) for years afterwards.

But this account of the life and death of one young man reminds us also of the dreadful sacrifices millions of people made in their fight against the evils of Fascism. Let us not forget.

Jim Walker

Introduction

Nancy Waddell was born on 7 October 1913, and during World War II trained as a nurse. She had to give up nursing when she contracted Hepatitis. She then went to work in a munitions factory at Charlesfield near St Boswells in the Scottish Borders. Prior to retiring, Nancy was for many years Secretary to the Officer in Charge of Galashiels Police Station. She died aged 96 years on 20 February, 2010, a kind and well respected lady.

On going through Nancy's personal effects, her nephew Ian Briggs, found a box containing numerous photographs and letters, and several journals written by Nancy's brother Ian Waddell, a Seagoing Radio Officer in the Merchant Navy during World War II. In among the letters was a note from Nancy:-

"In March 1942, Ian Robert Henry Waddell, my brother, born 6/4/21, was Second Radio Officer on the oil tanker, MV Narragansett, which was loading at Galveston, Texas, prior to sailing to join an east-bound convoy off Newfoundland. The attached correspondence is the only information which my parents ever received as to the fate of their only son.

On leaving school (Galashiels Academy) in 1938 or 1939 he trained as a radio operator at the Leith Nautical College, and joined the Merchant Navy, his home port being Swansea. He made several voyages, including one to Norway, where his ship was dive-bombed by German aircraft, but was beached by the crew before sinking. They shot the Norwegian pilot, who had previously brought other ships into a location of which German aircraft had the location & range. Subsequently he made several trans-Atlantic voyages before the final one.

He wrote wonderfully amusing and descriptive letters, which are contained here. I have never felt able to read or arrange them – though perhaps I will one day.

Ian was eight years younger than I, and I never really knew him as a person. I wish I had, as over the years many people have spoken to me of having known Ian, and all spoke of him with affection.

N. Waddell 30/9/98"

For the entire duration of World War II, personnel in the Merchant Fleet faced a multitude of dangers, not only from hazardous working conditions, severe weather at sea and mechanical failure, but from U-boats, mines, bombing by enemy aircraft, and shelling by surface raiders such as 'Bismarck' and 'Graf Spee', often with little or no protection. Despite all of these dangers Britain's Merchant Fleet kept Britain supplied with goods and materials which were vital for the country's survival and fight against the enemy.

This book tells the story of Ian Waddell's service as a Seagoing Radio Officer in the Merchant Navy during World War II. After training as a Radio Officer at Leith Nautical College in Edinburgh, Ian was employed by the Marconi International Marine Communication Company Limited, which acted as agents supplying Seagoing Radio Officers to companies operating merchant shipping. Ian wrote several journals detailing his experiences during and between voyages, in addition to the many letters he wrote to his family at home. He was also a keen photographer, and many of his photographs are reproduced in this book.

Ian was an intelligent and thoughtful young man with a wonderful sense of humour, which comes through in his journals and letters. Each is beautifully descriptive, and provides an excellent insight into the life and work of a young Radio Officer starting out on a new career aboard a merchant ship.

As far as possible Ian's story is told by reproducing the text in his journals, letters, and the photographs he took at school and at sea. No one could tell it any better. They describe in detail his work, his relationships with crew members, as well as the dangers he and his shipmates were exposed to from the stormy Atlantic Ocean. These were caused in the main by mechanical failure on the ships, and German U-boats, aircraft and surface raiders. It also includes a harrowing account of his part in a rescue at sea, and of happier times in his relationship with Monica Thomas, a young lady in Ian's home port of Swansea.

Ian Waddell was born on 6 April, 1921, in Galashiels, and educated at Galashiels Academy. He was bright, excelled at sports, and he was a keen photographer. He came from a comfortable background and his family was made up of Ian, his two elder sisters Nancy and Margaret, his mother 'Peggy', and his father Robert, a Sales Manager for Buckholm Mill, who travelled to the Continent frequently. The family home was 12 Abbotsford Road, Galashiels.

Ian as a young boy with Mum, Dad, Margaret (standing) and Nancy.

Ian's Sister Nancy (circa 1939).

Ian's Sister Margaret (circa 1939).

The family home at 12 Abbotsford Road, Galashiels.

Ian Waddell's parents Robert and Peggy, Christmas 1959.

A family group taken in 1980
Ian's sister Nancy is seated at the left of picture. His sister Margaret is seated on the right. His cousin Margaret Thomson (nee Walker) is seated second from right, next to Connie Walker, the wife of Ian's cousin, Jim Walker. Standing are, from left to right; Jim Walker, husband of Connie; Bobby Briggs, husband of Ian's Sister Margaret, and Bert Thomson, husband of Ian's Cousin Margaret.

Chapter 1 – Schooldays, Battlefields Trip & Premonitions of War

In the mid to late 1930's the threat of war was never far off and Ian reflected this by writing a thought provoking essay on the hostilities which were then taking place in Spain and Abyssinia:-

"27.9.37 – The Present Day Situation in the Mediterranean

Even before the guns in Spain started their crashing and stuttering cacophonies of death and hate, and pent up fury was loosed upon a war crazed world, trouble was bubbling and hissing in the devil's cauldron that expanse of blue peacefulness the Mediterranean.

Italy's unprovoked attack on Abyssinia disturbed the calm which more or less prevailed over the Mediterranean countries. All the little jealousies and hates in Spain were brought to a head by the outbreak of the Spanish War, now in its second year of disaster and destruction. Of late terror has spread to non-combatant countries.

Through the deadly medium of the submarine with its fearsome weapon, the torpedo, some unknown power has been indiscriminatingly attacking merchant shipping. There is a strong belief that these submarines are either given on loan to Franco from Italy, or are acting under the orders of Franco, the Insurgent leader, but it would be hazardous to state this fact without full proof.

An example of the danger to merchant ships is illustrated by the bombing of the British-owned oil-tanker (B.T.C.!) 'British Corporal', by either the Government or Insurgent aeroplane. Both by air and sea, then has war raised its ugly head. *(The 'British Corporal', a tanker owned by the British Tanker Company, was bombed and machine gunned on 6 August, 1937, off the Algerian coast by Spanish Nationalist aircraft. The ship survived the attack and none of the crew were injured. This led to a protest and a warning by the British Government to the forces of General Franco that any aircraft caught attacking British shipping would be shot down).*

These barbarous attacks could not go on indefinitely, as ships of different nationalities were being wrongfully subjected to piracy on the high seas. As protests to each side in the Civil War affected nothing, it was decided by the European nations to band together against attacks to their ships. A conference was held at Nyon, near Geneva, the leading powers in the conference being Great Britain and France. Nine other countries were invited to attend, but Germany and Italy would not be parties to the conference.

It was arranged that Great Britain and France should have allotted to them certain areas in the Mediterranean which they were to patrol with ships of war. The direct result was that immediately British and French naval dockyards were extremely busy putting depth-charges and shells on board their ships to combat the under-water raider. The orders given to the Commanders of these warships were that they were to shoot at sight any vessel not flying a flag or showing any nationality marks. These orders have been extended to aeroplanes, so that combatant aircraft will not find it so easy to bomb non-combatant ships. It is hoped that these measures will serve to make it comparatively safe for vessels to ply their trade between ports and to keep the terrible war in Spain from spreading to other countries, because of attacks on their ships compelling them to retaliate."

At some point it appears Ian developed a notion for life at sea, although it is never mentioned specifically. This notion may have been encouraged by his visit to a shipyard in March, 1938, which prompted another essay:-

"14.3.38 – A Visit to a Shipyard

A shipyard – surely this must be one of the most romantic places in any country! To witness a ship growing from a skeleton-like frame to a huge luxurious liner must be a very thrilling experience, especially so if one has played a part in assembling the ship.

I had the good fortune to spend a whole day in this land of steel plates and rivets. I saw ships in their infancy, ships growing larger, and, happy sight, I saw an almost finished luxury liner!

At six-thirty in the morning, I was carried in past the shipyard on the crest of a wave of shipyard hands. In a very short time the air was filled with the clang of hammers on steel plates, the scream of electric riveters, and the whine of drills. No one can imagine the terrific cacophony of a shipyard until one has been in, or near one. I was reminded strongly of a hive of industrious bees, when I looked round and saw that every man was carrying out his particular job with speed and precision. Everyone knew exactly what he had to do, and was doing it quickly and efficiently. Everywhere were signs of good trade returning after the slump. That all the stocks were occupied by semi or nearly completed ships, evidences that in ship building at least, good trade has returned.

Men were already greasing the slipway for the almost finished luxury liner, and just out from the slipway, dredgers were busy at work deepening the Clyde channel. I was told by the foreman of the shipyard, that the liner would undergo her speed trials off the west coast of Scotland. With what eagerness I watched the maiden voyage and career of that liner, I alone know.

I was privileged to see the inside of the liner. Men of all trades were engaged in beautifying the ship' interior. World famous artists were painting frescoes on the walls of a dining saloon. Electricians were fitting a new system of concealed lights. Carpenters were fitting furniture and wood-work everywhere. It seemed a pity that this beautiful ship was destined to be a film star's Atlantic ferry boat. So enraptured was I that I was nearly locked in, and so, after an ecstatic day, I left the shipyard for a whole more sordid world."

The last sentence perhaps reveals a premonition of the war which was to come, and all the signs were there. The arrival of 1938 saw the preparations for war increase. On 12 March, 1938, German troops marched into Austria and the country was annexed by Hitler. The British Government prepared plans for the conscription of men fit for service in the armed forces. Gas masks were being issued to the civilian population in the Scottish Borders and classes on how to fit them properly were being held in schools for adults and children. Gas mask drills were also being carried out in Borders Telephone Exchanges. In April 1938, Colonel Loch of St. Boswells was appointed Air Raids Precaution Officer for the counties of Roxburgh, Berwick and Selkirk.

In another thoughtful, and sometimes humorous, essay entitled **"The Simple Life"**, written in May, 1938, he reflects on modern day living as it was then, and discusses the advantages and the drawbacks. Some of what he writes can be identified with life today, particularly in the following passages from the essay:-

"16.5.38 – The Simple Life – do modern conditions make it possible, or, if possible, desirable?

The Simple Life – an oft quoted phrase, used chiefly by the wealthy city inhabitants, who, after a huge repast, are now suffering under the lash of dyspepsia. These mortals, writhing from indigestion, weary for the day when they will trip, fawn-like through grassy woods, and subsist on beech nuts and berries, foods which carry with them no aftermath of indigestion.

Some persons, disgusted with modern life and conditions have fled and secreted themselves 'far from the maddening crowd', but the number of hermits today must be relatively small. It is possible for people today to turn 'en masse' to a simple life? No, this evolution would take centuries in its entirety. The fact, then, that the Simple Life is not for our generation leads to the next point, is it desirable?

Hot-heads will cry 'Aye', and clamour for simplicity in modern life, but after sober reflection, one concludes the modern life does have its assets. Admittedly, they are almost swamped by its liabilities, of which modern warfare and the toll of the roads are only two examples, but think - we would be much poorer off without wireless, rapid transport, and modern medical science!

The obvious reply to this, is, why are all these put to bad use in warfare? Man's only reply can be that war has reared its ugly head ever since the beginning of the world. It has, perhaps, not been so coldly inhuman and ghastly as modern warfare, but there has always been war.

In retrospect, the 'Good Old Days' have always appeared worse than modern times, paradoxically enough! The olden days were simpler, but were they better than our time? Poverty, ignorance, oppression and hardship seem to have constituted the bygone 'Simple Life'. With the advancement of modern science and thought, most of these evils are being rooted out to make the modern life, if not simple, at least a better place to live in than before"

Ian's analysis of politics and politicians could apply today. In an essay written on 13 October, 1938, entitled, **'Is Consistency a Virtue?'** he wrote the following:-

"….But when 'consistent' accompanies someone's name, that is usually regarded as a mark in his favour. Politicians are notoriously inconsistent, in regard to their party beliefs. 'Veering' might be a good way of describing them. Some Members of Parliament have sampled almost every party, and the fact that they are upholding the policy of a certain party at present, is no guide that they will sink or swim with it, or even profess to have any connection with it, when public opinion derides that political party. Usually this is to the politician's interests as his livelihood may depend on his keeping on the popular side and thereby eking out a living. But such men are usually held in contempt by others, who cling to their beliefs through thick and thin."

Ian was also a budding artist, and drew many simple sketches reflecting on what he saw. Some examples of his work are shown on the next pages.

This is a sketch from a performance of 'The Gondoliers' performed by Galashiels Amateur Operatic Society in 1937. The text reads, "Some of the sketches I did at the 'Gondoliers' on Tues. night. But difficult in bad light (Preserve) IW '37". "Programme Boys eagerly discussing their night's haul." "Int. conversation carried on by members of chorus." "Inopportune applause."

This sketch appears to be a self-portrait of Ian as he grows a moustache.

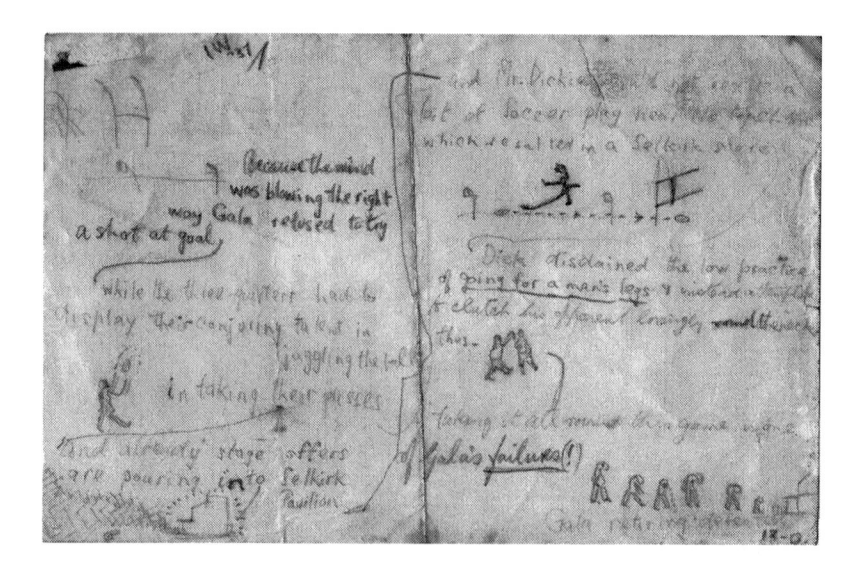

This series of sketches laments the defeat away from home, of Galashiels Rugby Football Club by one of its main rivals, the neighbouring team of Selkirk in 1937. It reflects the mood typical of a Scottish Borders rugby supporter when his team throws away the game and loses to a close rival. It is written in Ian's descriptive and amusing style. The text from left to right reads, "Because the wind was blowing the right way Gala refused to try a shot at goal. While the three-quarters had to display their conjuring talent in juggling the ball in taking passes. And already stage offers are pouring into Selkirk Pavilion, and Mr. Dickie could not resist a bit of soccer play near the touch line, which resulted in a Selkirk score." In a comment about the poor tackling he continues, "Dick distained the low practice of going for the man's legs *(the best form of tackling an opponent)*& instead attempted to clutch his opponent lovingly round the neck thus. Taking it all round this game was one of Gala's failures (!) Gala retiring defeated 13-0."

Ian also liked to write lines of prose and in 1937 he wrote the following passage in French. The translation reads:-

"The Seed

This little seed, which I hold in my hand,
one day will open up if it is put in the
ground and watered; (and) a hesitant shoot
will slowly grow through the earth which
covers it.

Then, if the sun warms it and the rain falls
on it, this green shoot will become a
beautiful tree with large branches covered
with foliage.

Buds will appear and swell, and then
scented flowers will start to bloom.

Nature holds no greater mystery than that
of boughs, branches, leaves and flowers
which grow from a tiny seed which one can
hardly see."

In July 1938, Ian was one of 850 schoolboys who went on the Scottish Schoolboys' Cruise to Norway on board the British India Motor Vessel 'Dilwara'. The 'Dilwara' was built in 1935 as a purpose built troop carrying ship for the British India Steam Navigation Company, but initially used for operating school cruises. She was recalled as a troop carrying ship for the duration of World War II and beyond, and finally scrapped in 1971.

On 26 July, he wrote to his mother who was in North Berwick:-

"Water, water, everywhere. So far very smooth, no qualms. No sleep hardly on Sat. night. Grub O.K. We get 5/3 *(£0.27p)* for Kroner. I am in charge of the Academy section; Joke, Knock, knock, 'Who's there? 'J'. 'J who' – 'Jehn'. Have not seen McCrorie since we left the dock. Could not see N. Berwick for mist when we passed. Passed Isle of May at 9.30. Pilot got off opposite Fidra. All well, Ian".

He wrote another postcard to his sister Nancy:-

"Just for a change I'm writing to you. This is Saturday 11 o'c, and we are going up the Lysefiord, if that means anything to you. We had a great day yesterday at Stavanger, as guests of the Stav. *(Stavanger)* Canning Industry. Taken to a picture house in aft. to see a film dealing with sardines etc. Before this in the morning, taken to a sardine canning place and shown over. At night football match, 'Dilward' boys v Stavanger boys. 6-1, Stav. Later marched to public park & Norwegian folk-dancing demonstrated. Some of the 'Dilward' boys danced an eightsome-reel & the dashing white sergeant. Took off sea joy on Mon. sea so calm; never felt at least queasy. At Tjaerland we walked 5 miles thro' driving rain to Boya Glacier, 5 miles back also in rain! Had to dry all my clothes in furnace room. That's as much as I can get for a penny *(cost of postage)* I'm afraid. Cheerio. Ian."

Little did Ian know that in less than two years he would have the narrowest of escapes in a Norwegian fiord when his ship was attacked and bombed by German aircraft.

In July, 1939, less than 6 weeks before the outbreak of World War II, Ian took part in the Scottish Schools' Cruise to Belgium and Holland. On his return he wrote a wonderfully detailed letter to his Mother, who was away from home on holiday:-

"12 Abbotsford Road
Galashiels
Sunday
Dear Mummy,

I got back last night by the Pullman, after a great holiday. We got into Harwich at about 6.30 on Saturday morning and after the Customs, got our train at 7.20. We had reserved compartments as far as York, where we had to change trains, but as our train got held up for about an hour, we missed our connection, and had to spend 1½ hours in York Waiting Room. But finally we got a train, and again had reserved compartments. We got into Edinborough, (or Edinburgh) at 9 o'clock, and I had a pie until we caught the Pullman home. The Turnbulls were meeting Welsh, so I was driven home, to find Nancy making a stew or a pie for dinner. After telling most of the outstanding events, I went to bed.

So now I'll try and tell you -

Friday 14. Train left Edin. 10.23. Had tea on train. Struck by beauty of Lincoln Cathedral. Boat left Harwich 10.25. As soon as the boat started another lad and I found ourselves in conversation with two affable gents. Think they were called Johnston and Campbell. Asked all about us etc. and then took us down to the 1st Class Smoke Room and gave us lemonade. Then walked round deck and showed us their cabins & finally gave us 5/- *(£0.25p)* each! – saying we were a couple of fine lads! One of them had a gypsum mine in Cumberland & the other had a yacht.

Sat. 15. Up at 7.45. Breakf. on board. Ashore and found Hostel. In Antwerp Zoo. Gargantuan lunch. In aft. climbed to top of Antwerp Cathedral. Ht. 402 feet, with 520 steps! Were we tired! At night got back to H. and had sing song with Germans. To sleep with the jabber of about 6 different languages.

Sun. 16. To Brussels. Tram to St. Andrew's Church. Arrived 11.30. Went in, in middle of hymn. Colin *(the Rev. Colin MacKenzie, a family friend)* just looked up & went on singing. After, met Colin & he went & got his 'millinery' off and walked down with us. Mrs. Mack. & Eliz. in Scotland. Former not well. He had to go off so we had lunch. Train to Ostend in aft. Bathe. Back to Antwerp singing 'Hail Caledonia'. Set upon by Germans wanting us to dance an 8-some Reel at Hostel. Bed.

Mon. 17. 21 Francs for Hostel. To Malines. In vegetable market where wholesale buyers buy from peasants. Interesting. Saw Van Dyke's Crucifixion in cathedral. Saw biggest carillon in Belgium *(a set of chromatically tuned bells)*. Used by Germans as an artillery point in war. To Ghent. Met Ayrshire lads in café. One knew Rev. Adamson. In Flemish Theatre. Later with all Hostel behind we marched round Ghent till we came to Market-Pl. where band was playing. It was a Feast-Day. Kennedy *(Donald Kennedy, a teacher at Selkirk High School accompanying the pupils)* went up to Band to play a Scots selection but best they could do was 'Horsy-Horsy', so had to do an 8-some R. to that. Marched back & our party went to a café. ½ hour late. Hostel dame said – 'Fe me powvais pas donner vos cartes' *(landlady refused to hand over party's documentation)*. We would have to had come home, for you cannot stay in Hostel without cards. But in morning Kennedy evidently succeeded in persuading her to give us them. Gave a peace-offering of grapes. We were fined 10 francs.

Wed. 19. To Ypres. At Lille Gate. In underground trenches. At Menin Gate where are carved names of 56,000 men who were never buried but just disappeared on the Ypres Salient. Wonderful monument. Saw them sounding 'Last Post' at 9pm. Opposite us was a line of Germans in white tunics who stood to attention and gave Hitler salute <u>while one of them took a photo when Last Post was being sounded</u>. Forcible language by some Glasgow Ex Servicemen round about us. They told us that a week or two ago some Germans had come and chalked 'Heil Hitler' on the Menin Gate Memorial! They had to be carried away! In War Museum. .

Thurs. 20. Walked to Hill 60. Passed Hell-Fire Corner which was shelled continuously for 4 years by Germans. Hill 62, 'Clapham Junction', 'Stirling Castle' (assembly points in war) and walked back down the Menin Road. Visited Hodge Crater Cemetery and Perth Cemetery. Pointed out where Passchendaele was. Can't realise that the countryside was bare. All trees have grown since war. Back to here last. Post again. Bed.

Fri. 21. To Bruges. To Zeebrugge in aft. In War Museum. Int. lecture on Mole Attack *(This was a raid on 23 April, 1918, on the port of Zeebrugge during World War I. The port was being used by the German Navy as a base for U-boats and other vessels, which were presenting a threat to Allied shipping. The aim of the attack was to block the port by sinking older British ships in the canal entrance, to prevent German vessels from leaving port. The raid failed in its objective, and 500 British personnel were either killed or wounded.)* Walked to end of 1½ ml. long Mole. Back to Bruges & saw the Hans Memlin Exhibition. Terrific. Wonderful paintings. Tell J. H. saw famous triptyones 'Mystic Marriage of St. Catherine', and 'Crucifixion'. Sing-Song in Hostel.

Sat. 22. To Brussels. In aft. to Mons. In War Museum. Back to B. met Colin at station (pre-arranged) and he took us round main streets of B. Stood us high-tea (10). Then he'd another engage. so had to go away. Very nice.

Sun. 23. Was on my own in morning. Spent it in the cheap-jack market. Very int. in aft. to Aviation Ex. Watched balloon being blown up for 3½ hours. The aviator seemed kinda nervous and had to say goo'bye about 17 times before he rose away up in balloon. Sing-song at Hostel.

Mon. 24. To Rochfort in Ardennes. Raining. Had terrible lunch in Hostel of <u>raw</u> ham sandwiches & milkless tea. In evening walked round town with rest of Hostel. In grottos.

Tues. 25. To Jennelle, & on to Namur. Spent most of day in waiting-room waiting on trains. Train to Dinant. There for 2 mins. & caught train back. Rotten day.

Wed. 26. Calamity. Charged 30 Francs for Hostels. This cleaned most of us out. Kennedy said, 'when we get to top of hill we will have 1 minute's silent hate!' Waited 2½ hours at station. Train to Liege. Rotten International Exposition most pavilions closed. Absolutely rotten show. Boosted up to stay at Angleur Hostel.

Thur. 27. Back to Antwerp. Spray & shave. Sang most of aft. & evening.

Friday 28. Last day. Got presents in town. Lunch. Took photos in aft. Farewells after dinner. 4 Dutch friends whom we'd met in Hostels came down with us to Boat. Sailed at 8pm. Last look at Antwerp. When moon came out, saw the phosphorescence caused by moonlight & ship's wash. Lovely white-green light. Bed.

Sat. You know what happened. So that's that. A great holiday. Hope you're having one as good. Sorry can't write very well in bed. Ian".

Whilst on that school trip the spectre of war could never have been far from the minds of Ian and his school friends, not only from what they saw themselves at the Menin Gate, but the thoughts of those around them. Five weeks after their return home, Britain declared War on Germany following the latter's invasion of Poland.

The Reverend Colin MacKenzie *(mentioned in Ian's letter to his Mother)*, a Church of Scotland Minister, working in Belgium, wrote a letter to Ian's parents:-

"18th July 1939

Mrs Mackenzie *(his wife)* and Elizabeth *(his daughter)* are in Scotland at the moment. The former has not been too well lately, and we hope the change will do her good. Living in the midst of 'crisis' has not been too good for any of us, and she certainly needed a holiday. She will come back (and Elizabeth too of course) sometime next month, provided the nightmare of war has not descended on us by that time. The Belgians have a pathetic belief that their country can keep neutral, though even now their army is almost on a war footing at the frontiers. Meanwhile I have become a kind of Air-Warden for the British Colony in Brussels, helping them to obtain gas masks, and along with a small body of business men from the British Chamber of Commerce trying to devise plans for the evacuation of British nationals. A difficult business, as the Embassy, though it approves, will not do a thing to help us, although they have a precedent of the French Embassy which already has such arrangements for their nationals. We all hope, of course, that it is work done in vain, and that there will be no war. If it does come, the best thing I can hope for is to be a refugee, the worst, to end my days in a concentration camp!

I was glad to hear from Ian about you all, and hope to get more news when I see him again. The boys seemed all very happy and enjoying themselves.

Kindest regards to you all, and many thanks for writing. I would be glad to hear from any of you at any time.

Yours very truly, C. S. MacKenzie."

Galashiels Academy School Photograph – date unknown.
Ian is standing at extreme right of picture on back row. His friend James Barbour is standing 3rd from left in middle row. Others, in no order, are W.S. Boyd, J. Gibson, J. Renwick, W. Carroll, C.M. Geddes, R. Murray, W. Yellowlees, Helen Angus, J. Paterson, Winnie Flynn, G.M. Coltman, Alex T. Shepherd, Dorothy M. Allison, Helen Herbert, & E.F. Lockie.

SCHOOLBOY CHAMPIONS

Galashiels Academy R.F.C., 1938, winners of the Border Schools Rugby Championship for the second year in succession. Mr. T. P. Wylie, Headmaster on right in back row, Mr Sandy Dickie, Sports Teacher standing on the left. Jock Gibson stands on back row third from right. Ian Waddell in middle row third from right. James Barbour, who also served as a Seagoing Radio Officer sits on Ian's right.

Ian left, with his friend James Barbour on right (youth in centre unknown).

Galashiels Academy Cricket Team 1938.
Back Row: Ian Waddell third from left & Alex Holmes fourth from left
Front Row: Ashly Turnbull second from left, James Barbour fourth from left,
& William Anderson fifth from left. Others unknown.

Ian Waddell at the high jump during a school sports day.

Caption: Scottish schoolboys cheer as they prepare to depart on a cruise to Norway. Including 100 Canadians, 850 of them, accompanied by 330 adults, left the Albert Dock basin, Leith, by the Fair maid on Saturday, and joined the motor vessel Dilwara in Leith Roads. Ian Waddell can be seen two thirds across from the left of the picture in the centre of the group.

Embarkation on the 'Dilwara'.

British India M.V. "Dilwara". 11500 tons. Cruising Services.

Hardangerfjord near Bergen, Norway.

Floien Funicular Railway.
Photographs by kind permission of Mr. J. Walker.

BELGIUM —
CHAOS IS COME AGAIN

Scottish Schools Cruise at Youth Hostel in Belgium
Ian Waddell is back row, second from right. His friend Welsh Turnbull standing on his right was killed whilst serving with the Royal Air Force.

International Group at Antwerp.

Antwerp Cathedral.

View from the top of Antwerp Cathedral.

Menin Gate at Ypres.

Menin Gate.

Ypres Cathedral.

Hodge Crater Cemetery.

Hill 60 Trench.

In Hill 60 Trench.

Relics of the War called Great.

Zeebrugge Mole.

Balloon at Brussels Aviation Exhibition.

Café Candid.

Goodbye Belgium – Selkirk High School party.
From left to right – Jack McKessock, George Blake, unknown, unknown, George Anderson, Donald Kennedy, Murray Ross.

Chapter 2 – Leith Nautical College and Ian's first posting – the Oil Tanker 'Oleander'

Following his education at Galashiels Academy, Ian trained as a Radio Officer at Leith Nautical College in Edinburgh, but it's unclear why he chose that particular profession. An acquaintance of the family remembers being told by Ian's sister Margaret that Ian was a keen amateur radio operator who had built his own short wave radio set and kept in touch with several other enthusiasts.

In part of a letter written many years later to her son Ian Briggs, and describing the war years at 12 Abbotsford Road, Margaret said, "Your Uncle Ian was by now in the Merchant Navy as a wireless operator. He had started his training before the war broke out. Like you he was not good at Maths, and I think that was why he chose the course. He was however excellent at English and art & there are some of his accounts of voyages still at Abbotsford." Seagoing Radio Officers were also being actively recruited at that time to serve in the Merchant Navy, and he was encouraged in that direction by his father. Whatever his reasons, it could not have been far from his mind the dangers he would face.

The passengers and crews of ships in Britain's Merchant Fleet were among the first to suffer at the hands of her enemies. About 7:30 pm on 3 September, 1939, only a few hours after the declaration of war, the British passenger liner 'Athenia', bound for Canada, was torpedoed by 'U-30', a German U-boat, off the west coast of Ireland. 19 crew members and 93 passengers, 28 of them US citizens, were lost. The British Admiralty also issued warnings to all British merchant ships that German submarines would regard them as warships and sink them without warning.

The sinking of the 'Athenia' touched Ian's home town of Galashiels. On 12 September, 1939, the Border Telegraph reported that Mr. and Mrs A. Nicol, and Mr. and Mrs. J. Pringle, who had been on holiday in Galashiels, c/o Shepherd, 16 Kirk Brae, were listed as passengers on the 'Athenia'. The Pringles survived the attack and were delivered safely to their home in Lawrence, Massachusetts. However it was reported that Alexander Nicol, aged 40, his wife Ethel, aged 33, and their 9 year old daughter Marion, from North Andover, Massachusetts, were lost. It was thought that the Nicols were near to where the torpedo had struck the ship.

Andrew Wilson from Galashiels was the Assistant Purser on 'Athenia'. Upon arriving home Andrew reported the ship had been struck by a torpedo about 7:30 pm near to the third class dining room resulting in many casualties either killed by the explosion, or trapped by the flooding. Andrew Wilson was one of the last officers to abandon the ship, and was rescued by a Norwegian ship which landed him and other survivors at Galway Bay in Ireland

On 19 September, it was widely reported that since the outbreak of war, twenty three British ships, including the Royal Navy aircraft carrier HMS 'Courageous', had been sunk by German submarines.

The Department of Radio Engineering and Telegraphy was inaugurated at Leith Nautical College in 1913, as a training school for Radio Officers for the Merchant Navy. Ian enrolled there in September 1939, after leaving school. The College boasted that, "The course of instruction leading to the Second Class and First Class Postmaster-General's Certificates is arranged to give a very wide and thorough training in the fundamental principles of Radio Engineering, so that students will be able to keep abreast of the ever-increasing developments of this latest branch of science."

Students were expected to provide themselves with the necessary text books, the total cost of which was not to exceed £1, and a pair of head-phones for personal use in telegraphy instruction. The College, as part of the course stated, "Careful tuition is given in Morse Telegraphy to ensure a high standard of operating proficiency. This includes preparation in the Acceptance, Transmission, and Reception of Radio Telegrams."

In his report to the Governors of the College in July, 1940, the Principal stated that, "Owing to the outbreak of war in September 1939, the number of students in attendance has been higher than ever before in spite of the fact that the number of regular seafaring students, i.e. mates, masters and engineers has been about normal. This increase is largely due to the abnormal demand for Radio Officers, and the Radio Department has been exceptionally busy during the session."

The Principal's report showed that of 56 Radio Telegraph Students in the 1939-1940 semester, 1 attained a First Class Pass, 12 attained Second Class, and 43 attained the Postmaster General Special Certificate. Ian attained the Postmaster General Special Certificate. No examinations for First and Second Class Certificates had been held since November 1939, due to courses being shortened as a result of the war and the need to increase the throughput of trainees for sea going duty.

Whatever his reason for choosing to become a Radio Officer, on 19 March, 1940, Ian sent a telegram to his parents from Edinburgh, which stated, "Passed staying the night = Ian". On 23 March he received a letter from the General Register and Record Office of Shipping and Seamen in London. The letter stated that he had been enrolled into the Merchant Navy Reserve, and that his name was being forwarded to operating companies and ship owners who were interested in the engagement of radio officers for the Merchant Navy. Things moved quickly and on 5 April, 1940, Ian received a letter from The Marconi International Marine Communication Company Ltd:-

"The Marconi International Marine Communication Company Limited

5th April, 1940
Mr. I. R. H. Waddell,
12 Abbotsford Road,
GALASHIELS.
Dear Sir,

With reference to our letter L/2 dated the 1st instant we have now received your medical report from the Glasgow Depot and confirm that our Medical Officer has passed you physically fit for service as a Seagoing Radio Officer with this Company.

Accordingly we presume you will now take the necessary steps to obtain your uniform and we shall be pleased if you will advise us immediately if you are available for appointment to our Seagoing Staff.

Yours faithfully,

THE MARCONI INTERNATIONAL MARINE COMMUNICATION

COMPANY LIMITED

S. Stansbridge

Assistant General Manager – SERVICE".

On 23 April, Ian travelled from Glasgow to London by overnight train and arrived at Euston at 6.40 am. Later that day he wrote the following letter to his Mother:-

"YMCA Canteen
Euston. 2.15 Wed.
Dear Mummy,

Shoved off from Glasgow at 9.30 last night. Didn't sleep so well, but got a rest. Hit Euston at 6.40, after having tea at 6 o'clock. Had trunk put into left L. and had brush up. Rain. Walked up and down neighbourhood round Euston. Came into Canteen at 7.45 and played 'Tomorrow is a lovely day' and 'Good Morning' – both appropriate on grams *(record player)*. Read a while. Went to Euston Sq. Stn. for Tube to East Ham – 11 ½d *(£0.5½ p)*. At Aldgate East I asked a gent about East Ham & he told me to get out & change. I did and eventually arrive at E. Ham. Subsequent enquiries proved that I should've stayed on the train. Howeva! In Marconi Office at 9.30 & filled in 100's of forms etc. At about 12 I was called, and …….. 'we want you to go to Plymouth. You'll get the 1.15 express tomorrow morning. It's the S.S 'Oleander' (that means 'Oleander'), & it's at Devonport Dockyard. You'll report to the Superintending Naval Stores Officer there, and you'll sign on the ship's articles then.' Enquiries elicited that the 'Oleander' was unknown to the R.O.V. man and a Radio Officer. He said, 'it must be a new ship'. So I got a voucher from Paddington to Devonport. Sleeper. Drew 1/- *(£0.5p)* Tube fare and 4/- *(£0.20p)* subsistence for today. Also got 1/3 of R'wy fare. Staggered out of office and got tube back to Euston (not without trouble!); bought a tube of aspirins (I needed them by now), came into Canteen and had 2 saus. & mash & b. beans & tea & bread. Now! Am writing this now. Feel fine. Will now get trunk over to Paddington. I'll let you know tomorrow where I've been sent to next! Plymouth Ho! Ian."

Arriving safely at Devonport on 25 May, Ian wrote home once more. The letter provides an excellent description of the experiences probably enjoyed (or endured) by most travellers in wartime Britain, and Ian's introduction to his ship:-

"Oleander
Thurs. nite
My Dear Mummy,

Well here we are at Devonport – it's rather misty here today.

To continue from where my last note left off … Got taxi from Euston to Paddington and received r'ly ticket (no sleepers!). Came out of Padd. and espied a Church Army Canteen. I went in and said I wanted a bath. The gent led me downstairs & there were the baths.

Had mine, scalding water, & very much refreshed stepped briskly up the stairs to the eating section. Had sandwiches and orange & lemon juices. After a while the gent derriere *(behind)* the counter came across & asked if I came from Edinburgh, his town. He was an ex-soldier, refused this time thro' medical. Leaving, he said, 'lang may yer lum reek wi' ither folk's coal.'

Cleared out and caught bus to Paramount Cinema in Tott. Ct. Rd to see Conrad Veidt and Valerie Hobson in 'Contraband'. Very good. There was also a stage show on, complete with Al Bollington at the organ.

Emerged at last & slipped onto my bus again. Took trunk out of pawn and had it shipped aboard the train. Found an empty comp., so settled down for long journey. Left at 1.15 and arrived at Devonport at 7.10 or so. Again dumped trunk in bond and went for a daunder round the town. (and now my eyes are refusing to stay open any longer, after about 4 hours sleep in 2 days. More tomorrow – g'nite.)

6.30 Friday evening. To continue – I wandered round for a few hours and when it was time I reported to the Superintending Naval Stores Officer, but not before a conductor on my bus stated, on enquiry, that the 'Oleander', a coal boat, had sailed two days ago!

I said, 'Oh' in a curiously flat voice. Howevah, the N. S. Officer sent me to the Fuel Organiser, who sent me to the 'Oleander', a tanker of about 7½ thousand tons.

I rushed back, first to the wrong station, and then the correct one, got my trunk, had a taxi take me to the Dockyard (Naval), and in a short (long) time I was on the gangway pushing silver onto my John.

Well there she was. A cheery lad saw me standing theah and probed that I was the new Sparks, and would I go up theah. I would and did. The 1st W *(Wireless)*. Officer was leaning out saying, 'I'm Humphreys'. So I replied that I was glad to meet him. He showed me to my quarters, very comfortable, with elec. fan & reading lamp & plenty of locker space & good bed.

We then proceeded to the *(Radio)* Cabin via the Old man's Cabin. Very good apparatus. The Old M. covered his eyes when I stepped into his room. You see I was wearing the Yellow Peril *(Ian's bright yellow pullover)*. 'Bit bight eh sonny?' (He calls all his officers 'sonny'). I laughed easily, or something, and in a bell-like voice announced who I was. He didn't seem to mind much, so I retreated on being told that I should have to go ashore with him in the afternoon to sign on.

Had a look at the Cabin & Humphreys dodged round helpfully. He is an extremely sound guy, one of the best. Is very keen on photography, and has a film tank and materials in his room! Coincidence.

Lunch followed. Soup meat, peas & pots. Sweet & coffee. Grand. Met the other officers, great crowd. Did some unpacking & then went ashore, in an R.N. *(Royal Navy)* car, to the Shipping Federation Offices to sign on, at £4 a month, which is the ship's pay. Rest you get from Marconi & tanker allowance.

I'd better say that the 'Oleander' is a Government tanker, a ship of the Royal Fleet Auxiliary, chiefly used for oiling our fleet. Now don't get jumpy, we're not at Norway yet! The destination is very secret, but 2nd Engineer said – Imagine where the biggest accumulation of the Fleet is just now *(a reference to the Allied landings near Narvik in Norway)*

After signing on I had a wander round Plymouth, saw the Ho where Drake --- *(reputedly played bowls in 1588 as the Spanish Armada approached the English coast)* and came back for tea. Now I shouldn't be telling you this – but the 'Exeter' is alongside us being repaired, and she needs it! Phew!! *(On 13 December, 1939, HMS 'Exeter' had fought against the German Pocket Battleship 'Graf Spee' at the Battle of the River Plate, off the coast of Argentina, suffering extensive damage that resulted in a long refit).*

When I'm not writing this I'm having long chats with Humph. or somebody else. We're landing oil just now – have been all day, will go on all nite and most of tomorrow. Helped to fit batteries in the morning. Lunch – soup, cold meat, turnips, French beans & pots, sweet 'n' coffee.

In cabin some of the afternoon, accustomising myself to the gear. There's a method of sending inside the cabin, but with no radiation *(method of practicing telegraphy without transmitting outwith the ship).* So we sent a few messages to each other. He said on completion of my sending – that's oke.

Discussed our cameras. That's why this letter was never finished. And also because to go ashore necessitates knowing the password, & the village is 3 miles away. Maybe tomorrow I'll manage, but meanwhile I'll keep on writing.

We have a Royal Marine aboard to look after the guns. Also we have rifles outside the Cabin.

I'd imagine it'll be cold at ..a..a..o. *(possibly Ian's code for Narvik in Norway where the Allied landings were taking place)* if that's where we're bound. Today has been lovely, - a sun that's actually hot. Devon's nice. A street called Pennycomequick and bronzed inhabitants who say 'I thang you', just like A…n A…e., and 'yez zurr', just like Uncle T. Cobbeley, or was it Richard of T. D? The talk at table is usually of ex-members of the ship and incidents at so & so. Very amusing most of it.

I think we are pushing off by Sunday noon (or Zaterday noon, wi' H. Humphreys, Ian Waddell, 'Happy Shaw', Will Astley, H Russell, W. Sharpe, Old Uncle F. Harvey an' all) but if I know definitely I'll of course let <u>you</u> know. But I'd keep it dark. Because you see, we're under the Admiralty, and where we go there'll usually be H. M. ships. So Your Courage, Your Resolution, and Your Careless Talk will keep the fox at the garden door, or sump'n.

I think I'm going to like it a lot. Un' buy the way – Humph. says the trunk is much the best way; not 2 suit cases. You haven't enough room with cases, he winces. His trunk is twice my size of trunk and even then it's cramped.

(My eyes are going again, so more on Sat.)

Sat. morning - Wakened at 8.10 – Your tea sir. Up for breakf. Cereal, curried ham & egg. And now it's raining very hard, so there's no hope of going ashore just now, so I'll keep on writing! 'Oleander's been painted yellow, while in refit. She was built about 1922 I think.

Thank Nancy for the toffees. I never thot they'd be so welcome. Just been down in the Engine Room. Going ashore to post. Cheerio. More later. Ian."

Ian's excitement at going to sea, along with the thought of having a meaningful war occupation, comes through in his letters to his family. On 4 May, 1940, he wrote a letter to his Mother:-

"0020 (or 20 past midnite)
Saturday morning
Somewhere at sea
My dear Mummy,

This may seem a peculiar time to be writing, but it's all very simple.

Under orders, we've had to keep a continuous radio watch, and my hours are midnite to 6 and midday to 6. This will be my fourth 'middle watch', so you can imagine that I'm waiting for port, (land!), with great impatience. Six hours on and six off is not conducive to clear sparkling eyes all round. But I'm hoping that we'll reach port before 6 am, and I'll be able to close down.

We transmitted yesterday! A message was sent to us earlier in the day and later they asked for acknowledgement. The Old man was asked, the mains put on, motor started up, and in about 45 seconds the coast station sent 'thanks', and we shut off, having sent our acknowledgement. When I say 'we', I was an interested onlooker, but I had taken down the request for acknowledgement before that. I know how to start up and transmit now."

Ian was also turning into a budding author, and in the same letter he wrote a passage describing some of the tedium of the voyage.

"Here's an excerpt from my new book, as yet unpublished – '... 6 mins. to 1, ship's time. The grey and black tones of the receiver stood out under the bench lamp's glare. Reaction 46, anode tuning 10 --- Prickly-eyed, the Radio Officer read the name tabs on the instrument – Marconi International Marine Communication Co. Ltd. London.

The ship's bell outside – only 5 hours more. Eyes strayed across the log to the list of stations. On one page 6 call signs had been stroked out. Did that mean ---? Funny that they should be cut off like that, must ask the Chief about that tomorrow *(meaning possibly that the ships allocated those call signs had been sunk!)*. Tomorrow – only 4 3/4 hours yet. Mustn't divide up hours. Makes it seem longer.

Somebody sending figures, far away. At last a message, code groups. Followed it thro' to stave off boredom' Cheery isn't it."

Ian went on in the letter to describe his introduction to the ship and to some members of the crew, and to the ship's guns which would be used as a defence against enemy U-boats and aircraft. He also describes the monotony of being on an uneventful radio watch through the night:-

"We had roast duck yesterday! It was good. Had stuffing and vegetables too. Haven't had breakfast for some days now as I sleep on till lunch time when I've been on watch.

The gunner had a long chat with me before I turned in last night. He showed me the guns, explained just why the shell left the barrel, and pressed shells into my hands. He has the most Bow Bell'ish accent I've heard. 'You could 'it 'em with a 'ammer when the pins in.' Then he hauled out the cordite charges and furnished the fact that the ash from a cigarette would ---. I would look suitably unimpressed and hedged away to get some sleep. All his remarks are concluded with 'see', whereupon you nod your head sagely and say 'ah'.

The 3rd Engineer comes from a place near Dunfermline, and has been down by Selkirk, Gala, Hawick, etc on holiday. I'm beginning to think that there must be at least one Scots engineer on every ship in the world.

Before we sailed, the Chief and I went ashore and bought 1 pkt. Lux, one pkt. Oxydol, two cubes of Reckitt's blue, and one pkt. Robin Starch. This to wash our dainties. We haven't got round to it yet, but probably will when we reach port.

Everything goes on smoothly, including the ship, the weather even is irreproachable.

I wrote Auntie Ruby, and told her, to tell you where to write to, but in case she hasn't written, here it is: –

R.F.A. 'Oleander', c/o G.P.O., London.

The 3rd mate tells me confidentially, that R.F.A. really means Ready for anything. At sea you lose count of the days, and apart from scraps thrown by the Old Man who has a radio, no news of current happening percolates to us. A world apart.

Only one radio is permitted to operate on the ship at a time. This is because sensitive direction finding apparatus could pick up our position by the oscillations of the radios. And that wouldn't do us no good, no 'ow.

0200. Propping up of eyelids with matches is indicated now. Time staggers on complete with leaden feet. My hours when a normal 8-hour watch is being kept are midnite to 6, and 4pm to 6pm.

Did you have Mr. Henderson over? Was David there?

0300. No message worth logging since midnite. Very quiet.

0404. Still grinding away.

0500. In the last lap now. I've opened the port and outside the sun is shining.

0600. At last! I'm away to put the strain on all parts – in other words, to sleep. I dunno when I'll get this posted, but it'll be as soon as possible.

You may as well write, because altho' I don't know <u>when</u> I'll get your letters, I shall no doubt get them some time.

Cheerio, Ian.

5.45. Just had tea. Did my washing today. Shirt, vest, socks, hankie. In cold water! Am drying them by means of the fan and radiator. And we're in port!"

Ian's first voyage on 'Oleander' finished at Scapa Flo, prior to leaving for Norway. He was not allowed to say where he was on his letters home, nor was he allowed to send picture postcards in case this provided useful information to the enemy. Letters from home were a welcome distraction from the routine of the ship, which is indicated in the following passage from his letter to his family written on 11 May, 1940:-

"Dear Family,

I'll describe the scene today. After breakfast the Chief and I took a frame piece of the transmitter down on deck to scrape and repaint it.

I was bashing away, then a drifter came alongside, and the 3rd Mate went over. I looked up and there he was, holding the mail. Suppressing a desire to rush over and tear his burden from him, I pseudo-nonchalantly continued bashing.

About five minutes later the 3rd reappeared and jerked his head back. This I divined was an indication of mail for me. Whistling nonchalantly again, I strolled over, up the ladder, and when I was out of sight, rushed to my cabin. There on the table was 'The Signal' and another letter postmarked Leith.

Thinking that you had enclosed a letter inside the magazine, with nerveless fingers I tore it open. Nothing. Again I went thro' it. Nothing. 'Ah well' I said, or words to that effect. Opened the other one. From a screwball dame in Leith *(no indication of who this was, but perhaps an acquaintance from his time at Leith Nautical College?)*. No importance. I think I said 'Ah well' again and went back to my bashing.

Five minutes after resumption, the 3rd again appeared, this time holding an envelope. He shouted something, but I didn't hear – I was on my way up to him. There it was. Knocking off bashing, I snatched the epistle(s) and screamed again to my cabin. Spent about half an hour reading & rereading the letters. All thro' the day I've been delving into my pocket and having another glance at them.

The foregoing may give you some idea of the welcomeness of mail. It's rather a strain writing, because you have to think out everything beforehand and avoid 'careless talk'. But now we are leaving and going on a job. 'Oh?' you say. Sorry *(this sounds like Ian apologising for being unable to tell the family where he is and where he is going).*

By this time Ian was growing a moustache, much to the amusement of his shipmates. In the same letter he describes their reaction, in a poem written by Shaw, 'Oleander's 3rd Mate. "The following appeared on the dart board today:–

*'We have a man aboard this ship
Who has some hairs upon his lip
Two to the left and three to the right
It is a most distinguished sight
Far be it from me to mention his name
Or wonder how it came
To such vast proportions
And kept in train by what contortions.'*

I may mention here that I am the only hirsute person on board. So the 3rd Mate has immortalised the event. He also professes glare and blindness when I've the yellow peril on."

In another indication of some of the monotony of life aboard ship, and how cut off ships' crews were from news from home and elsewhere, he wrote, "I was in a bad way off for reading material so I sent off letters to Dumfries, A. Belle, and Mrs Ballantyne, asking them, if they were in the habit of getting a magazine regularly, to send it on to me! But if nothing turns up from these appeals, I shall graciously allow you to send me some magazines. A gramophone, one of the worst, is grinding out 'Danny Boy' from the Stewards' room. This happens every night. They have about 3 records."

After mooring at Scapa Flo, 'Oleander' set sail for Harstad in Norway, where British troops had landed in an effort to secure key points in Norway. Ian would have his first real taste of war on arrival there.

Leith Nautical College as it is today in Commercial Street, Edinburgh.
Photograph by Harry Scott.

Ian Waddell with his friend Peter (last name unknown),
14 April, 1940, on graduating from Leith Nautical College.

Ian Waddell and his friend Peter in Uniform.

Shaw, 'Oleander's 3rd Mate, author of the poem about Ian's moustache.

A ship's gun.

Chapter 3 – Ian's first taste of war. Bombing of 'Oleander' and loss of HMS 'Courageous'

On Sunday 12 May, 1940, 'Oleander' left the Firth of Clyde as part of Convoy NS.3 with 5 merchant ships. On 13 May, 1940, she left Scapa Flo for Harstad in Norway to support the Allied landings at Narvik, arriving there on Wednesday, 22 May. Among the other ships there was HMS 'Glorious', an aircraft carrier of the Royal Navy, with another son of Galashiels on board, 17 year old Boy Telegraphist, William Jeffrey Ormiston.

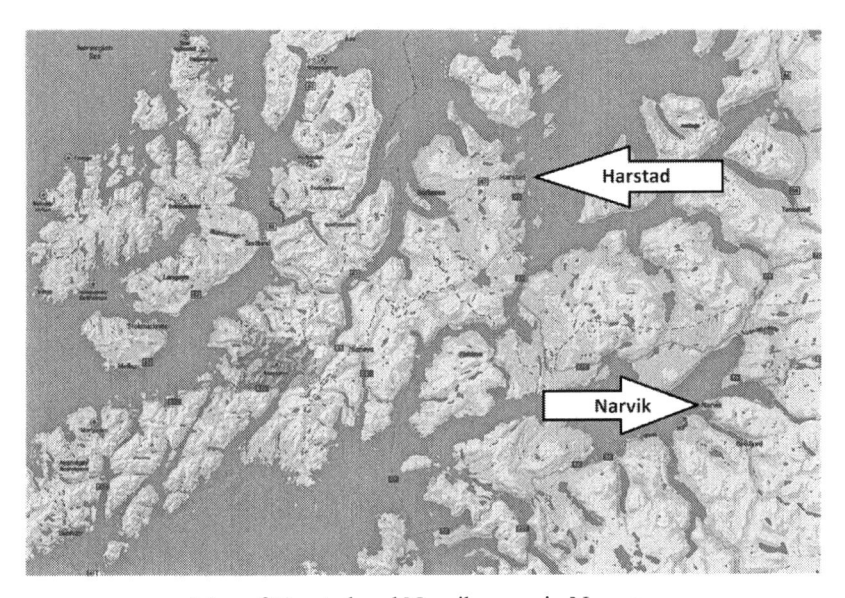

Map of Harstad and Narvik areas in Norway.

Ian kept a log detailing the voyage that gives a compelling insight into life aboard a merchant oil tanker, which was considered a prize target for enemy bombers and submarines:-

"Monday, thirteenth day of May - Left Scapa at 7 a.m. under convoy of two destroyers and one flying boat. Other ships, cargo and tanker join up in line ahead, astern of us. We are the Commodore ship.

Breakfast at 8.30. After this the Chief started his watch. I retired, read a little of the 'Club of Queer Trades' *(A collection of stories by G.K. Chesterton first published in 1905)*, and then curled up on my bunk.

At about ten minutes past twelve, 'crump, crump, crump'. I levered myself up, and two more 'crumps' shook the ship. Everything that happened next was automatic. Falling over the bunk's side, I feverishly pulled on my shoes, combed my hair, of all things, grabbed my wallet from a drawer and a coat pocket, and then made for the upper deck. An excited 'depth charges, that's what them are', from the gunner's room confirmed my guess.

Up on deck, I paused to scan the heavy sea. The ship rolled and heaved crazily. The Chief also opined that these had been depth charges. Ahead, the destroyer, emitting whooping siren blasts, was altering course. Thinking perhaps an extra pair of eyes would help, I climbed up onto the bridge. The Old Man, in an obscene pullover and blue beret, was peering through binoculars. Seeing me he said that I'd be better see to my wireless sonny. As I could always take a hint, I regretfully climbed down.

Soon action began. The 2nd Mate pulled an Aldis out to the port wing. The lamp clicked and blinked to the ship astern. As much as I could translate was 'stand by for action'. The Bosun rushed past, face convulsed, shouting, 'Get the cover off the four-inch gun'. The 1st Mate told the steward to get the gun crew to the aft gun.

Men rushed along the cats-walk, lifebelts streaming behind. The gunner, pulling on a khaki greatcoat, ran to take charge of the gun. Soon he was back, having forgotten the firing cartridges. "Ah there, gunner!"

At the top of the stairs, the Chief and I chatted to the 3rd Mate who had come down from the bridge to fortify himself with a gin. He, of course, professed 'nerves' and made us laugh by conveying the tumbler to his mouth with simulated trembling of his hand. But his normally fresh complexion was greyer than usual and a spot of red burned on both of his cheeks. He soon left us to go back to the bridge. He'd said that the destroyer had spotted the sub, but we had seen it first.

The helm was put hard over, and rolling drunkenly the ship came round in a hard circle. One destroyer raced down on the port side, her submarine hunting pennant fluttering wildly. The other came in on the starboard. Both of them darted to and fro in an effort to place the sub.

Suddenly overhead, a flying boat with welcome British cocardes roared defiance at the unseen enemy. This flying boat must have been recalled by the destroyer to help in the search.

I noticed many dead fish floating belly-up past the ship. Killed by concussion from the depth charges, they provided a meal for the seagulls.

The Chief Engineer joined 'OS' *(name unknown, but possibly the 3rd Radio Officer)* and I. His fortification had been whisky. He thought the explosions were his propeller shaft breaking, then went on to tell us how he'd seen two subs in the last war.

On the horizon I noticed an object like a stick. Drawing the Chief's attention to it, he thought it was a very peculiar object. He reported it to the bridge and left with the assurance that an eye would be kept on it, while I put on the phones in his absence. It turned out to be a dan. buoy used in fishing!

The only apparent action taking place now was by the destroyers which were still oscillating to and fro. Things quietened down afterwards and the 1st Mate gave the wash out sign from the aft gun position. The erstwhile gun crew trooped back to their accustomed jobs, so that soon the stewards had lunch ready. The lunch gong reverberated thro' the ship drawing those who could get away down to the mess.

Conversation during lunch was a little artificial, but appetites were not impaired. After lunch I relieved 'OS', and my first message was a safety signal from the Admiralty warning that mines might be laid off the Norwegian coast without warning. I took down the message, but when 'OS' came up we checked it on the map to find that it was too far south to affect us."

Tuesday 14 May, 1940, was an uneventful day, however Ian's journal goes on to describe him suffering a severe bout of sea sickness and the level of 'sympathy' he received from his shipmates:-

"Friday, seventeenth day of May - The unaccountable lapse in chronicling may be attributed to indifference, but more truly to mal de mere *(Ian suffered from sea sickness)*. Why did I ever leave home!? Subsisted on tea and toast. One morning I asked the cabin boy, hereinafter to be called my protector, for a cup of milk. Yeah, yeah, sure. In 15 minutes he was back with a tureen of bread cubes in warm milk. Something about says it's a feed as well as a drink. Golluped down some of it.

This morning I asked for a glass of cold milk. Sure, yeah, yeah. Soon he was back with sweet milk, quite good.

The middle watches during these five days don't bear telling. On the first day I was rendered hors de combat, the steward came in, wiping his hands on a towel and ghoulishly enquired, 'feeling all right Sparks – not sea sick'. I struggled up on one elbow, to say oh not bad, no not sea sick, ha ha. Then enquired what was for lunch. Believe it or not he said pork chops. I think he realised the awful import of this for he gave a feeble oh, ha ha and left. Covering my staring eyes with a shaking hand, I fell back, P.C.'s Ohhhh.

Went up to relieve 'OS' at lunch, and when he came up he said hurry and don't miss your pork c. Then planked down a yellow covered sweet & began to eat. Subsequent elicitation proves that he was not aware of my condition.

Was up for lunch today. With t.u. lip I took my place at table. The Old man said how was Mr. W. this morning – ready for a pork chop? Ha, ha. In an endeavour to enter into the s. of the t. I turned round and said I think, not so bad, ha, ha. Banter was then loosed on me. Shaw had composed another epic, quite kind this time.

Lapse of chronicling of two days.

Sunday nineteenth day of May - One week out. Still we don't go into Narvik. Heard Winston last night. Eat my food now. The zig zag clock. Refuelling at sea yesterday. Bored today. Go in tomorrow!

Monday twentieth day of May - With two other ships and three destroyers we make for that 'smudge of land'. Full speed all day. More revelations of Merchant Navy from 'OS' 'Ropeners'. 1/2½d *(£0.06p)* and G' *(a guinea or £1.05p)* a day for food. No faus for Gold Coast, no heating for Gulf of St Lawrence. Load lines too low. 'There was once an honest ship owner--! No watch this morning – not called.

Tuesday twenty first day of May - On watch. At 0225 I saw land for first time since the 13th. Looks like an island. Today should be exciting. I think we've entered the fiord. I see a destroyer on the starboard with merchant vessels, on the port great rocks wreathed in mist. Very light at quarter to four. We go in line astern. Wonder if we'll see the 'Effingham'? *(The cruiser H.M.S. 'Effingham', transferring troops to Bodo to help stem the Germans advancing on Narvik, ran aground in Vestfiord. 'Effingham' was later torpedoed and abandoned)(http://www.naval-history.net).*

Now at five thirty it's getting misty. At six we run into a bad mist. Engines stopped. I'm off to sleep.

Wednesday twenty second day of May - Similar to the first diary report is today's – land. And much the same as Bergen was. Square multi-coloured houses clustered round the water surrounded by wooded hills. It is Harstad. Nice place – before last night raid. Seventy bombs, one hit, petrol tank. I can see the fire from here.

Duty boat comes alongside. "Any mail?" But it is outward-bound mail. Boat manned by battle-romper-clad tommies. Army, Navy & Air Force here.

A ship that we had stores for has been hit and beached. A tanker in an air raid was half sunk, so it was towed out to the middle of the fiord here & scuttled.

This is a local Hell's Corner. From tales of ships sunk & scuttled to shrapnel going thro. 2 bulkheads. Rowed over to the 'Broomdale' with Shaw, met Sparks & "Sparks"- latter jittery. So is Captain. Chatted to Assistant Steward from Greenock. Species of shrapnel. Bombers are evidently after the tankers. Will look for further developments with interest.

Well here they are. At 6.30, bang from destroyer. Things quietened down, then at 9.30, bang, bang, plus blast on siren and red flag. Good barrage put up drove plane off. Fire still burns on shore. After exiting day, go to put the strain on all parts. Another one while I'm in pyjamas. No guns. Just drone of planes. All clear.

Thursday twenty third day of May - Have survived 24 hours anyway. Posted first letter. French cruiser refuelling from us. Typical Continental odour emanates from it. I long for Belgium Matelots much more free'n'easy than ours. Peeling potatoes onto deck.

Well here we go again folks, with another thrilling episode. Four fifteen sirens & bangs. One plane at first liberally peppered. Then seven. Phew! Then the bombs. Phew again. First on the port of the 'B.P.' *(British Petroleum Company)* ship. Blew the barge up. Then all round. Pheeeeew, bang, and the blast of air. Clambered about from mess to cabin and lavatory, looking out of ports.

The 'B.J.' *(possibly the tanker 'British Justice')* got hers soon. Plane goes over, and all round the ship, fountains of water. She lists to starboard. Her rudder is out of action. Again she is singled out. At least she gets under way and beaches herself. Boats are lowered & the men abandon her.

Sight of plane coming overhead of us. About 50 yards astern, crash! Scurry to mess to see other side. She's over the top of us now. Will the next one be for us? 3rd Mate decides that we're the next on the list so into the Centre castle we go.

Observe faces of occupants. Any joke greeted with high laughter. People talk to prevent a hiatus. Half-hearted chaffing of the small deck-hand. All clear. Go up to bridge & watch abandoning of 'B.P.' thro' telescope. Tea – very welcome

Observations of afternoon's raid – jittery gunner, whine of bombs coming down enables you to watch then duck; pom poms' quick metallic cough; destroyers & cruisers cruising under fire.

Best scene – after power dive, a Junkers screamed across harbour, very low, to intense concentrated fire. From the 'British Governor' shells could be seen parabolically making for the plane. Glinting copper streaks followed by a puff of brown smoke. One of these must have got the plane, as smoke belched from her. Clearing the mountains her engines went clackety, bang, pop. Circled round & we lost sight of her. After raid saw a British plane, presumably looking for her.

Others – salvo of bombs along shore. Nearness of explosion to cruiser. Ring of explosions round the 'B.P.' Another warning at 10.45. One plane, driven off before it reached us. Another four over at 11.15. Driven off.

Friday twenty fourth day of May - Awakened at 2.15 by explosions. One very near, off forecastle, shook me in my bunk. Lay a while, and as fire got fiercer, climbed out. In mess doorway, when one, 50 yds. on starboard, rattled the old bones. Worst so far. Squatted on floor when it burst.

Into the centre castle we go. Mr. Henry regales us with a commentary, very lurid. Explosions on port side, bad ones. Rattle of shrapnel.

Cleared off for a while. Pumps had found 3 bits of shrapnel. Got one. All clear. We and the 'Brit. Gov.' are the targets this time. Saw ring of rubbish caused by bomb thro' port just after explosion.

3.30 get back to bed. It's getting hotter. The rats dive out of the sun and let go. Know when they're low as soon as pom poms begin hacking.

Sign of nerves around. It'll be hell if things continue as bright as this. Not so bad first few times, but when your range is determined, and your anchors down, I'm reminded rather too forcibly of a sitting bird.

They reckon that the first bomb of yesterday's raid was dead where the 'Broomdale' should have been. She sailed the night before. The 'B.J.' supply-troop ship is on the beach badly down at the head. Us next?

Seven o'clock more explosion. Once again I get up, dress, and issue forth.

Bad one astern of us, shook up everything. Plane leaves a plume of white smoke right above us. This is interpreted as a guide for the other aircraft. Much foreboding and criticism of us lying out here in the open.

Had breakfast. At half past 10, siren again. No shots. All clear.

Twelve fifteen another warning. Before that went, aboard destroyer to get biscuits in her canteen.

Latest reports say that 2 Gloster Glads. were up during last warning. That should help. Might see an air battle now.

Men on trawlers reckon that most of townspeople of Harstad are pro-German.

About 7.15 again. Bad one this time. Low clouds made anti fire difficult. Junkers 88. Twin engine, tapered wing sod. Banked steeply and I saw four eggs let go. Blast, blast. Shaw & Cap. swear destroyer blown up. Later proved false. Again the 'B.J.' troopship attacked. Two marines killed in yesterday's do on her, they say. Land batteries pretty effective. As soon as crumps start, gunner beats it below. Not a nice attitude at all for a Marine. He's a mass of nerves. Babbles incessantly to people. Not manly. 'O.S.' jittery from yesterday. Is off his chow badly. Complains of ineffectiveness of anti!

If we'd gone over to Hell's Corner as planned tonite, we'd've been blasted. Big brute the plane. Go aboard the destroyer for chocs etc. Well stocked up now.

Saturday twenty fifth day of May - At 6.30 and 8.30. Popular prices. The 'B.J.' again. 9.30 once more. One plane. Repeat performance at 10.30 and 12. Two of three planes. Junkers 87 *(Stuka dive bomber)* and a Dornier flying pencil *(twin engine medium bomber)* from Trondheim I think. Amazing spectacle – power dive on the 'Vindictive'. Let go two. Missed and climbed away. *(H.M.S. Vindictive, originally a cruiser converted to a repair ship and* *used as a base ship during the Norwegian campaign).* Subjected to terrific barrage. Our turn next. Rattle of shrapnel & blasts. See tracers go thro' the wings. Power dive on destroyer. Blam, blam in reply. Smoke belches out from plane. Escapes round mountain. Heads for home.

One egg whined down & failed to explode. This is a long raid; until 1.30 at least. 15 raids in 96 hours. One every six. Feeling that this has all happened before somewhere. Must be the films. Blasé! Only the blasts that shake the ship indicate that this is not the screen. Retraced letters & rewrote some of them. Shrapnel from Shaw.

Only 1,300 tons away. Another good odd. Do we stay here until empty or blasted? Warning at 4.30. Another at 7. And another at 8.30. The poor destroyer has come alongside us twice now & has had to sheer off. The Lieutenant shouts to me each time – back in half an hour. The food question is very acute on board her. No bread or meat. She says that in the last dive on her the Junkers loosed 33 bombs on her, most of them burst in mid air, others missed.

Sunday twenty sixth day of May (Day of Rest) - Quarter to three. Short warning & shots. Go leisurely out. To forward end of alley amidships. Overhead two silver Junkers 87's. 15 seconds later terrific blast. Rush headlong into alley. Crash, ---- bounced up & down in alley, glass & crockery falling all around. Tossed about like proverbial cork. All others bouncing about too. Awful noise. Pick ourselves up. Go to door. All the deck sprayed with treacly oil. Steam escaping aft. Skid back to cabin. Shambles. Lump burning on bunk. Books sprayed over floor. Grabbed essentials, wallet, pay book, camera, films, greatcoat. Up to deck.

Rushing about rampant. Boats being lowered. Took photos of wreckage. Greaser reeling about. Damaged internally. Photos of boats. Steam hissing very strongly. One bomb under stern, one amidships each side. Steam pipe cracked.

Into starboard boat. Pulled away. 'Dulciebelle', Aberdeen, picks us up. Into hatch. While making for shore, blasts of bombs – very close. Ashore. Whine of bomb. Dodged into shed. Wooden walls! Very close. In town somewhere. Up to town. In cellar.

Trawler men. Tales of hell endured in this hole. Stood outside with Chips. Bluejacket queries if we are 'Oleander's' crew – go back on board! Get down to quay. On board with Naval chappie.

Survey wreckage. Engineers' cabin the worst. Also foc'sul bad. While rooting about 'Brit. Gov.' comes alongside to take off oil. Air raid warning! Didn't feel so good then. Into centre castle. Others of crew mutter about 'trap'. Bombs near us. Passes thro', after others come on board. With 'Man of War', 'Oleander' is pushed stern first onto beach. She is cracked in 3 places in deck. Crack down port side amidships. Down in engine room, 3 feet of water. Wireless cabin blown about. Auto top drawer hanging out. Transmitter valve broken. Tried receiver. She works. Packed kit half into trunk. It all went in, quite easily.

While on 'Man of W.' another raid when we were shoving stern ashore.

All kit aboard trawler. Broken record lying on deck – "My fate in your hands"! Chatted to Hockings, a member of the crew of 'M of W.' Got 3 subs.

Eventually rowed ashore with bedding. Into camp. Chatted with an ex-Super Ikonta owner. Get down to shore to meet other officers. Went up to officers' mess. A Captain redolent with "actually" & "look here" dispersed drinks. Very decent. Arranged for sleeping accommodation in loft above soldiers. Asleep at 2 o'clock.

Monday twenty seventh day of May - Up at 8.30. Breakfast in mess. H and eggs cooked by our cook. The Lieutenant talking with us estimated that ours were 1000 lb. bombs, and not the usual 500 lbs.

The pilot who brought us in & anchored us where we were has been arrested this morning. He put 3 tankers where we were. All bombed. (Our pilot) – the pilot who ran the 'Effingham' onto a rock has been shot *(H.M.S. 'Effingham' struck a rock and ran aground whilst on transport escort duty. The rock was marked on the navigation chart, but had been obscured by a pencil mark made by the navigator. She was later scuttled and sunk)*. Saw the place. Just in harbour. 30 women shot for spying yesterday. Namsos is seemingly the worst place. Out to ship again. Brought baggage & food ashore. Toted it up to lorry.

Down to Naval Barracks. Lunch. In afternoon back to ship. More food brought down to quay. Went in 'puffer' to ship. Food & blankets. Suddenly word from shore – 12 bombers coming. The crew pushed off & we made for jetty. Left some on board. They rowed. Into hospital ground. No warning. Back to 'puffer' & 'Oleander'. Finally got all food aboard and made for 'British Governor', a British Tanker Co. ship. Got food & bedding aboard. We're in the hospital. Not casualties! Had a much needed wash. Under way at 11.15. Bed.

Tuesday twenty eighth day of May - Wakened by 'O.S'. at some unearthly hour to go on watch. When I did get up, I was an hour late! Had breakfast. Our watch at 12 till 4. Continuous 3 operator watch.

Saw the 'Eskimo'. Her bow blown completely off. Dodged 7 torpedoes. Got the 8th. Talked to a survivor from the 'Curlew'. He swam ashore. Bombed in narrow fiord. *(H.M.S. 'Eskimo' had her bows blown off by a torpedo. Temporary repairs were made to the ship which returned to Newcastle-on-Tyne for full repair. She survived the war and was scrapped in 1949).*

At last fighters are up in Harstad. The Naval C.O. has reported that the fighters had to be sent as A. A. guns were of little use against bombers. How true!"

The war was raging in theatres other than Norway, in particular Europe. In a letter to his family dated 26 May, 1940, Ian says, "The news we hear of the fighting on the Western Front gets more depressing. But I still say they'll be halted", indicating that there was still some optimism that the German advance in Europe could be brought to a halt. The German Army had by that time broken through the Allied lines and was making its way to the Channel ports, splitting the French and British Armies. Following that on 28 May, King Leopold of the Belgium, without any warning to the British or the French Commanders, surrendered his army and the British and French Armies began to evacuate from Dunkirk.

Overcoming the tedium of routine life at sea was also on Ian's mind and the need for news from home. In that letter he also says, "Write soon and get anybody else you can think of to write too so as to make the next mail I get a large one. Cheerio, Ian".

The worry felt by the families of those in harm's way is, to some extent, reflected in a letter to Ian from his Father:-

"Sunday, June 2, 1940
Dear Ian,

I think it was last Sunday we wrote to you and as it is into the third week since we had your last letter, are wondering how you are & what you've been doing. Hope it won't be long before we hear from you.

News came this last week of the capture of Narvik *(by the Allies)*, and we wondered if you had a hand in it! I enclose a picture. There are no picture pages in the paper these days, just an occasional odd one.

You will get the news I expect, & will have heard how we've been let down again by King Leopold. The getting of our men out of the trap has been a terrific ordeal.

Mummy is away this weekend to Dumfries. Tomorrow would have been a holiday here. Mr. Hodge had a bundle of Penguins *(books)* posted to you from Edinburgh. You will be having a heavy mail to deal with when you get it.

I was talking to Ian MacDonald's father yesterday & asked about his Radio Officer son. He has been at it for about 10 years, & is away to S. America this time. He says a convoy is the safest of all.

Lovely weather we've been having. The lilac trees & the Rhododendrons are in full bloom, the garden stuff is coming on splendidly.

Perhaps you would like to see a newspaper so I will post you the Sunday Times tomorrow. It will keep you in touch with what is being written about current happenings.

Now I'll push off to Church.

Kindest regards & Good Luck.

Cheerio, Yours, Dad.

P.S. – Mummy got your first allocation from Marconi & has put it in bank."

Ian survived Harstad, but there is no record of his return to the UK, although he did get some well earned leave. A letter dated 10 June, 1940, from F. M. Harvey of 34 East Acton Lane, London, referring to a lost luggage claim, hopes that he will enjoy his leave. And in a later letter Ian states, "Collected about £8 pay, from 1.6.40 – 31.6.40 (Full pay for the month's leave!)"

Whilst Ian and his colleagues on 'Oleander' had a narrow escape, the crew of the aircraft carrier, HMS 'Glorious' were not so fortunate. On Saturday, 8 June, 1940, 'Glorious' and the destroyers escorting her, HMS 'Ardent' and HMS 'Acasta' were returning to Scapa Flo. The flotilla was intercepted by the German battlecruisers, 'Gneisenau' and 'Scharnhorst' in the Norwegian Sea, about 300 miles west of the Norwegian coast. All three ships were sunk with the loss of over 1500 officers and men. Among the missing was William Jeffrey Ormiston. It was later sadly confirmed to his parents, James and Agnes Ormiston, that he had been killed in action and the following report appeared in the local newspaper:-

"PRESUMED KILLED – Boy Telegraphist William Jeffrey Ormiston, aged 17½ years, elder son of Mr. and Mrs. Ormiston, 180 Glendinning Terrace, who has been reported missing since June, 1940, has now been presumed killed. Official intimation to this effect was received by his parents last week. Boy Ormiston joined the Navy in June, 1938, and after serving on HMS 'Caledonia', was transferred to HMS 'Glorious'." *(Border Telegraph, 28 October, 1941).* William Ormiston is remembered on Panel 39, Column 3 of the Plymouth Naval Memorial in Devon.

On a more positive note, the Border Telegraph carried the following story about a native of Peebles and his 14 year old son:-

"Escaped from Belgium – Peebles Natives Experiences - Mr. Charles Morris, a native of Peebles, has reached the home of his brother Fred in Mall Avenue, Musselburgh, after being six days on the road in Belgium and France, making his escape, says the 'Evening News'. Mr. Morris, who has lived in a village outside Brussels since the last war, is accompanied by his 14 year old son, Robert. His wife, who is Belgian, and her mother, remained in the village.

On learning that the Germans were only three hours distant, Mr. Morris made up his mind that as a British subject, he had better get back to this country. He and his son set off on bicycles for Calais. Progress was slow, for there were many refugees. Often roads were blocked, and the refugees had to turn back and find roads not closed to them. Calais was eventually reached, but there were no boats leaving for home.

Refugees Machine-Gunned. Mr. Morris and his son then made for Boulogne. 'On the road, five or six kilometres ahead of us', said Mr. Morris, 'I saw a German aeroplane machine-gun refugees. I did not see any casualties, but what I did see was old people with their throats cut. They had been unable to go on, and had thought they were better to commit suicide than fall into the hands of the Germans.'

At Boulogne Mr. Morris was advised to go to Dieppe. When about half-way there he was turned back to Boulogne. He and his son had covered about 300 miles since leaving their home outside Brussels. The night in Boulogne was spent in an air raid shelter. In the morning escape was made on a British destroyer.

Mr. Morris fought in the last war, and it was upon being demobilised in 1919 that he returned to Belgium to marry a Belgian girl." *(Border Telegraph, 4 June, 1940).*

The Destroyer HMS 'Beagle' refuelling from the 'Oleander'.

Getting 'Oleander's' lifeboats launched
(note the oil on the surface of the water).

Rowing the lifeboat away from 'Oleander'.

'Oleander' after being bombed.

'Oleander' lying low in the water after being bombed by enemy aircraft.

'Oleander beached after being bombed by enemy aircraft.

'Oleander's' Galley after bombing by enemy aircraft.

Ian's cabin after 'Oleander' was bombed by enemy aircraft.

Members of 'Oleander's' Crew wearing life jackets.

'Oleander's' Officers ashore after abandoning ship.

'Oleander's' crew ashore at Harstad following bombing by enemy aircraft.

Ashore at Harstad.

William Jeffrey Ormiston killed in action, 8 June, 1940, whilst serving on board HMS 'Glorious'.

HMS 'Glorious' sunk by the German battlecruisers 'Scharnhorst' and 'Gneisenau' on 8 June, 1940.
(Pictures by kind permission of W. B. Ormiston)

Chapter 4 – The 'Battle of the Atlantic' and the 'U-boat peril'- Jedburgh man's ship attacked by U-boat.

This chapter sets in context the dangerous working environment of those, like Ian Waddell, serving in the Merchant Navy during the 'Battle of the Atlantic' throughout World War II, and provides a chronological summary of several of Ian Waddell's Atlantic crossings whilst serving on various ships.

The chapter also summarises the dangers to Allied shipping from the German Air Force and Navy, particularly Germany's deployment of U-boats, as well as the other hazards such as severe weather, faced daily by the Merchant Navy.

Following the experience of World War I, where deployment of German U-boats had been particularly effective, the British Admiralty from the beginning of World War II, organised most Allied ships crossing the Atlantic into convoys for greater protection. Unfortunately the Royal Navy was desperately short of ships suitable for convoy duty, and the Admiralty had to rely on converted merchant ships and trawlers to provide additional convoy protection vessels. Even then other factors such as the British withdrawal at Dunkirk in May and June, 1940, meant that protection of convoys came second to protecting the British mainland from the threat of invasion by the Germans. Protection from the air was also limited, seen as being less important than the strategic effort of bombing Germany as the war progressed. This led to a dramatic increase in losses of shipping in the second half of 1940, and the beginning of 1941.

In 1939, the German Navy was not strong enough to take on, in set battles, the might of the British Navy, still the most powerful in the world. The German strategy therefore was to defeat Britain by ruthless attacks on her merchant fleet and those of other countries supplying her. This was achieved by the deployment of U-boats, long range aircraft, and surface raiders such as 'Bismarck', 'Prince Eugen', and 'Admiral Graf Spee', which alone sank 9 merchant ships during the first 3 months of the war. Extensive mine laying and the use of armed merchant ships were also tactics employed by the German Navy.

Until July, 1941, Atlantic convoys approaching or leaving the UK were escorted by the Royal Navy only when they were within about 150 miles to the south or west of Ireland. There was usually no Allied warship or air cover for the majority of the Atlantic crossing, and the U-boats exploited this 'Atlantic Gap' weakness to the full. Following the fall of France in 1940, U-boats based in French Atlantic ports began to wage unrestricted warfare on shipping in British coastal waters as well as deep into the Atlantic.

This was known as the U-boats 'Happy Time', and they operated in hunting packs with devastating results on the largely unprotected Allied convoys. During the period June to October, 1940, over 270 Allied ships were sunk by U-boats. In October, 1940, Convoy SC 7 alone lost 20 of its 35 cargo vessels with the loss of 141 lives. The British Navy began to employ a more offensive strategy in an effort to combat the threat posed by U-boats by forming hunting groups based on aircraft carriers to patrol the shipping lanes. However the tactics employed to achieve this had not been perfected and the U-boats, for the most part, continued to remain elusive. The aircraft carrier HMS 'Ark Royal' narrowly avoided being sunk by torpedo on 14 September, 1939, and 3 days later 'U-29' sank a second carrier, HMS 'Courageous' off the west coast of Ireland. A month later 'U-47' penetrated the British base at Scapa Flo in the Orkney Islands, and sank the battleship, HMS 'Royal Oak'.

The Royal Navy had fitted many of its smaller warships with 'Asdic' equipment which used sound waves to locate submerged submarines. The equipment was housed in a metal dome beneath the ship from which sound waves were transmitted. The time that passed from the sound wave hitting the submarine until the echo was heard by the operator indicated the range of the submarine, and the pitch of the echo revealed whether it was approaching the ship or moving away. Whilst revolutionary for its time 'Asdic', in its early stages, did have its limitations and operators needed weeks of training to make its use effective.

Following the fall of France, German aircraft also posed a real threat to Allied shipping. Long-range Focke-Wulf 'Condor' or 'Kurier' aircraft, based near Bordeaux, ranged up to 600 miles, bombing Allied shipping and directing U-boats to their location. In the first two months of operation these aircraft alone sank 30 ships. It was only a lack of effective co-operation between the Kriegsmarine (German Navy) and the Luftwaffe (German Air force) that prevented these attacks from becoming more effective.

For Allied sailors Atlantic convoy duty was drab and monotonous. The British merchant fleet was very varied and many ships were in a poor state of repair because the owners would not, or could not afford to maintain them properly. Convoys were placed under the command of a Commodore, usually a retired regular Navy Officer. However, experienced Merchant Navy Masters were occasionally appointed as Commodore, or Vice or Rear Commodore, in case the first appointed Commodore became incapacitated for some reason. Working conditions varied according to the type of ship, and there was no continuity of employment for the sailors in the Merchant Navy. When their ship was sunk, their pay was stopped, and the practice continued until an order from Winston Churchill rectified the matter, and a Ministry of War Transport was created to administer the Merchant Marine and British sea ports.

The convoy system overall was a success with the majority of convoys never coming under attack. Despite this, the danger of attack was always present and losses were none the less heavy in terms of personnel and shipping. "But every day those men spent at sea they never knew when their luck might change" *(Rear Admiral Sir Kenneth Creighton, [1956] Convoy Commodore, WWII)*.

Ships of 'SC' convoys comprising of slow moving vessels which seldom made a top speed of 8 knots per hour faced the most danger. On average these convoys lost 4% of their number. Ships straggling from the convoy because of mechanical problems or other reasons were particularly vulnerable as U-boats, wary of escorting warships, would try to work their way to the rear of the convoy to pick off any straggling merchant vessels. The convoy also presented dangers of its own making. Many of the ships were old and 'lumbered' rather than sailed, and with so many ships in close proximity to each other collisions were not unknown, especially in poor weather.

When convoys were attacked, courage and discipline was required on the part of the merchant seamen to remain at their posts. Engine room crew in particular were at risk as U-boats would target that area of the ship in an effort to sink it or at least slow its speed. The engine room was also the most difficult part of the ship to escape from being mostly below the water line in the depths of the vessel. Oil tankers were prize targets for the U-boats, and crews knew they would most likely be burned alive if the ship was torpedoed or shelled. Ships carrying iron ore would also sink rapidly if damaged because of the weight and density of the cargo. Despite knowing about these dangers morale among merchant seamen remained high and most felt they were doing a job of work to support the Allied war effort like so many millions of others.

Following his time on 'Oleander', Ian Waddell was assigned to the 'Fylingdale', which had already made several Atlantic crossings, as well as supporting the Allied landings at Narvik. Although 'Fylingdale' survived the war it was lucky to do so. Whilst Ian was serving aboard 'Fylingdale', among others, it formed part of the following convoys crossing the Atlantic *(The following information is by kind permission of www.uboat.net and www.convoyweb.org*:-

Convoy OB-184 left Liverpool bound for Canada on Monday 15 July, 1940, dispersing on 19 July. There were 31 merchant ships in the convoy with 2 escort vessels. The 'Fellside' straggled from the convoy and was sunk on 17 July, by 'U-43' about 500 miles west of the Scottish coast with the loss of 12 crew members. 'Fylingdale' arrived off Quebec on Tuesday 30 July, 1940.

Convoy SC.1 left Sydney, Nova Scotia for Liverpool on Thursday 15 August, 1940, with 40 merchant ships and 6 escorts. The 'Eva' straggled because of unsuitable coal, and was sunk on 15 August by 'U-28'. HMS 'Penzance', an escorting sloop, was sunk on Saturday 24 August by 'U-48', and Ian provides a full account of the incident in Chapter 6 of this book. The 'Blairmore', which like the 'Fylingdale' had stopped to pick up survivors from 'Penzance', was torpedoed and sunk by 'U-37'. On 28 August the 'Elle' was hit by a torpedo from 'U-101', and was eventually scuttled by the Royal Navy. 'Fylingdale' arrived in Belfast Lough on Thursday 29 August, 1940.

Convoy OB.220 left Milford Haven on Thursday 26 September, 1940, bound for Canada, with 31 merchant ships and 5 Navy escorts. The

'Hemminge' straggled from the convoy and was sunk on 30 September by U-37 about 250 miles west of the Irish coast. The convoy dispersed on Tuesday 1 October, 1940, and on 2 October, the 'Kayeson' was sunk by 'U-32' about 500 miles south west of the Irish coast. Although the crew were seen to take to the life boats, all were lost. 'Fylingdale' arrived in Sorel, Canada, on Tuesday 15 October, 1940.

Convoy SC.9 left Sydney, Canada on Thursday 24 October, 1940, bound for Liverpool, with 31 merchant ships and 8 Navy escorts. No ships were reported lost and 'Fylingdale' arrived in Milford Haven on Sunday 10 November, 1940.

Convoy OB.256 left Liverpool for the USA and Canada on Sunday 8 December, 1940, with 35 merchant ships and 4 escorts. 'Fylingdale', due to join the convoy, did not sail because of repairs carried out at Plymouth to a damaged propeller. It was a narrow escape. On 14 December, the 'Euphoria' and the 'Kyleglen' were both sunk by 'U-100' with the loss of most of their crew.

Convoy OB. 260 left Liverpool with 29 merchant ships and 5 Navy escorts on Monday 16 December, 1940, bound for Canada. The convoy dispersed on Thursday 19 December. The 'British Zeal' was attacked by 'U-65', east of the Cape Verde Islands. Although damaged, the 'British Zeal' managed to reach Freetown where temporary repairs were made to the vessel. On Friday 20 December, the 'Carlton' was torpedoed and sunk by the Italian submarine, 'Pietro Calvi' off the west coast of Ireland. On 25 December, the 'Jumna' was shelled and sunk by the German raider the 'Admiral Hipper' west of Cape Finisterre, North West Spain. 'Fylingdale', arrived in Boston on Friday 3 January, 1941.

Convoy SC.20 left Halifax, Nova Scotia, for Liverpool on Wednesday 22 January, 1941, with 48 merchant ships and 7 escorts. On Tuesday 4 February, the 'Calafatis' and the 'Dionne II' were attacked by German bombers with the loss of 18 lives from the 'Calafatis'. The 'Dionne II' was subsequently sunk by 'U-93' with the loss of 27 lives. The 'Empire Engineer' carrying steel ingots was torpedoed by 'U-123' and sank with the loss of all hands within four minutes of being struck. On 5 February, the 'Ioannis M. Embiricos' was bombed by German aircraft and sunk. On 6 February, the 'Maplecourt' was sunk by 'U-107'. The Germans saw the crew take to the lifeboats, but they were never seen again. 'Fylingdale' arrived in Barry Roads, Bristol Channel, on Monday 10 February, 1941.

Convoy OB.296 left Liverpool on Monday 10 March, 1941, with 40 merchant ships and 7 Navy escorts. The convoy dispersed on 15 March. On Tuesday 8 April, the 'Tweed' was attacked and sunk by 'U-124' south west of Freetown with the loss of three lives. 'Fylingdale' arrived in Halifax, Canada, on Sunday 30 March, 1941.

Convoy SC.29 left Halifax, Canada, for Liverpool on Saturday 19 April, 1941, with 46 merchant ships and 18 Navy escorts. No ships were reported lost and 'Fylingdale' arrived in Belfast Lough on Saturday 10 May, and onward to Swansea on Thursday 29 May.

Convoy OB.333 left Liverpool on Monday 10 June, 1941, with 39 merchant ships and 7 Navy escorts. On Saturday 21 June, the convoy dispersed in mid Atlantic, about 1000 miles east of Puerto Rico. No ships were reported missing and 'Fylingdale' arrived first at Quebec on Wednesday 9 July, and then on to Sydney on Saturday 12 July.

Convoy SC.38 left Sydney for Liverpool on 22 July, 1941, with 30 merchant ships and 18 escorts. Foul weather and ice were the enemies here. The 'Agia Marina'; the 'Armathia'; the 'Boltonhall'; the 'Dimitrios Chandris'; the 'Empire Bunting'; the 'Empire Hail', and the 'Senata' were all forced to turn back after colliding with icebergs. 'Fylingdale' arrived in Belfast Lough on Thursday 7 August, 1941. On 10 August 'Fylingdale' sailed from Belfast Lough with Convoy BB.59 and arrived in Swansea on Sunday 17 August.

Ian's next posting was to the 'Treminnard', a general cargo vessel.

Convoy OS.6 left Liverpool for Freetown, on the coast of West Africa, on Thursday 11 September, 1941, with 31 merchant ships and 9 Navy escorts. Although this area was a favourite hunting ground for German submarines, no ships were reported lost. 'Treminnard' sailed on independently and arrived in Bahia Blanca, Argentina, on Monday 20 October. 'Treminnard' sailed on to Sydney, Canada, arriving there on Thursday 11 December.

Convoy SC.60 left Sydney on Tuesday 16 December, 1941, with 23 merchant ships and 14 Navy escorts. No ships were reported missing, and 'Treminnard' arrived in Belfast Lough on Wednesday 31 December.

Ian's next posting was to the Motor Tanker, 'Narragansett'.

Convoy ON.63 left Milford Haven on Sunday 1 February, 1942, with 34 merchant ships and 11 escort vessels. On Thursday 5 February, HMS 'Arbutus', an escorting corvette, was torpedoed and sunk by 'U-136' with the loss of all the crew. On Friday 13 February, the convoy dispersed about 350 miles west of Nova Scotia. On Saturday 14 February, the 'Empire Spring', a British Catapult Armed merchant ship, was torpedoed and sunk by 'U-576' with the loss of all the crew. 'Narragansett' arrived in Galveston, Texas, on Friday 13 March, 1942, and then sailed on to Port Arthur, arriving there on 17 March.

On Tuesday 17 March, 'Narragansett' sailed from Port Arthur, independently for Halifax, Nova Scotia. She was due there on Friday 27 March, the intention being that she would join a convoy sailing for the UK. On Wednesday 25 March, about 400 miles east of Hampton Roads, Virginia, 'Narragansett' was torpedoed and sunk by 'U-105' with the loss of all of the crew.

Whilst they may have been the enemy, no one can doubt the courage of the German submariners, who had their own type of close camaraderie. Life was dangerous and unpleasant for the crews of the U-boats. U-boats were hot, cramped and smelly, and almost unbearably claustrophobic. Personal hygiene was problematic because of the overcrowded conditions the crews had to endure. Typically 25 men would share a space measuring 12 feet across, sharing it with 22 foot torpedoes and other equipment. Each bunk would be used by two or more men on a shift system. The diet consisted mainly of tinned food, mostly always tainted by the taste of diesel oil.

Contrary to British propaganda at the time, German submariners did not routinely machine gun the crews of the ships they had attacked and sunk, although there is one documented case of a German submarine commander firing on survivors. He was tried, and eventually executed, at the end of the war. In the early stages of the war in particular, German submarine commanders were willing to go to some length to assist shipwrecked crews with offers of food & water, medical attention, providing directions, or even towing lifeboats to safety, as illustrated in the following story from the Border Telegraph:-

"TORPEDOED BY GERMAN SUBMARINE – JEDBURGH MAN'S EXPERIENCES

A Jedburgh man, Chief Radio Officer James Bain, is home on sick leave after having been torpedoed in the Atlantic. In an interview at his home in Castlegate, Jedburgh, he described his experiences. He said, 'Our boat was bound for an eastern port when, without the slightest warning, we were torpedoed by a German submarine about 1.45 pm one Saturday near the end of 1940.

I had just come out of the starboard alleyway and was going up to my room on the lower bridge when the ship was struck on the port side. It seemed to me as if a most terrific electric shock was passing through me. I was thrown on the deck and when I recovered I saw the deck full of holes all around me. I found my hand had been wounded, how badly I didn't realise, and also my foot was very painful. Thereafter I struggled up to the bridge, where I met the Captain, who told me to send the S.O.S. out.

I was in such a mess he did not know me at first, and when he saw my condition he ordered me to the boats immediately. However I staggered to the radio roof to send a message. The door was jammed, but ultimately we forced it open and sent out our signal. I think the aerials must have been smashed, because the submarine did not hear us. There had been six of the crew of thirty nine killed, and after the rest of us had been put into the lifeboat we got away from the ship and waited to see her go down. It was a sad sight.

The submarine then came up and fired a shell, which went over our heads. The men swore, they were fiercely angry, but there was no trace of panic in their faces. However the submarine was not shelling us, but our ship. They fired six shots, two missed and four hit.

After the ship had sunk, the submarine ordered us alongside, and the commander ordered our Captain and all wounded men aboard. I was surprised when the German doctor and his assistant commenced to bandage my hand and arm. He did not touch my foot, however, he gave me two spare bandages. I wondered if we were to be kept prisoners, but after handing down a big aluminium kettle full of fruit juice, a flask of water, another big drum of blackcurrant juice, two big hams, a bag of bread and cartons of Turkish cigarettes, they put us in the lifeboat again.

The German commander, who seemed a decent chap, gave our Captain a chart with the course to Freetown marked on it. When we sailed away the submarine crew lined the decks and gave us a hearty cheer and wished us good luck. We were thirty six hours in the boat, having travelled 120 miles before we sighted a British boat, which rescued us and landed us at a West African port." *(Border Telegraph, 4 March 1941).*

German offers of humanitarian aid changed somewhat following the 'Laconia' incident in September 1942, when several U-boats draped with Red Cross flags, and towing lifeboats as well as carrying survivors on their decks were attacked by an American bomber. This caused several casualties among the rescued survivors and damaged one of the U-boats, but even following that incident German submarine crews tended to abide by the custom of the sea to assist mariners in distress when the occasion arose

The danger from German U-boats dominated Allied shipping from the outset of the war until mid 1942, when more Allied naval escorts were deployed, with much improved weaponry and submarine detection equipment, as well as improved tactical deployment. The tide really turned in favour of the allies in April and May of 1943, when the U-boat packs suffered unsustainable losses at the hands of Allied ships and aircraft. Nonetheless it was a close run thing and Winston Churchill, the British Prime Minister later said, "…the only thing that ever frightened me during the war was the U-boat peril."

Losses among the Allied Merchant Marine and U-boat crews were huge. Allied losses were 2,200 merchant ships lost, 2,003 due to U-boat action, 100 Allied Naval Vessels and 600 RAF Coastal Command aircraft. At least 30,000 merchant seamen were killed in addition to the many hundreds of service personnel who were also lost. German submariners' losses were as grievous as those of the Allies. Of 750 U-boats which saw service in the Atlantic, 510 were lost by the end of the war, and of 27,000 U-boat men who served in them, 18,000 (2 out of 3) died in action. *(Liverpool Maritime Museum, Battle of the Atlantic Exhibition)*

An Armed Trawler, possibly HMS 'Man O' War' (FY 104), launched in 1937 and taken over by the Admiralty in August 1939. Armed with one 4 inch gun.

Chapter 5 – Ian's appointment to 'Fylingdale' and first Atlantic crossing to Canada.

The first record of Ian joining the Steam Ship 'Fylingdale', a cargo ship built in 1924, is in a letter to his Mother dated 8 July, 1940, and posted in Cardiff:-

"Cardiff G.P.O.
Mondaynite

Flash – here we are again. Sheffield 4.35. Sent wire. Gloucester train 5.20. Arrived about 10. Cardiff train 10.35. Cardiff 12, time I stated on telegram! Office just over from station. Signed book. In about 3 mins. called in. 'This is Mr. O'Conner'. The lad I had chatted to in the waiting room. He'll be about 20 no more. Had lunch with him. Back to Depot which place is pleasantly crazy. But decent guys, and things done. Ship is 'Fylingdale', a cargobote. We join her at Port Talbot tomorrow. Stay in O'C's digs the nite.

Advance reports from the Union man state the 'F' is not very big, but all rite. Probably <u>not</u> separate accommodation for us. Howeva. Very secretive - Union man says 100 to 1 it's Montreal. Keep it dark. Collected about £8 pay, from 1.6.40 – 31.6.40 (Full pay for the month's leave!). Allotment should arrive soon. The Union man took charge of my N. H. cards. He posts them to the proper authorities. Going to see play – 'The Light in Heart'. Will write tomorrow. Ian."

Ian wrote a follow up letter to the family on 9th July from the Walnut Tree Hotel in Port Talbot:-

"To continue. Had a good sleep last nite. Breakf. 5/- *(£0.25p)* for bed & b. Taxi to station. Most cars down there are gas fed. Train to P. T. *(Port Talbot)* to Shipping Office. Signed on. Down to docks in taxi. Met the ship. Oh! About 3000 tons gross. Coal was being loaded. Oh! My room hasn't the cat's swinging amenities but still, when one settles down -- tin hat & life jacket all there for me. Chatted with various mates etc. Reports state – very happy ship. Extremely nice Old Man. Good food. So I think it'll be allrite. The Union guy's tip was correct.

O'Conner's from Dublin, 22 – looks 17. Nice guy, very. Here's address – (Ship's name) c/o Headlam & Son, Ship's Owners, Whitby, Yorks.

After looking over the scow we came up to the hotel and had a huge lunch altho' it was kinda late. Welsh people are nice people. Habit of saying – 'thassrite' very hilly down thea.

Saw Cardiff Arms Park yestereve. Got nasty shock in Marconi Office yesterday – enquired about 'City of Wellington'. 'Oh yes', averred one guy, 'sunk off Finniestair.' Asked Union man. Not true. So he's alrite Pierre. Circulate my address around & pour in the mail. Postage is 2½d or maybe 3 *(about £0.01½ p)*. Enquire & see – 6 weeks maybe. Cheerio, Ian."

Whilst in Port Talbot Ian began another journal, and the dangers merchant ships faced was not always whilst they were at sea:-

"Saturday 13th July – Round about midnite, the sirens in the town let go. Klaxton croaks aft, bringing gun's crew out, as we happen to be the sole ship in the docks which is allowed to man an ack-ack weapon.

Hear planes high up. Blast on a steam siren ashore split the night. Everyone is puzzled, but I think it is an auxiliary warning for ships. I go up to the gun platform just as telephone tinkles. The Captain wants to know what the steam siren means. Gunner is unable to elucidate.

Slipped on the tin hat and meandered up to pantry. Old Man's old lady, Mrs. Butch, steward & wife, O'C and myself. More of the 'Oleander' centre castle atmosphere of jokes and high laughter. Get tired so I go back to my cabin and at 12.40 all clear screams."

At 12.30 pm on 13 July, 'Fylingdale' left Port Talbot en route for Montreal via Milford Haven and Liverpool. There she joined Convoy OB-184, and on 15 July sailed with 31 other merchant ships and 2 escorts. Danger was ever present, along with the monotony of the ship's routine. On Tuesday 16 July, Ian wrote in his journal, "Another sub warning. We're entering danger area now. Sleep with boots on. 'Arnadora Star' got hers around here" *(On 2 July, 1940, the 'Arandora Star', a passenger ship was sunk by 'U-47' about 125 miles west of the coast of Ireland, with the loss of over 800 lives. The ship was carrying German and Italian internees, and German prisoners of war and their military guards, as well as the crew) (uboat.net)*. On 17 July the 'Fellside', which had straggled from the convoy, was sunk by 'U-43' in approximately the same area with the loss of 12 crew members.

On Thursday 18 July, 1940, he wrote, "Depressed & headachy. What with reports & mal de *(a bout of sea sickness)*, life's just grand". On Friday 19 July, he logged, "Another sub report. She got a Norwegian behind us this morning *(the ship was probably the 'Gyda', carrying about 2000 tons of salt, sunk by 'U-58' northwest of Ireland. After being struck by a torpedo the ship sank within one minute with the engines still running. The Master and ten crew members were lost) (uboat.net)*. However we seem to have made half the journey". 'Fylingdale' arrived off the coast of Canada on Sunday 28 July, en route to Quebec, and Ian wrote, "And it is a good morning. Land on both bows plus sun. Fine".

That day Ian wrote home describing his first Atlantic voyage and his life on the ship. The letter also provides an insight to the need that most personnel serving away from home had for letters, newspapers and magazines providing home news. The opening greeting of his letter was unusual!:-

"St Lawrence,
28th July '40
Dearmummydaddynancymargaretandanybodyelse,

Today finds me sitting atop the wireless room, listening to Bob Crosby's band. A thoughtful former R.O. has wired up the roof for phones, and we c'n sit up in the sun and enjoy music from the set down below.

Much water has flowed under some bridge or other (and also us) since I last could write you. For fifteen days we've ploughed thro' grey water and for some of these days I've felt nostalgia badly. But that can't be helped much. So – The ship _is_ a happy one, and the Old Man's fine. The food _is_ fine, and the cabin _isn't_ too bad.

One of the first meals aboard was kinda funny. We hadn't sailed, so the various wives were still aboard. It was teatime and at the beginning there was one of those aggressive silences that demand an answer. So I barged in with some remark or other. But the conversation fainted again so I leapt forward with restoratives. The wives replied in a few well frozen words. So I held my end of the conversation up till it was practically perpendicular. The minutes passed in Indian file. The audience strummed their catarrhs. At last the party broke up, allowing me to stagger, stricken, to my cabin.

Now about this cabin. After I'd done a bit of washing up and bought a shade for the light, it wasn't too bad after all. Only when I stuck Mummy's foto up I got me thinkin'.

One night at a dance out of town, an RAF guy averred that I was me. He was a Gala chap, one of these people you know all but their name. Chatted a while to him. He was pleased to see a hometown face, such as it was. Said he'd write home and mention that he'd met IRH down in the wilds of s. Wales. I also fell in with a coupla RAF guys. One from Middlam (is that rite?), the other from Edinburgh. It's a small world or sumpn.

The trip has been uneventful, notwithstanding sub reports. For my 'two hot baths daily', I go down with my bucket to the bowels of the engine room. There, amid flashing pistons and thundering cranks, I have a very pleasant wash. It's nice'n warm too. When the 3rd Engineer is on watch he explains the workings of the engines to me, but I primarily go down for a bath!

One of the apprentices had a 21st birthday recently, an occasion celebrated by the cook baking him a cake. A most peculiar cake. It had as its main ingredients, treacle, spices, a tumbler of rum currents. Atop of it was icing and in pink shaky writing, 'Many Happy Returns'. We all had a portion, but for all the ingredients there wasn't much taste.

Once at midnite the engines broke down. It was queer, rolling gently in a swell, waves washing against the sides. In ten minutes we were ploughing on again.

As I came off watch one night, Cappy averred that I was a Narvik veteran too. Slipped him a resume. He'd been up loading one just before Norway was invaded. He was called up to London & congratulated for bringing 8 Dutch ships out of Narvik by the Admiralty recently.

He threw out an appeal for lite reading. He was delighted with the 'Strands' I gave him, largely becos there were Wodehouse yarns in them. P.G.'s his favourite author. He slipped me 13 Readers Digests in return. I supply most of the ship with lit now.

I should look up Stephen Leacock in Monty. Will have a look at McGill University. I'm going to send a wire when we get ashore, and also I'll write Bill Carroll, as I've an idea that this is the burg *(Scottish burgh town)* he came from. I'll tell him to write to the house, and you c'n forward them. I don't think we'll get any mail over here, but it'll be waiting for us when we get back. Remember the 'Telegraphs', & J.H.'s 'Lifes'.

We've just picked up the pilot, and I c'n see on the banks a lotta villages, each with its own church.

Have you spread the address round the Aunties? I'll postcard them from here. Also inform Mrs. Ballantyne, (Picture Post was to be her contribution), and get Marg. to tell Miss Whamond so that she c'n send the magazines she promised me, & Dumfries, I hope, continues the 'Strands' for me & Cappy.

Just now we're doing watches, 8am-10, 12am-4pm, 8pm-10pm, G.M.T. Canadian Summer Time is five hours forward from Britain. I don't think the exchange rate is so good as it might be out here.

Wednesday 31st July

We just got in this morning, and I'd come off watch. I was washing myself when the door was pushed against my back. Preparing to leap out & brain somebody, I was amazed & delighted to see the 3rd Mate thrust some letters into my hand. I c'd only mutter 'Gee, tanks', and feverishly tear open the missives. Seven in all. Most of them postmarked 15th or 16th July. But what I did like was the quick delivery from shore.

From my port I c'n see big CPR *(Canadian Pacific Railroad)* locos, with clanging bell and peculiar whistle. Pretty wooden houses too, in bright colours. I've intended going ashore tonite. As I put my head thro' port 3rd M. comes along says 'Keep your head in, they'll think it's a cattle boat'. He's suitably punished.

Cappy has come aboard. He says we can go ashore, only half the crew have to stay aboard. I'm <u>not</u> the crew! He's got some Canadian currency, so hi-ho. If you be interested, I'm looking bronzed & fit & well.

I can now wash a pillow slip, a necessary procedure here, as they seem to issue one set of linen for one trip. Next will be the turn of the sheet – a big job in a basin.

This really is the end now, I'm going ashore to post it. Cheerio, Ian"

On Tuesday 30 July,1940, 'Fylingdale' anchored near Quebec, where Ian learned of a particular tragedy. On Wednesday 31 July, he wrote in his journal, "Cappy tells of telegram waiting for Skipper of the 'Chelsea', *(Robert Harrison)*, which was loading next to us in Port Talbot saying his wife and kid had been killed in an air raid on Hull. 'Chelsea' is making for Monty *(Montreal)*. Tuff luck". (*Later, on 30 August 1940, 'U-32' attacked Convoy HX-66A, 58 miles west-northwest of Cape Wrath and sank the 'Chelsea'. Eleven crew members were rescued, however the Skipper, Robert Harrison, 22 crew, and a gunner were lost) (uboat.net)*.

Happier news was received on Thursday 1 August, when it was learned that the 'Fylingdale's 'Old Man', Captain Pinkney, had been awarded the O.B.E. On 27 July 'The Times' reported, "AWARDS TO MERCHANT NAVY - O.B.E. - PINKEY, Captain John Short, Master, S.S. 'Fylingdale'. When Germany invaded Norway, 'Fylingdale' and other British ships were ordered by the Admiralty to proceed to sea at once without escort. Captain Pinkney showed great enterprise, determination, and skill in guiding an unescorted convoy of about 40 ships safely through Norwegian waters".

On 2 August, Ian, O'Conner and the 3rd Mate went ashore to the Army and Navy Club, and Ian persuaded the band to play his favourite tune, 'Begin the Beguine'. They were joined by, "Three dames accompanied by mother, later joined by father", who had been at the World's Fair *(held in New York)*. About 1.30 am "Whole party of Mum & Dad & dames & us pile into Chev. *(Chevrolet motor car)* to look for eats. Find place like Sloppy Joe's. I have egg salad. Others various hamburgers. Then on down to ship. Get on board & asleep about 4".

'Fylingdale' sailed to Sorel to load with grain. Ian, O'Conner, and the Second Mate went ashore again:-

"Our last place was all French-Canadian, necessitating my remembering of such phrases as 'Combien', and 'bin est la plume de ma tante' etc. But we got by. Last nite we were ashore there. O.C., 2nd Mate & I met up with 3 dames who spoke English not so bad. We struggled away in ponderous English until I started crooning 'Frere Jaques'. 'Ah you spik French?' With an easy nonchalance I ground out 'Un peu' *(a bit)*, so for the rest of the nite they, in not so hot English, and I in worse French, chatted grimly about the weather, the town and anything else that could be translated into manageable phrases.

The doll I was with was an interpreter in a local factory, but there can't have been many English to practice on. Her Uncle, whose office we passed, was a Notaire & Advocate. His office is next to the jail! They have their hangings in public in that part of the Province. There was this dame, her sister, and a friend from Rhode Island (where the chickens come from), that latter being the best English speaker. All very Entente Cordialish."

Ian's last day ashore was Tuesday 6 August, after which 'Fylingdale' set sail for Sydney, Nova Scotia, to take on coal for the return voyage to the UK, and have its radio equipment inspected and modified. Much of Ian's time was spent on routine ship's maintenance, with lots of reading, sunbathing and listening to the BBC News to relieve the monotony.

'Fylingdale's destination was Greenock, then on to Belfast, and it set off in Convoy SC.1 with 40 other vessels on Wednesday 14 August. 'Fylingdale' was the 'guard ship' in the front line of the convoy, which meant that an 8 hour radio watch had to be kept. Much of the beginning of the voyage was uneventful, however Saturday 24 August, Ian and 'Fylingdale' would become involved in a dramatic rescue.

The Steam Ship 'S.S. Fylingdale'.

Chapter 6 - Sinking of HMS 'Penzance' and rescue of survivors

'U-37' was a Type IXA U-boat in the service of Nazi Germany's Kriegsmarine, and designed for ocean going operations. The boat was commissioned in August, 1938, under the command of Kapitanleutnant Heinrich Schuch, one of the German Navy's most experienced commanders. Initially it operated from its base in Wilhelmshaven, but with the defeat of France its base of operation moved to Lorient on the Bay of Biscay, which was more suited for operations in the Atlantic.

On 17 August, 1940, following repairs, and under the command of another experienced commander, Fregattenkapitän Victor Oehrn, 'U-37' began its seventh patrol off the coast of Ireland. On 23 August, 'U-37' sighted and sank the Norwegian steam ship 'Kernet', the British steam merchant 'Severn Leigh', and on 24 August, the British steam merchant 'Brookwood', all of which had dispersed from Convoy OA-200 on route from Britain to Canada.

At 19:05 hrs on 24 August, at a position south west of Iceland, 'U-37' reported sighting a large tanker which was part of convoy SC-1 on route from Britain to Canada. 'Fylingdale' was part of that convoy, escorted by HMS 'Penzance', a Royal Navy sloop, commanded by Commander Allan Wavish. At 19:36 hrs Oehrn logged that he could see 3 groups of ships about 1100 metres distant. About 30 were medium sized vessels with one destroyer (HMS 'Penzance') at front, but no defence at the rear. At 20:38 hrs Oehrn fired one torpedo from 380 metres, which struck HMS 'Penzance'. The German torpedo sliced the ship in half and 'Penzance' broke in two and sank quickly. Depth charges in 'Penzance's' stern section exploded, killing some of the crew who had survived the torpedo strike and who were now in the water. The explosions also caused damage to 'U-37'.

As a result of the attack on HMS 'Penzance' 90 men, including Commander Wavish, were lost. 13 survivors were picked up by 'Fylingdale' and 7 by the S.S. 'Blairmore'. 'Blairmore' was later sunk at 01:46 hrs on 25 August by 'U-37'. Five crew members were lost and the 7 survivors from 'Penzance' had to abandon ship once again. Survivors from 'Blairmore' were picked up by a Swedish merchant ship and taken to Baltimore, U.S.A.

Ian wrote a very descriptive, and sometimes harrowing, account of the aftermath of the sinking of HMS 'Penzance'. His account begins:-

"At 6.40 (18:40) *(Ian's timings are at odds with those of the U-boat Captain, possibly caused by confusion on the part of one or another over which time zone they were in)* siren croaks on bridge. Steam siren from Commodore follows. Scurrying about. Shouts. O.C. dashes in 'Got one ahead of us'. I stick on watch. Next report – it's the escort vessel. Mine seemingly. I sit. Thump shakes ship. Must be the gun. It's a lovely day with a heavy swell.

Sub all rite. Large patches of reddish colour on surface made by depth charges going up. Guns crew swing 4" round. That smell I know from Harstad, permeates cabin. Boat's crew going over side for survivors. I shiver! Good thing we had gun & boat drill today. Shouts. Cap shouts 'starboard'. His calm voice helps. 4 men & 2nd & 3rd Mate in boat. Despairing shouts of men, covered with oil some with life jackets on swimming and shouting 'help!' Wreckage drifts about. 'Come on', shout survivors. Drenched in oil. Boat pulls away. Pick up guys. We stop in case any get sucked in by the screws. The destroyer has disappeared entirely, nothing but oil & wood.

Must be a lot killed. 'Help' floats over water. Stench of oil over everything. Boat from another ship pulls towards men unable to be packed into our boat. Their cries of 'Help' aren't nice to hear. 'Full astern. Keep your eyes open for any men near the propeller'. These commands from Cap.

Still picking people up. Cries become hoarser & more despairing. A horrible scream drifts in my port. A man who shouts in an Oxford accent is clinging on a piece of wreckage. 'I can't hold on much longer'. Cap shouts 'Hold on Joe, we're coming'. His voice croaks – 'Ahhh'. A ghastly sound. 'Hard astarboard, full astern' to swing her round. A feeling of impotency sweeps over me. 'Can I help him?' Command is repeated. He's still hanging on. It's now 25 past 7. These guys have been in the oil-smeared water 45 minutes.

No more cries. The officer has been picked up. Heavy sea & choppy sea delays boat's manoeuvring. Cap says 'It's been an explosion on board'. The last survivor lets go piece of wood & is hauled aboard lifeboat. 'How many men are aboard?'

Smell of oil is sickening. Ship's bell clangs 2 bells uncontrolled. All men are now picked up. An oil soaked lifebelt floats past. A call for ropes to enable boarding is issued. 'Roll out the barrel' drifts over water. Survivors have started singing! Boat pulls alongside, 2nd Mate at tiller.

No signals on wireless. Are we in minefield? 1st Mate's face is ruddy & troubled. I put on a lifebelt rather tardily. Men are helped down to engine room for baths. We've 12 on board. But the others? One chap factitiously asks for a glass of water. Some in bad condition, others walk. All soaked in heavy brown fuel oil.

I oscillate between cabin and bridge. One lad is hurt. Hauled up with rope & laid on hatch. His face is brown (oil) & red (blood). Steward attends to him. Cuts jacket with carving knife. Poor guy shivers uncontrollably. I help to haul in boat. Then go down to engine room. Most have lain down on gratings, still shivering. I'm asked if there is a doctor on board. The surgeon is pointed out to me. He's in a bad way. I roll fags for men until baccy runs out. One guy on top of depth charge when it went up. Must've been a torpedo. I sweat oil. Rush around dispensing water & clothes. I find a ready market.

10.18 pm – Hear snatches of what happened. It <u>was</u> a torpedo. Hit her dead in the boilers.

Sunday 25th August - Capt's story – He heard the siren go & rushed on deck to see the 'Penzance' in half, bow & stern pointing to the sky. Then depth charges went up.

3rd Mate on watch – 'Penzance' was 2 cables *(approx. 400 yds.)* away on our bow. A sheet of flames spread from amidships laterally, followed by dense pall of smoke. He sounded the klaxon.

I clothe the gent who was clinging to the wood with my vest, learning that he couldn't've held on any longer as cramp was creeping up his legs.

I roll fags feverishly with my own & other people's tobacco. Funny how this morning we were bemoaning how little baccy we'd left. Now tins appear like magic. Men have given generously of their clothes. With paraffin, oil is washed off those who can have it applied. Bad burning cases among them.

I finally land in O.C.'s room where surgeon is laid on deck. He sounds pretty bad so I'm detailed to watch him all nite. So I settle down to nocturnal vigil. He's pretty bad. Shuddering screams & groans interspersed with 'Oh God', 'Jesus', 'Make them cut me up & get it over', etc., rent the almost deadly quiet now pervading the ship.

I am kept pretty well occupied. Cries for water, hot water bottles, morphia, condensed milk, pillows & washing down send me dashing about. He has lucid moments when he tells me what happened to him. He'd just turned in, shedding his jacket with £19 baccy money & £19 personal & his glasses etc. when she struck. He rushed up ladder & made a dash for the aft battery. But now ship was sinking quickly & he was trapped in a water filled battery. 'My wife will be a widow,' he thinks. By pushing against stanchions & stays he manages to get out of the trap & immediately shoots to the surface. This caused the 'bends', one of the causes of his condition. He struck out in the oil drenched sea, grabbed hold of some wreckage, to be later picked up.

Even more lurid is that tale of Thomson a sturdy lad with beautiful white teeth. He was sitting in the mess room with his mate having tea when blow fell. Vessel heeled over to starboard, bringing piles of gear down in front of door which slammed shut. Crawling from underneath a mass of bodies he saw porthole. 'Well here goes!' Managed to squeeze head & shoulders thro' remembering old adage that where a head can go, a body can also. It was not until ship lurched again that he was thrown clear thro port in water where he swam strongly. So good was he that he swam right to our ship! As he neared side he thought he'd try a stylish overhand stroke as an impressive variant to the breaststroke he says. He & Barker are the least hurt. Two nice lads.

Next comes account of Sub Lieut. Boyle. Here mention must be made of an event. Cap is introduced to him as a fellow Whitbyite & says 'Are you

Commander Boyle's son?' He is. Cap says he was thinking of the Commander that afternoon, really to wonder if he c'd tell him the procedure for going before the King!

Boyle was playing deck golf on the quarterdeck with another officer when they heard a snort. 'That must be a whale', he exclaims. 'No it's a tin fish!' he shouts when he sees it break surface 100 yds. away. 'Hard a starboard', but bridge crew just stare at him. It's too late. Ship was going too slow to swing & torpedo strikes amidships under bridge where magazine is. A sheet of flame is all he could see. Boyle is helped in the water by Barker. Before war, he was ADC to Governor of Trinidad but hostilities recalled him from the Diplomatic Service. He is washed by the Chief.

Then Sub Lieut. Langley an RNVR lad tells all. On bridge at the time, his recollections were of bridge a mass of flames so he dropped 30 feet into water. Came up to see ship towering above him, coming down, but she slips away under clear of him. He wonders if this is him so looks down for wavy RNVR braid. Not there. He's puzzled, then remembers he has on his waterproof. His shoes've been blown off. The depth charges exploding when the men were in water has caused the greatest amount of damage as instanced by the fact that a charge will destroy a sub 28' away from explosion. It's a mercy the other charges on deck were set to 'safe'.

Grim stories from the boat's crew of several heads, arms and legs floating past. I also ascertain that the red which was intermingled with oil patch was blood. Probably of stokers who were wiped out to a man. Over 90 lost including Captain. She's a sloop, not really meant for escorting but for policing in Red Sea & generally showing the flag. She's been out in the W. Indies for 18 months. This trip 5 days leave was to've been granted. Torp. came from port side on after quarter, diagonally.

One chap aboard here had been in crow's nest! Others badly burned on face & hands. Thomson, Barker, O.C. & me roll fags most of the morning. We use ½ lb of baccy & produce about 200 fags or more. Hand them out round ship to sailors.

When I go on watch at 6 there is a destroyer, the 'Highlander'! painted in very businesslike black & grey. Zig zag. A little later two more destroyers appear & take up their positions. We have signalled across to the Highlander asking if he has a doc. on board & could he slip us some cigarettes. He shoots a line with that special gun of theirs so that soon we have plenty of fags aboard. These ships must've beat it out here hell for leather & it's very comforting to have them too."

Ian's journal also narrates the story of the 'Penzance' sinking and its aftermath, including a moving account of a burial at sea. This narrative is no less descriptive and begins:-

"**Sunday 25th August** - Day of rest but not for us. As one can imagine I didn't snatch much sleep from 6.40 onwards. Attend to my patients in O.C.'s room. An AB *(Able Seaman)*, Mumford, has been brought in and laid on the settee. His requests are varied – from cow's milk to cocoa, from water to scrambled eggs. He gets them all. Doc gets more morphia as spasms come on again. He diagnoses cases brought before him from his bunk, asks questions & advises.

The arrival of the escort cheers considerably. About teatime the 'Highlander' drops depth charges which shakes us up. Still no word of the 'Blairmore' which with us picked up survivors. An explosion was reported last night by some & it is feared that she's been potted. Glasgow ship. We have disobeyed orders by stopping to pick up these men & Cap'll probably have to answer for it. But I'd rather have taken a chance in getting these guys aboard than beating it, because the rear ships of convoy would've been too late. We must've been directly above the sub. I drift round hearing vignettes of life just before the knife & what various chaps' plans for leave etc. Dry notes on radiator.

Monday 26th August - 'Harstad' anniversary again. A busy day of attending to patients. Get up after solid 12 hours sleep. Doc has been bathed, this operation bringing his hair into its true colour – red. Much washing has been done of clothes used by survivors & they look quite presentable in their borrowed rig. In the afternoon preparations are made for firing a line across to the Commodore to facilitate the officers' statement to be given to the Admiral, but he semaphores that he'll get it at Greenock.

Butch fires at what he thinks is a mine but which turns out to be a float. Submarine positions continue to pile up as also messages of sinkings. It's thought that the 'Blairmore' has beat it for the nearest port. There are now 36 ships in the convoy. We started out 40.

We drop out of line & stop to enable doctor from destroyer to come on board by boat. Reports say 2 serious cases – Paymaster & Mumford, internal injuries, others not so bad. Also serious cases are Alexander, who's badly burned & sustained broken leg & Doc. The doctor is staying on board. O.C. & I listen to Radio Eirean. I optimistically do some ironing and get to bed at 12.20.

Tuesday 27th August - Wakened by O.C. for breakfast. Tells me that the Paymaster, McDonald *(Sub-Lieut. Roderick Alan Stuart MacDonald, aged 27 yrs. from Virginia Water, Surrey)* died last night at 7.30. He like the others, was given morphia as soon as the Doctor came on board. He passed out unconscious. Munford has the same symptoms so he's not to be told of the death. Preparations go ahead for burial. Canvass bag is sown, & fire bar wrapped up. A Union Jack was sent over from the destroyer.

We all dress in uniform. At 11:30 I help carry the stretcher down to deck & place it on the plank where it's draped with the flag.

Lieut. Boyle reads the service & eyes smart and swallowing of hard lump start. 'In the midst of life we are in death. Man hath only a short time to live', and other phrases sound over the deck silent but for the throb of the engines. Furtive dabbing at eyes shows how deeply we are all moved by the passing of a man whom we never knew, and who is now to be slipped away. My only dealing with him was to give him some morphia to drink the first night. But the combination of fuel oil and internal injuries caused by the depth charges proved too much. At the finish of the Lord's Prayer the plank is tipped ready. The telegraph rings on the bridge to stop engines & now everything is silent. Just before 'and now we commit his body to the deep, to turn to corruption', the body moves forward, as if impatient of leaving this world. When the phrase is completed the Lieut. gives the sign for the plank to be tilted, the flag is removed, & the canvas sack slips over to fall with a light splash into the almost calm sea. Captain gives the signal to 3rd Mate on the bridge who blows 3 blasts on his whistle to conclude the service. We drift off, muttering totally irrelevant small talk, trying to forget this thing.

Soon an RAF flying boat circles overhead & we have yet another guard. The Red Ensign is raised once again to the top of the gaff and life proceeds again aboard.

At 12:30 I'm shaken by the sound of the Klaxon again. O.C. dashes in again & grabs the phones, allowing me to slither out to see 'what's to do'. On port bow I see something like a whale spouting water, but Cap. has thought it was a sub. His orders are shouted thro' the telephone to the gun platform, 'Range 400 fire'.

After a slight pause, while the gun layer waits for the target to swim into his sights, the 4" booms out to be followed by a burst of yellow smoke 200 yds. over the target. 'Down 200, fire!' Next shot is nearer, and 3rd shot nearer still. 'Cease fire'. Boyle semaphores across to Commodore 'target we fired at was whale'. Reply – 'Well done'. We retort – 'Thankyou'.

In afternoon watch I get an SOS from 'EVA', a Norwegian formally in our convoy, but who has now been torpedoed ahead of us in 57dg 48 mins & 11dg 50 mins W. Semaphore this to Commodore, as we are the only ship keeping watch on this period." *(The 'Eva', carrying lumber, left Sydney with Convoy SC.1, but straggled due to unsuitable coal. 'Eva' was only able to do 6 knots and was sailing alone when she was sunk by 'U-28' about 60 miles east of Rockall. One crewman was lost, but the survivors made landfall on the Isle of Barra. A Finnish ship, the 'Elle' was also lost from the convoy after being torpedoed by 'U-101'. All the crew survived and were picked up by HMS 'Leith') (uboat.net).*

My patient the doc got up today. Two destroyers have gone to deal with the sub. The remainder of this eventful day is without incident. At nite I help to flash alter course signal to the Drakepool. Turn in at 10.

Wednesday 28th August - Rose late & pottered around till dinner. In the afternoon watch at 3.40 I felt a thud shake the ship. One of the destroyers had dropped a depth charge. Steam whistles blew telling the convoy to execute the emergency turn. 2nd Mate wound the Klaxon, bringing the gun's crew out to man the 4"

Most of the afternoon we've run into big patches of oil. Reports tell of wreckage & a lifebuoy floating past, also white woodwork such as a neutral bridge might have been painted. The escort vessels dart about, converging at the rear of the convoy, but nothing more happens. We're due in Belfast tomorrow nite, so roll on Belfast Lough. When I think of the mail waiting for me - !

Thursday 29th August - Rise late once more. Have bath. Land on either bow - good. On entering the Channel, the convoy forms up in line astern because of mines. Heavy BBC interference enables us to enjoy music while keeping watch. I help Thomson the Yeoman of Signals survivor to try to contact one of the destroyer escorts to relay a message to Commodore asking if we may break convoy to proceed independently to Belfast as we have a dangerously sick survivor in need of urgent hospital attention.

We are unable to reach the vessel by either lamp or semaphore so eventually we break off to be followed by destroyer whose Captain tells us to go into Belfast. We see a group of merchant seamen on her decks, survivors from some neutral vessel, mebbe the 'Eva'. So we groan along at 3 knots, and incidentally keep continuous watch, messages from which are chiefly air raid warnings (Blue). Due in around 6."

On Friday 30 August, the survivors from 'Penzance' left 'Fylingdale' to receive treatment for their injuries. Ian wrote:-

"We dropped the hook & waited. Alongside was a Russian ship with the hammer & sickle at the rt hand corner. Soon the 'Albert Faroult', ex Le Harve, comes alongside skippered by an RNVR Sub-Lieut. Arrangements are made to transfer the survivors. First Mumford, delirious & not expected to survive, is handed across the planks. Then Alexander, the cheery Leading seaman with the classical features. Next Brooks of the burnt face, now septic and puffy, and Crofts, the irrepressible one, who cracked jokes at most unamusing times. F'r instance when Cap was bathing his face he quips "- Mother'll say – 'what? Been fighting again?' Doc is wearing McDonald's pants.

The officers & other now fit 'Pirates of Penzance' shake hands all round & thank us warmly. As the 'Albert' pulls away, Boyle calls for 3 cheers for us, & Cap. asks us to slip them (hip 2 & hooray) 3 in reply. So there they go waving mightily, after almost a week since the catastrophe. The ship seems empty & quiet without them now, these brave men whose duty it was to protect us, but fate had reversed the order."

At the next meal time the sinking of HMS 'Penzance' is the topic of conversation. On 30 August, Ian wrote in his journal, "Stories of survivors are still told. How the E.R.A. *(Engine Room Artificer)* in the water looked up to see two depth charges secured by twine over his head, thought, 'well I'll have to go now'. How others, exhausted, found new hope & strength from nearby pals shouts not to give up. How Barker was smacked on the head by the ship's hull as she heeled over. How, when one saw the track of the torpedo, thought 'How unfair, when all aboard are due leave'. How most of them when the depth charge went, thought, 'So this is the end'. Hundreds of accounts, too many to chronicle. Cap's succinct statement, 'the blood of Nelson must still flow in these men's blood', aptly sums up the whole affair."

In the same journal entry Ian wrote, it seems with some pride, "And so, at the middle of this book is the finish of the first trip I make on the 'Fylingdale', a ship that has given Adolf quite a few headaches so far. I hope we exist long enough to give him some more". That same day he learns that 'Oleander' was scuttled in Harstad after her oil had been offloaded onto another ship.

The German Kriegsmarine was the enemy, but there can be no doubting the courage of submarine crews, nor can the dangers they faced be underestimated. Victor Oehrn was one of its most experienced U-boat Commanders, having enlisted in 1927, and after service on light cruisers, joined the U-boat arm of the service in 1935.

Following the sinking of HMS 'Penzance' Oehrn logged that he was planning to attack other vessels, however an explosion nearby forced him to dive to 30 metres, and also to avoid any overhead aircraft. Suddenly a large explosion, probably from one of 'Penzance's' depth charges, damaged 'U-37', causing a sudden loss of electricity and water to enter the boat. 'U-37' also suffered a loss of some instrumentation, and its rudder jammed at an angle of 25 degrees down. Due to the damage, Oehrn decided that any further attacks would be made at night.

Oehrn recorded the following entries in the log book of 'U-37' relating the sinking of HMS 'Penzance'. It provides some insight into the tension felt by him and his crew during the action and immediately afterwards:-

"16.00 - Large tanker in sight to starboard, coming on very quickly. Position 40. Boat *(U-37)* has difficulty staying on edge of line of vision. To port, several smoke clouds. Boat *(U-37)* must dive. Convoy to port in very sharp formation, letting us approach from the front without difficulty. 3 columns at intervals of approx. 1000m. Some 30 medium-sized ships, just the odd one or two around 8000 tons

In front, is a destroyer, otherwise nothing else to be seen on watch. Convoy steers 90 degrees, then 40 degrees. Boat *(U-37)* directly in front and sails as planned between the middle and left hand columns. Destroyer sails middle and short runs, back and fore, changing position, turns several times straight onto me, then stays in position 0, 6-800 metres away and turns a little.

Seconds of tense anticipation. Will he turn again, will he yaw *(move slightly to the side of its intended direction)*, has he seen me? I am clear to fire and dive deep. His distance away from us gets greater. Fire from 300m. Hit in the rear third. He breaks up completely and sinks more quickly than the smoke cloud disappears. The delight in the boat is spontaneous. I almost have to push them about to bring back order.

Then I up periscope and see that the boat *(U-37)* is positioned well between the columns. The first ship is in position 60-70, about 1200m away. I am looking out the best and most favourable when there is a really loud explosion nearby. I look around....nothing. I think that it was a depth charge on the deck of the destroyer exploding. No danger for our boat.

Then I decide, at least briefly, to go down to 30m. Though improbable, it could be an aerial bomb. 25m. I go down below and just arrive when there is cracking and splintering all around. The light goes partly out. In the control room water hisses and spurts out. The boat *(U-37)* lists forward. The tower crew come down and report that water is coming in. Might be no longer watertight. As a precaution the tower should be abandoned. All pressure gauges and instrument dials fail except the deep pressure gauge and the Papenberg-instrument in the control room.

The forward depth-rudder jams hard down. 25 degree list. The noise from the spurting water is such that we have to shout loudly. Our ears notice no rise in pressure. There are no reports of water breaking in. In these seconds my whole body tightens up; the awareness that, in the next moments quick decisions will be necessary hits me hard.

I stand in the control room and try to form a picture. Each man stands at his place, stands firm and stays at his post and says nothing. 'All clear!' announcements come from bow and stern. If, up until now the crew has had to rely on me, now I have had to rely on them

Gradually the spray and hissing die down. The boat pulls itself together. Peace and quiet reign. The hit was not as severe as that from the aerial bombs north of Scotland, but in the boat the effects from shattered glass and broken instruments are greater. For me, the greatest impression is that of the comportment of my crew. I can only describe them as courageous—and none lost his sense of fun. Perhaps they were aerial bombs. Meanwhile, while the convoy sails on over us, the boat will be brought back to order."

Following the attack on the 'Penzance', Oehrn detailed the damage done to his boat. The forward torpedo tubes were damaged and full of water; half of the compressed air system and half of the battery cells were out of action making an emergency dive impossible; the forward rudder was jammed; several gauges were out of action and a third of the lighting was out. 'U-37' lay on the bottom to avoid detection by any other escort craft, and after hearing the convoy move on, despite the damage, Victor Oehrn decided to follow the convoy in the hope of mounting a night attack using 'U-37's rear tubes. Oehrn fired the last of 'U-37's rear tube torpedoes at an unidentified tanker, but missed. However Oehrn was not finished and about 22:30 hrs on 25 August, on route to Lorient, 'U-37' sighted the British steam merchant 'Yewcrest'. Oehrn decided on a surface attack using 'U-37's deck gun. 'Yewcrest' returned fire from her on-board gun, however after an exchange, 'U-37' scored a hit between 'Yewcrest's funnel and crane. 'U-37' scored more hits on the steamer and the crew abandoned ship. One crew member from 'Yewcrest' was lost, but the remainder were later rescued by the destroyer, HMS 'Highlander'.

Despite the successful attack on the 'Yewcrest', 'U-37' was so badly damaged that Oehrn was forced to abandon the remainder of his mission and return to dock in Lorient. 'U-37' was thereafter withdrawn from front line service and assigned to training units until the end of the war. It was eventually scuttled in Sonderburg Bay off the coast of Denmark, on 8 May, 1945.

In November 1941, Oehrn was appointed to command the Mediterranean U-boats, but in July 1942, he was severely wounded and captured. He survived his wounds and returned to Germany in October, 1943, after being released as part of a prisoner exchange. He spent the remainder of the war undertaking a number of staff appointments and was awarded the Knight's Cross, the highest made by Nazi Germany during World War 2, to recognise extreme battlefield bravery or outstanding military leadership. He died in Bonn in 1997 at the age of 90.

On 31st August, 1940, Ian sent a telegram from Belfast to Galashiels saying, "Arrived after thrilling crossing. May get home shortly. Ian". Ian's greatest delight on reaching Belfast was the mail waiting for him from home. The joy of receiving those letters comes through in a letter to home:-

"Belfast
3rd September
Dear All.

If the impossible could happen: that I should have a surfeit of mail, then I'm bowed down now. I jumped about the deck as we moved in, in a frenzy of impatience, then when all seemed lost I lurched into the saloon and there they were dishing it out. 2nd Mate got tired of calling out the name on the envelopes so he just said 'You'd better take the lot. I did, and spent the next coupla hours reading & rereading.

Among them was one from Peter. He didn't say anything about his ship being torpedoed but in a letter from Alma, she mentions that 'it was pierced by a German arrow'. He had 4 day's leave and is now away on a 12,000 tonner.

For obvious reasons I'm not going to say anything about the trip, except that it wasn't too healthy.

First day ashore here I met George Wright, a lad who was at college with us, and as he's to be here a while as well, we knock about together. I think everything has arrived – the Telegraph, sweets, Lifes, & cigs. from Mrs. Bally., the latter also from Mr. Hodge. For all this, my friends, I thank you one and two.

FLASH – 2nd Mate has just flung 2 letters at me. Time 11.40. Hoora. Time off to read them; they're from Daddy & Marg. First answer – No. I've plenty of cash 'nk you. Also 'nk Mr. Hodge for same. 2nd – I'll probably bus out down to Carrickfergus this aft. or so. It's well down the Lough from Belfast. 3rd – I'll try & go up & see her (Mrs. Hunter) sometime. 4th – I hope to get home from where I originally started from P.T. *(Port Talbot, Wales).*

That's all folks, see you soon, Ian"

On Thursday 12 September 'Fylingdale' docked at Swansea and Ian left for some well earned leave at home.

HMS 'Penzance'.

German U-boat – 'U-37'.
(Photograph by kind permission of Deutsches U-boot Museum)

German U-boat – 'U-37'.

Oehrn (on upper left of picture) with crew of 'U-37'.
(Photographs by kind permission of Deutsches U-boot Museum)

Crew of HMS 'Penzance' *(uboat.net)*
* indicates those logged by Ian as being picked up by 'Fylingdale'

* **Alexander, W.A., RN, Leading Seaman**
Allen, Charles A., RN,23, Leading Signalman
Ansell, Frank Charles, RN, 23, Stoker 1st Class
Barber, Frederick Corris, RN, Steward
* **Barker, J.R.H., RN, Leading Seaman**
* **Boyle, D.G., RN, Sub-Lieutenant (Rtd)**
Brinston, Douglas Vernon, RN, 19, Able Seaman
Brookes, E.R., RN, Able Seaman
Brundell, Reginald William, RN, 20, Telegraphist
Budd, Albert William, RN, 28, Leading Telegraphist
Buddery, J.B., RN, Chief Engine Room Artificer
Butler, Joseph, RN, 23, Able Seaman
Byrne, Michael, RNR, 42, Stoker
Carter, Albert Edward, RN, 27, Able Seaman
Cock, James Francis, RN, Petty Officer Supply
Coles, Ernest Frederick, RN, Petty Officer
Collins, Leslie James, RN, 30, Leading Seaman
Cook, Charles George, RN, Leading Stoker
Court, George Albert Edward, RN, 32, Petty Officer Stoker
Courtney, George Chesney, RNR, 35, Lieutenant
Cowling, Joseph, RN, 21, Stoker 2nd Class
Crane, John William, RN, 19, Able Seaman
Croft, W.E., RN, Able Seaman
Denham, John William, RN, 34, Leading Steward
Draisey, John W., RN, Lieutenant
Elliott, Richard, RN, 34, Petty Officer Stoker
Friend, Arthur Cyril, RN, 31, Engine Room Artificer 2nd Class
Galton, Jack Valentine, RN, Leading Seaman
Gaughran, Cyril Thomas, RN, 40, Commissioned Engineer
Grimes, Francis Vivian, RN, 22, Ordinary Seaman
Harrington, Thomas, RN, Stoker 1st Class
Harvey, Robert Charles, RN, 36, Petty Officer Stoker
Hatch, Edward, RN, 23, Stoker 1st Class
Henderson, Gilbert, RN, 21, Able Seaman
Hepburn, Thomas Joseph, RNVR, 22, Engine Room Artificer 4th Class
Hines, George Arthur, RN, Stoker 1st Class
Horrocks, Alfred George, NAAFI, Canteen Manager
Howard, Bertie Victor Percy, RN, 28, Stoker 1st Class
Hughes, J.F., RN, Surgeon-Lieutenant
Hurt, Frederick Gordon, RN, 28, Gunner
Hutchinson, John, RN, 26, Leading Cook (S)
Hyde, John, RN , Leading Seaman

Jacobs, William Ronald George, RN, Able Seaman
James, Geoffrey Arthur Westwood, RN, Able Seaman
Jolliffe, Wilfred Crayden, RN, 29, Able Seaman
Kenworthy, Ernest, RN, 20, Stoker 1st Class
Kitching, Wilfred Francis, RN, 28, Leading Sick Berth Attendant
* Langley, J.F.T., RNVR, Sub-Lieutenant
Lawrence, Everett Agustus, RN, 19, Stoker 1st Class
Layland, Dennis, RN, 20, Able Seaman
Litt, Alfred William, RN, Stoker 1st Class
* Macdonald, Roderick Alan Stuart, RNVR, 27, Sub-Lieutenant (S)
Macpherson, Douglas Ian, RN, 21, Able Seaman
Marklew, Edward, RN, Stoker 1st Class
Marshall, Frederick Maurice, RN, Signalman
Martin, Kenneth, RN, 19, Telegraphist
McGahey, John Arnold, RN, 24, Supply Assistant
Medforth, Walter, RN, 34, Petty Officer Stoker
Mensforth, George Browell, RN, 21, Able Seaman
Mercer, Philip Augustus, RN, Stoker 1st Class
Mirrlees, Henry, RN, Assistant Cook (O)
Misson, Frederick Henry, RN, 38, Chief Stoker
Moon, William Frederick, RN, 34, Petty Officer Stoker
Morgan, Albert, RN, 37, Able Seaman
Morrison, John, RN, Stoker 1st Class
* Mumford, P.J., RN, Able Seaman
Murphy, John James, RN, Stoker 2nd Class
Nankivell, William Eddie John, RN, 28, Petty Officer Telegraphist
Newell, William, RN, Stoker 2nd Class
Nicol, Charles Forbes Alexander, RN, 30 Able Seaman
Noble, Frederick, RN, Stoker 1st Class
Norman, Stanley Arthur Thomas, RN, Able Seaman
Peckford, Francis Charles Roy, RN, 20, Ordinary Seaman
Percy, Maxwell Claude, RN, 20, Stoker 1st Class
Ricketts, George, RN, 39, Leading Cook (O)
Roberts, Sydney Charles, RN, Stoker 1st Class
Sage, Reginald George, RN, 22, Stoker 1st Class
Seeds, James, RN, 25, Leading Stoker
Sewell, Richard Edward, RN, 39, Chief Petty Officer Writer
Shepherd, Kenneth, RN, Able Seaman
Simpson, Sidney Herbert, RN, 41, Stoker 1st Class
Sims, Nelson William, RN, Able Seaman
Slade, Frederick Alfred, RN, 34, Petty Officer
Smart, Joseph Henry, RN, Engine Room Artificer 3rd Class
Smart, William Henry, RN, 20, Able Seaman

Smith, N.H., RN, Leading Stoker
Smyth, John Herbert, RN, 32, Lieutenant
Snoad, Alfred Lawrence, RN, Leading Seaman
Spooner, Frederick James, RN, 35, Petty Officer Stoker
* **Thompson, K.W., RN, Leading Signalman**
Tompsett, Cyril Jack, RN, Petty Officer Stoker
Trent, Frederick William Harry, RN, 40, Leading Stoker
Trevethan, Claude William, RN, Cook (S)
Vallis, Sidney Herbert, RN, 28, Steward
Van Tromp, William Alfred, RN, 41, Shipwright 1st Class
Veal, Oliver William, RN, Able Seaman
Ward, Ralph William, RN, 20, Stoker 1st Class
Watson, Arthur Charles, RN, 37, Chief Engine Room Artificer
Wavish, Allan John, RN, 43, Commander
Webster, Reuben, RN , 33, Petty Officer Stoker
Windsor, Alfred Leonard, RN, Leading Stoker
Wood, James Henry, RN, 35, Joiner 1st Class
Yates, William Arthur, RN, 19, Able Seaman

Chapter 7 - Second crossing of Atlantic to Sorel, Canada - near hit from German bomber.

At the end of his leave Ian returned to re-join 'Fylingdale' in Swansea. On 21 September, 1940, he stayed overnight at a hotel in Crewe. In a letter he complained of overcharging and having to pay 11 shillings and sixpence *(£0.57p)* for accommodation, 4 shillings *(£0.20)* for breakfast, and a service charge of 1 shilling and 6 pence *(£0.07 ½)*. Ian said, "This is exorbitant & there should be a law about it".

About that time a Galashiels mother received word of her son, captured by the Germans in France. The Border Telegraph carried the following article:-

"PRISONER OF WAR WRITES HOME – Mrs. George Kennedy, 64 Overhaugh Street, Galashiels, has received a post card from her son, Pte. Hunter A. Turner Kennedy, R.A.M.C., who is a prisoner of war in Germany, informing her that he is quite well. Needless to say, Mrs. Kennedy was delighted to have this communication from her son and know that he is well. Pte Kennedy, who was previously reported missing and later officially stated to be a prisoner in Germany, joined up in November and went to France in January. At the time of his enlistment he was in business as a baker and confectioner in Overhaugh Street." *(Border Telegraph, 10 September, 1940)*. Hunter returned to Galashiels' and became one of its personalities as well as continuing to be a well respected baker and confectioner.

Ian boarded 'Fylingdale' on Sunday 22 September, where a letter of appreciation was received from the father and sister of Sub-Lieut. MacDonald. He had survived the sinking of HMS 'Penzance', but died of his injuries on board the 'Fylingdale' and was buried at sea.

On Thursday 24 September, 1940, 'Fylingdale' set off on a voyage to Canada via Milford Haven loaded with Welsh anthracite. She joined Convoy OB.220 with 31 other merchant ships and 5 escorts. As Ian settled into the ship's routine he wrote in his journal:-

"**Fri 27** *(September, 1940)* - Day starts off with report of sinking. As usual main items are sub posns. & warnings. At dinner I query re survivors *(from HMS 'Penzance')* – learn that doctor is at sea again, didn't get his 14 days leave he yammered about. Boyle, Cappy saw in Whitby often, received a silver match box from Langley, had letters from McDonald's father & sister. He went out very bravely. No fuss.

At tea, spirited argument as to advisability of going to bed with or without clothes, in present circumstances. Learn that blankets & brandy have been put in the lifeboat. When I come off at 9, I'm struck more than ever by the immensity of the task of keeping position in darkness with no lights, high wind, rough sea, zig sagging.

Sat 28 – Wake up with bloodshot eye. During day see wreckage floating past …. Dance music is played to me during watch, the Beguine looming large. This is a good thing. Hear Kenway & Young at nite.

We have now entered the Valley of the Shadow i.e. the danger zone. She bounces about a bit now as the Atlantic in encompassed. We're still too far back from our position in the front line for everybody's liking. Sore throat".

Submarines were not the only hazard faced by merchant ships on the dangerous Atlantic voyages. Many ships were several years old and prone to technical and mechanical difficulties. 'Fylingdale' had been built in 1924 and was propelled by steam engines, as opposed to diesel fuel in more modern ships. Its top speed was only 11 knots per hour, and as a result it had to join slow or 'SC' convoys made up of ships with a similar or poorer performance. It was these convoys which suffered most at the hands of the U-boat packs.

The severe weather, which the Atlantic could hurl at ships crossing it, was another. Thoughts of being sunk by a U-boat and having to take to the Atlantic in an open boat, and in rough weather, were never far from the minds of a ship's crew, thoughts reflected in Ian's journal:-

Sun 29 - We have fallen far behind the convoy owing to coal difficulties. On 24 hour watches while on our own. Depth charges blow off in the morning – 6 of them, flung by trawler. This seemingly inspires firemen to new efforts, for we forge ahead much faster! We are making for a point where we hope the convoy'll be in the morning. In the evening, with the convoy still on the horizon, the destroyer comes down & shouts – 'You must try to get up into position before dark.' We signal that we've been hindered by coal worries, but are doing better now. The cocky signaller aboard acknowledges receipt of each word before 2nd has spelt it out. Then, astern of us, she winks back – Drive on Steve! – a little joke much appreciated, for it breaks the tension of a rather trying day. Good old 'Vanquisher' *(HMS 'Vanquisher' a Type D-24 destroyer).*

Mon 30 - Curry & rice today! Still on 24 hour watch, but we catch up the convoy at 4 o'clock much to everybody's relief. Back to 8 hour shift. Two reports of bombing & machine gunning in the Atlantic today, together with usual sinkings. Cappy still tells funny stories.

Tues 1 - Oct. Awakened by 2nd's shout of – 'A ship's been torpedoed' – I look out of port, to see pall of grey smoke on horizon. Later in morning, position of sub is given where smoke was. – another gone. Tanker probably, by smoke. Escort go to see & don't come back. I take a 42 & a 92 Group message – both to decode! In the evening, sloop appears on horizon signalling desperately to Commodore who doesn't see him. We do, and tell him of the sloop's appearance. She then gets message off her chest and hops off.

Little later flags go up – cancel dispersal. We rejoice, as this'll mean no 24 hour watch, but hopes are rudely dashed, as dispersal takes place under cover of darkness. Too bad.

Wed 2nd – Ship alongside us in convoy got hers this afternoon 'Kayeson' *(Kayeson was steam ship carrying general cargo and coal. It was unescorted when it was sunk by 'U-32', on 2 October, about 500 miles west of Ireland. The crew abandoned the ship in lifeboats, but were lost) (uboat.net).* Weather gets tough. Wind pipes. Just nice for open boat. Lotta SOS's.

Thurs 3rd – A snorker of a wind today & plenty of waves, making the old can jump about. But do I mind? No! Took photos in afternoon. Going to cut Great Circle Track *(the shortest distance on the surface of the Earth between the ship's departure point and its destination)* tonite so beware the Ides of March. Subs abound thea. A beautiful nite for a row. Rain, high wind, big waves. Yum yum. These continuous watches become rather irksome.

Frid 4 – Cap slips in to enquire after the supply of lite lit *(reading material)*. I make up an assorted bundle including Winsom Winnie which he devours. We're now trying 4 on, 4 off watches. Up to date I've made 15/- *(£0.75p)*.

Interesting post script to 'Chelsea' skipper – killed by explosion of torpedo on way home after announcing that he didn't care what happened to his wife 'n kid" *(see entry 31st July, 1940).*

Sat 5 – Sleep from 12 till 4. Now in Great Silent Zone – no sigs. Have bath – the benison of hot water! Also my weekly shower. Dobey a little in afternoon. Large tot, in fact two tots at nite, first this trip; other times I've been on watch. Learn about Free Masons – 'you always have a job' etc. This sounds a good thing. Where's the catch? Today I realise that I welcome the not-too-violent rolling & heaving of the ship. My sea legs must've matured at last. Supping soup slopping in plate is a sight not now sick-making. One gets used to everything in time, doesn't one? Leaning over at a 60 degree angle on the bridge I chat britely about sea lore. Ha ha.

Sun 6 – Gale increases in fury, whipping up 40 foot waves, but ship rides well. Just right length I'm told, & doesn't get too far into them. I now roll nautically (very) on the bridge & eat large dinners while canted at 45 degrees. Hot dog. Soon I shall be able to spit out of the side of my mouth. But we do only 3 knots because of seas. Notice a BTC *(British Tanker Company)* ship 'British General' got hers today; if sea at 24 degrees W is same as out here at 38 degrees or so, God help 'em. We was lucky." *(At 18:55 hrs on 6 October, 1940, the British General, which had dispersed from Convoy OA-222, was sunk by 'U-37' about 550 miles west of Ireland. The master and 46 crew members were lost. 'U-37' was the same U-boat which had sunk HMS 'Penzance' on 24 August, 1940, some of whose survivors were rescued by 'Fylingdale') (uboat.net).*

Mon 7 – Weather continues – 3.3 knots. 80 miles today! Today she's rolling more than usual. Puzzle – do I need more than 4 hours sleep? And it is cold! 40 – 60 foot waves today. I retire about 7 as usual leaving note for 3rd to waken me at 8. But he doesn't see it so O'C decides to let me sleep on. I get up there at 12 and put in 8 hours solid!

Tues 8 – Much calmer today, but fog springs up for a little in aft. A msg from ship being pursued by unknown vessel. Raider!

Wed 9 – We go along very smoothly now & are due in Belle Isle Straits at 8.15 tonite. The 4 hours sleep, plus cat naps throughout the day when off watch, have turned out to be quite sufficient. My trouble has surely been oversleeping! For luxurious cabins with H as well as C we stick a steam pipe into a bucket of water & lo! In a few minutes there appears hot water. Very tasty. Take Ice Report from Belle Isle, noticing a chill as we forge on. Ice in neighbourhood. The stove in messroom is now alight giving out a cheery heat & blaze to which I'm drawn in aft. At nite take photos of nap school in progress & lose 1/- *(£0.05p)* in that silly game, pontoon. Very cold on watch till 12.

Thurs 10 – Up brite 'n early to observe sunrise (& also to go on watch) above Belle Isle. See ice. Listen to Maritimes on watch. Serials. An ordinary 8 hour day now to Quebec. We bowl along merrily – no blackout. Have huge tea of curried salmon 'n chips, chutney & beetroot. Cor! Nap 'n pontoon still flourish.

Fri 11 – I open one of the envelopes from Doc. Lang & find on the Card'stack – 'To introduce & commend to you Ian W., a wireless operator. He is a young member of my church & the son of one of my best Elders.' Hot dog!

Sat 12 – Belching up the smooth waters of the St Lawrence, running into fog in the aft. Pick up Pilot at Father Point *(Point-de-Père),* learn that Monday is a holiday – no work.

Sun 13 – Drive on thro' heavy rain all day. Pass the Montgomery Falls – highest in N. America, to get alongside at 3 o'clock. Sparse mail – Margaret & Lazell, postmarked 20th & 22nd Sept. More later I suppose. Write passes – have tea – get $5.90 ashore with O'C. Up to Hts. of Abraham & barge around. Have malted milk shake, dames – Joe's Place – supper in the Old Homestead Resus. Walk back after having failed to make a taxi driver understand where to go, largely owing to the fact that we didn't know.

Town v. quiet, but Thanksgiving Day tomorrow. We're near a huge silo. Work of unloading starts at 7, goes on till 12."

On Tuesday 15 October, 1940, 'Fylingdale' moved on to Sorel, near Montreal, to pick up a cargo, and sailed for the UK via Sydney, Nova Scotia. Ian's journal entries continued:-

Fri 18 *(October, 1940)* – Gets very cold. Snow. Wind. Rough sea. Cold (mine) is worse so I get 3 aspirins & bottle of cough mixture from Wilf. Wrap up and turn in.

Sat 19 – Rough today. Retract statement re sea legs! Miserable. I improve a little at nite. Write a letter. Listen to Wilf. Bed.

Sun 20 – Hear of big total of sinkings last week. Also of subs out here. Good program at nite. Charlie McCarthy with E. Flynn & R Gardiner, Jack Benny, Walt Winchell."

Ian also described how cold it was. "Did I mention it was cold? It's been so cold that when we talked, the words came out of our mouths in pieces of ice, and we had to fry them to see what we were chatting about. Normal garb – vest, shirt, 2 pullovers, scarf and jacket, plus mitts & helmet worn on top of the head. Steam heaters full on & ports closed! To get hot water for washing we take our bucket of water to bathroom and put steam thro' it. Water scalding hot in about 3 minutes. Very tasty".

'Fylingdale' docked in Sydney on 21 October. At 1 pm on 24 October, loaded 6,200 tons of grain, she steamed homewards as part of Convoy SC.9 with 31 other merchant ships and 8 Navy escorts. Ian continued his journal entries in which he describes a period of duty on the bridge in the teeth of an Atlantic gale:-

"Thurs 24 *(October, 1940)* - Cap & O'C go ashore for conference. I clean up cabin. Leave at 1 for Milford. Amen for orders. In front line starboard of Commodore. On watch, smell of paint is very trying. Black out to be strict. If light shows orders are to call up & if no answer, fire on it. Signal to 'Cranford Chine' who has her navigation lights on!

Fri 25 – A Greek, the 'Liley' starts sending to Commodore that she has a broken legged man aboard & must go back to Sydney. This orgy of sending goes on for a while until 'Deptford' goes down beside her. Later, I think, she turns back for Sydney.

Sat 26 – Emergency turn executed, & after this, Commodore Aldis's across to us – Cease W/T watch except for 'Rugby' *(Rugby Radio Station was located near the village of Hillmorton, near Rugby. It was used by the British Government in World War II to provide worldwide radio coverage to Allied ships and submarines).* Hot dog! We must have been oscillating or sumpin. So long days stretch ahead of nuthin to do. Well well.

Sun 27 – Waken up at some ghastly hour with sheets *(of rain or sea water)* on deck as usual. I don my waterproof on its maiden voyage to savour the delight of being on the bridge of a tramp in an Atlantic gale. Rain beats on the old face, almost embedding itself in it. Cheeks are whipped to a ruddy glow. Oh! Pretend to help with flags up top. Gorsh. Wind tears at you, rain screams into you. The hooks joining the flags break & 2 flags are left hanging at end of jumper stay *(a stay or tackle set up especially in heavy weather to* *prevent a ship's yardarm or boom from jumping).* Tiny, clinging to mast is hoisted up to top of where he reaches out to grab recalcitrant streamers. He is rewarded with a drink. All this was done while the ship rolled & bucketed. Very nice. I help in pulling halliards" *(a line or rope used to hoist a sail, flag, or the yardarm of a ship).* Ian then describes going to the engine room, "....down to the bowels. Am taken thro' to stoke hold. Then to 'tunnel' where screw shaft goes thro'. An unenviable place to be around in when fish *(torpedoes)* get at you. The engineers, they are the tuff lads.

Mon 28 – Morning after the night before. Butch calculates there'd be 80' waves last night. One had stove in the woodwork on lower bridge, both sides".

Ian continued to work on a ship's magazine, 'The Fylingdale Filings'. This magazine, designed by Ian, was intended to provide a light hearted glimpse of life aboard the ship. The articles from the magazine reproduced below give an insight into Ian's imaginative sense of humour:-

FYLINGDALE FILINGS
With which is incorporated the Pickering Pig Breeders' Gazette
EDITORIAL - NUMBER 1. VOLUME 1

The reasons for this rag are many. Such a famous ship, (see Parliamentary report in our companion paper The Daily Wail – '....the Fylingdale….. that ocean greyhound'….. Mr. A. V. Alexander), needs an outlet for her suppressed talent.

I learn that the firemen's fo'csl seethes with Kipplings in the making. Probably the apprentices could dash off an article on how slave-gangs are run. Somewhere aboard an, as yet, unrecognised artist may lurk.

So let your contributions pour in. Articles need not be typewritten, ha, ha, but should be preferably on white paper of approximately the size of this number.

I should add that we have no blue pencils in the Editorial Office.

GO TO IT."

"THE BOMBING AT RANDOM BY OUR NEUTRAL CORRESPONDENT

I was at Random yesterday when the forces of Hit and Miss paid us a visit. Very little damage was done, though there were a few casuaties, two of which proved fatal. The victims were Mr. Willie Nillie, and Miss Carriage, both well known local inhabitants, who were caught napping – literally killed in their sleep.

General Nuicance, who hurried over from Slow-on-The-Uptake, rendered valuable assistance in clearing debris from the public urinal.

Our Spitfires, on getting aloft, thrashed the enemy at Random, the few remaining planes retiring like whipped dogs to their master, Mr. H. Goering.

Mr. Asinine Bray-Bray (affectionately known as Haw-Haw), furiously denied this above outrage."

Whilst the humour relieves some of the tension, the danger from the U-boats was always present as noted in his journal:-

Tues 29 *(October, 1940)* – Glass up a bit today *(weather barometer indicating improvement in weather)*, but still rough. Not troubled in the slightest by motion. Hear news – 45 ships in a week. Uh, ah. Ship rolling drunkenly & very heavily. So what!

Wed 30 – A routine day! Breakf., a spell on bridge, read, dinner, doze, 3 o'c tea, read, tea, news, read, retire to cabin & read. Great isn't it? Two sunk today. Still rolling a bit".

Thurs 31 – Wake up feeling cold. Find that the steam heater's off. At break learn that the heaters will be forced to remain off ad infinitim, i.e. the end of the voyage. Reason – valve or sumpn gone. We shiver. We're now the outside ship, as the 'Cranford Chine' has moved astern of us. Not so good *(Being on the outside edge of the convoy put the 'Fylingdale' in a very exposed position and more vulnerable to torpedo attack by U-boats or surface raiders).* In aft. reports tell of a cloud of smoke on horizon where ship had been. Sloop dashes away to investigate. No more word.

Fri 1st Nov. *(1940)* – Sloop fired 8 rounds this morning, evid. for practice. Direct ops for a while on bridge. Charge Aldis lamp battery. Go down increasingly often to Eng's mess for warmth. Take a 92 group message!

Sat 2nd – Still going N. Now only 15 ships in convoy so we're now Vice Commodore. 8 knots. At night eavesdrop on Band Wagon, an almost forgotten treat. Consider buying radio.

Sun 3 – Nuthin much in morning or aft. We're now making easting. Reckon that next Sun. we sh'd be in Milford. Strange ship on horizon. Have bath & dress up in clean clothes.

Mon 4 – Fun'n games start today. At break. was stretching to a close, a thud shook the ship. With one accord claws ceased conveying comestibles cavernwards. O'C says britely 'Somebody's got it.' We all rush bridgewards. Sloop has slipped some depth charges to a tin fish. Sirens blow for an alteration in course & ships execute emergency turn. Sloop races about busily. Gun's crew is manned aft. 'Depthford' blinks to Commodore. Some profess to her having sent 'sunk…', but it may've been Sunday, or sunfish. Things quieten down again. Later the lookout reports ship on starb. beam. Signal this to Commodore, who thanks us. The telescope tells that it is an escort corvette, & it's nice to have her. She darts about on our starb. Another charge mumbles underwater, with Commodore hoisting 'submarine operating in vicinity'. But nothing transpires. Aft passes uneventfully.

Tues 5 – Guy Fawkes Day, but a quiet enough diem. Notable only for appearance of Polish destroyer H 37, followed by 2 more. Am awakened in aft. by blasts from hooter. Emergency turn executed but nuthin transpires. Get 2 sub messages. Hear that Leith 'n Edinburgh's been bombed?

Wed 6 – So Roosevelt got in eh? *(on Tuesday 5 November, 1940, the incumbent President, Franklin D. Roosevelt, the Democratic candidate, ran for, and won, a third term of office).* Day is notable for number of depth charges dropped. We've now 6 escort vessels! And a flying bote. Cap tells me of concert on radio from Edin. of Polish sojers singing 100 Pipers etc. & performing on bagpipes.

Thurs 7 – Hear that 'Melrose Abbey' is being bombed. But it's a ship somewhere off N. Ireland. We've a Hamden bomber flying round us now & 7 escorts. *(The 'Melrose Abbey' was a steam merchant ship owned by Frederick Jones and Sons, Cardiff. All the ships operated by the company were named after British abbeys).*

Fri 8 – Land both bows. Day starts off with sig. for Commodore – 'Attack from aircraft may be expected'. So a busy morning is put in by me, attending to signals, messages & all the paraphernalia of the bridge. A Coastal Command crate roars over us low down, & if we'd carried out our orders to fire at aircraft within 5000 yards, he'd've had a warm time. Take a 190 group msg. from Rugby! This followed by a 42 group one. Spend aft. & evening decoding it. Briefly it says that R/O's are to assist in signalling duties when off watch in convoy. Facilities are to be provided for training us (in flags & semaphore I expect). Hot dog! Go on continuous watch when convoy breaks up. At night terrible weather – rain, wind, worse than the Atlantic.

Sat 9 – Great deal of signalling today. Msg from 'Empress of Japan' being bombed off S W Ireland. One engine out of commission. Next msg says aircraft returning. Course for Skerries. Presumptuous Trawler escort dictates our instructions we've already given out.

Sun 10 – Arrive Milford about 8. Get Pilot in but no instructions. Day wears on until tea time when trawler brings envelope – Falmouth! About the farthest point from Gala. Later reports say of going further than F. merely calling there for orders. Mebbe onto Southampton or London! The news has depressed Cap considerably who'd counted on the Bristol Channel. Mate regales him with horrific stories of ships dashing their brains out there due to tides & winds. All agree it will be fun'n games going round there. Reports of machine gunning off Scilly Isles today does nutn to reassure them. Chief in a bad way. After dark I slip up to W/T room for music. Am disturbed by power plant aloft *(aircraft engine noise)*. Curious note. Barge out – Mate claims he saw red lite on it, but I couldn't see the navigation lites our planes burn. Apprentices report 2 'things' drifting down alongside a ship. As trawler skipper warned us to look out for magnetic mines this seems it. But as this was unconfirmed, well –

Later I'm attracted by big flashes in distance followed by weaving searchlites. Hear plane, see shells burst, screw Klaxton (for which I've been waiting!) & things move. Gun's crew closes up aft, the Hotchkiss up top is manned & Old Man tumbles up. Searchlites search, but plane over so they shut off. After a spot of watch I retire, with clothes, for we've an early start tomorrow. Heard of Chamberlain's death.

Mon 11 - At breakf. learn that port is closed because of mines. So the apprentices did see them *(reference to possible sightings the previous night)*. I'll say it is. At the end of dinner a big bang & thud shook us. Dashed out to see, about 50 yds away, a lakebote envelope in smoke. A mine which the trawler had found by means of her trawl wire. She gave 4 blasts as if in triumph, but it must've shaken her. Tuff lads. But at 4.15, while on my bunk, a terrific blast bashed the ship. My toothbrush flew across the room & I was jumped about. Hurried out to see the 'British Diligence' wrapped in smoke. Some kinda mine had exploded under her stern. Onlookers tell of a blinding red flash with spray & mud from bottom flung about. A black stain floats over the water. The tanker had picked up her anchor, as she was dragging, & was moving to another spot when mine spoke. If somebody in engine room hasn't been hurt, or if plates haven't been sprung then she's lucky. As it was, our engine room staff were lifted off their feet.

Altogether, six mines have gone off today. Very stormy weather, indicative that we might finish up on the beach like the Greek which blew 2 anchors. I replace my toothbrush". *('Fylingdale's movement card for that date contains the following entry. '11/11 Underwater explosion while at anchor. Caus List 185 11/1').*

Tues 12 – Wakened early by bang. Don't do anything about it, but at breakf. learn that numerous bombs have fallen nearby. A pleasant haven. Weather still stormy.

Wed 13 – Wakened at 5.40 by bang. Look out, see nutin, turn over. 3 mins later another bang, louder disturbs me so I, once again, look out, this time see a searchlite. Pull on a few duds, dawdle out, collide with apprentice rushing to tell 2nd mate that there's a bomber overhead dropping bombs. With numerous airy laffs & 'this is my meat' expression, get up to bridge. Discover we've fired twice at plane, flying very low over us. If only, the second time 'they hadn't trouble with the breech theyd've got im'. Thinking of ½ the Navy unsuccessful 5 day barrage at Harstad, I smile inwardly or sumpin. 2nd is greatly incensed that he wasn't called at first so's he c'd've Hotchkissed the Hun himself. Mate's maxim had been evidently to hope that everything would turn out allrite & hadn't sounded the Klaxton.

After a talk from the gun's crew, I rebunk, finally being dragged out for breakfus. (2nd table!). Stores are exhausted, a fact we vainly try to impress on examination bote & others. An orgy of Aldising goes on throughout day.

Inefficiency has been the key note of this 4 day delay here. Am worried that old focs'll *(folks)* be worried about us being one of the sunk ships in the Jarvis Bay do. *(On 5 November, 1940, HMS 'Jervis Bay', an armed merchant cruiser, was sunk in the north Atlantic by the German pocket-battleship 'Admiral Scheer', while trying to protect 37 merchant ships in convoy HX-84. 'Jervis Bay' was the sole escort and due to her action most of the ships in the convoy scattered and escaped in the night. 190 men were lost. 65 did survive and were picked up by a Swedish vessel).* Now 21 days since leaving Sydney. After the ruch outa Quebec & Sorel we're stuck here! As 2nd is bunking in wireless room so's to be near his beloved gun, I've to git at 8. Stagger along to Chief's & persuade him to tune in. Quite a good evenin's listenin' after that.

Thurs 14 – Another hectic morning of signalling with little or no result. A situation verging on the ridiculous is caused when we signal our store list to examination bote – '10 pounds pork, loin, 20 lbs sprouts, 1 lb yeast' etc. Cap is about off his head with this lash-up. At last, at about 3.30 by asking ex bote if we c'n go even saus *(source)* stores, he gives us the O.K. which could've been given far sooner. The anchor is started to be hauled up. But it has fouled on anchor chain. An earnest group headed by Cap goes forward to look at it. When they begin again to haul up, the windlass *(winch)* creaks with strain. The frame is split. Cap raves. Tell the ex bote this news but he still won't come alongside. They finally manage to haul the hook ½ way into the pipe & we sail at 4. We lick along in fine weather. Full moon nite. Hear 'Howdy folks' on radio. Still haven't had bath.

Frid 15 – Run into some weather at Lizard but arrive Falmouth at 4 pm. First thing I see is the bow of ship sticking up out of water in front of harbour. Still flying her convoy numbers. Pilot comes on after we're thro' boom & then we learn of new toy – the vibration mine, activated by thrash of screw. This is what I said caused explosions in Milford & for once I was rite. The sunk ship got hers yesterday evening as convoy passed out. So did 13 of the crew. Another view of ship's superstructure greets us inside the harbour, a ship which was bombed outside, set on fire, & rushed in, where she sank. Learn that 'Rangitiki' in Milford was in 'Jarvis Bay' do. On watch hear bombing of 'Apapa' in 16 degrees W, 54 degrees N. she's on fire in last message *(On November 15, 1940, about 200 miles west of Ireland, S.S.' Apapa' was struck by four or five bombs from an attack by a single 4 engine German Bomber, believed to be a FW200 Condor. 229 passengers were rescued, but 5 passengers and 18 crew were lost)(Convoyweb.org.uk).* Slip Pilot telegram which I hope'll go O.K. Render up camera to bond & exp. *(exposed)* film to security police who've come aboard. Says they'll forward prints. Cap goes ashore until 10.30. We go to Plymouth where windlass will be replaced, 10 – 12 days. Hot dog!"

On 16th November, 1940, Ian sent a telegram to his parents simply stating "arrived safe". It would appear Ian was granted leave and went home, but there are no details documented about how he spent his leave. On Sunday 24th November, he began the journey south to rejoin his ship.

The threat from the menace of the U-boats was known not just to the men and women of the Merchant Marine, but to the public at large through the newspapers they read. On 6 November, 1940, the Border Telegraph carried an article reporting comments made by the Prime Minister in the House of Commons:-

"Speaking in the House of Commons on November 5, the Prime Minister referred to the recent recrudescence of sinkings by U-boats in the Atlantic approaches to Britain. He spoke of the 'gigantic task' of the Royal Navy, with the strong naval forces we have to maintain in the Mediterranean and elsewhere, and the threat of invasion necessarily depleting the number of escort craft available for the protection of our innumerable convoys. He mentioned, too, that the lack of fuelling bases for our destroyers and aircraft in Ireland placed a grievous burden upon us." *(Border Telegraph, 6 November 1940).*

Italy had entered the war on the side of Germany and the ability of U-boats to operate from the Channel ports meant they could range further into the Atlantic Ocean and placed more strain on the already overstretched Royal Navy. On the plus side the Navy was inflicting losses on the U-boat fleet, and the USA had supplied 50 old destroyers to be crewed by the Royal Navy for convoy escort duty. However this was the period of the U-boats' 'Happy Time', as described in Chapter 4 of this book, and the losses to Allied shipping were heavy.

Chapter 8 – Christmas on board 'Fylingdale'– Ian meets Monica.

Ian began a new journal on 24 November, 1940. It began with a narrative of his trip from his home in Galashiels to Swansea, which was repeated in a letter to his family on 28 November, written in his usual amusing manner. The letter presents a fascinating insight into the trials of servicemen and the general public as they moved about the country on the rail network, and 'enjoyed' the catering and rest facilities available at that time. It also describes the hospitality shown by some families to servicemen who were complete strangers to them:-

"Swansea
28.11.40
Honoured Family,

With many recriminations for cutting train catching so fine, I was borne Carstairwards. Train came along in 10 minutes for Crew. I munched a pensive sandwich or three on the way to Crew, which was reached at 4. There I looked up my old friend, the Wyman bookstall dame, for local info. Elicited that there was a pub and a milk bar. Checking my case, I minced into the upper light where a bus shook me to where I'd asked – 'the centre of the town'. Arrive there to find a square and little else. Tried one street & then another with no success, then espied a board directing the foolhardy to a Canteen. By following the pointing finger I came to the door which gave into stygian *(murky blackness)* gloom. Feeling round, I at last found the right entrance. Barging brashly barwards to the unblinking stares of clumps of sojers *(soldiers)* I flashed my most winning smile to the earnest, mouse haired, bespectacled nippy *(waitress in uniform)* and asked for tea (meaning a large family size tea). But all there was displayed consisted of a cold pie, and sandwiches. Making do with these scrumptious goodies, I retired to a table, the cynosure *(attention)* of all eyes.

I fell back exhausted after a few desultory bites and concentrated on the magazines; to read, I mean. Nearby a group of sojers attempted to repair a grammo. *(record player)*. Chatted to RAF sparks, who was formally at Swansea Wireless College.

Soon the earnest female who sold me the delicacies came over with a pile of mags for me. She was rewarded with a gracious grimace. Later I idled thro' to next room where ping pong and billiards were played, where I'm accosted by the earnest female again who came up with some tale of me being like her nephew, and was I enjoying myself, as I'd looked lonely, or some rot. Goes on to say – would you come home with me? I started a little, but thanked her gravely, saying nothing definite. She then pressed me to playing ping pong with another gent who beat me.

As the evening wore on I espied a face I knew – a soldier marked RAOC *(Royal Army Ordnance Corps)*. (O.K., take it easy, it wasn't Jimmi). Slipped him the usual line – so you come from Gala too eh? He assented readily enough & we got talking. He comes from Tweed Terrace, where I've seen him at odd times, but I don't know his name. Gave him local news, & he tells me about France & sinking of 'Lancastria'. *(The 'Lancastria' was a passenger ship requisitioned by the Admiralty in April 1940. She was off the French coast and taking part in the evacuation of British troops and other personnel from St. Nazair. The ship was bombed by the German Luftwaffe, rolled over, and sank within 20 minutes. She had an unknown number of people on-board, estimates vary from 4,000 to 9,000. Over 4,000 lives were lost, possibly many more).*

I had been thought French in the canteen & credited with very good English, but soon put the canteen cuties correct. Only they had some difficulty with the rich Scots brogue or sumpn.

Evenin' wears on & Gala guy leaves for an appointment, saying that if I'm here at 9.30 he'll take me to station. But the joint closed at 9, and as I filtered out, the earnest f. enquires – well, are you coming? With a helpless acquiescence I'm led down the street. Arrived at door, thro' which I'm pushed to find white-haired mother & Kaiser-moustached father listening to 9 news.

I'm introduced as a young gent who has some time to wait for a train, and made to sit in the best chair. On hearing that I'd be charmed to hear the news we all fell into silence, enabling me to study room. It is papered in the usual vile pattern & hung with the usual ghastly fotos of grandparents heavily hirstute. Cluttering up the mantlepiece were pics of relatives in uniform etc., including the one allegedly resembling me. A foul lie of course. The news finished we all chatted about that and this. Only thing was that I could scarcely make out what the 70 odd father was saying. However, with a judicious use of nods and ayes, I got by. Then the e.f. (I'm rather afraid she was called Lizzie or Bessie) darted about from recesses 'n things, preparing supper – meat sandwiches (I'd had rather a surfeit of s' that day, hadn't I?), cheese, choc. biscs. & tea. To this groaning table I was led, groaning too, but by having 3 of everything, I filled out again.

Various people bust in at odd times, causing me to spring to my feet & shake hands fervently. As time bore, sorry, wore on, I started making efforts to escape. An autograph book was pressed on me to write something in. After that, the e.f. slipped me some more sandwiches for the train & told me where to get the bus. With many protestations of gratitude I stumbled away, to discover that there were no buses, a position necessitating a 15 minute walk to the canteen outside the station.

Inured to stately entries now, I pushed into a room full of forces asleep. I picked my way among inert corpses & dozed a while. Feeling famished around midnight, I went thro' to eating place. Scrambled eggs on toast & oxo was soon dispatched & at 1.40 I started for the station. De-locking my grip, I imperiously called for a porter who took me up'n down lifts & thro' subterranean tunnels to various platforms until we found the right one.

Into a crowded compartment I went, occupants being 3 sailors, one RAF (black) and one RAF (white). Due away at 2, the train didn't go till 2.30. Soon the sailors unpacked food. One thing was a large chocolate covered cream-cum-jam Scribona cake, of which I had 1/3. Mucho buono. I passed some of my sandwiches until we all fell back distended. A nightmare journey punctuated by countless halts & jars went on until dawn broke; it always does. I'm not very clear about the various stations, but I remember going into Swindon, stopping, & then coming out in the opposite direction. Outside Bristol we halted about 3 times, usually for an hour. Reason was that the place had been visited the nite before, with a detrimental effect on the station. Once we stopped on a banking, where down below was a hole with a notice saying unexploded bomb. But with much shouting we sidled into a platform at 2.15. Left at 2.30 after some liquid nourishment(?)

One of the sailors was on the 'Hardy' at Narvik time (Warburton-Lee etc.) The 3 matelots & I had great fun most of the time from Crewe to Plymouth, which place we hit at 6.30 pm. As I staggered along the platform in search of the other Filings whom, I'd learnt were on the trains, I heard a voice crying in the wilderness – 'Fylingdale'. Getting to the root of this, I found a gent from the Sailor's Home, which place, he said, was to be our night-time resting- place. Reason for this being that the ship had sailed that afternoon (steady now) to anchor in the Sound. We were pushed into taxis & whirled to the Home, where rooms were given to us & later the biggest feed served to us that I've ever had. Egg, bacon, sausages & chips. Hot dog!

This was all Cappy's doing, who, having realised the impossibility of our arriving on time had made these arrangements. His reward shall be in Heaven."

Ian learned that the repairs to the ship had been completed ahead of schedule, as had the unloading of its cargo, hence its early departure from the quay. The 'Fylingdale' would also have a new Captain, by the name of Armstrong for the next voyage, to allow Captain Pinkney to take leave. Captain Armstrong joined the ship on 4 December. 'Fylingdale's next crossing was to be to Boston, Massachusetts, USA, and Ian was delighted.

There is a gap in Ian's journal between Sunday 24 November and Friday 13 December, 1940. However he did write letters to his family during that period describing how he spent his time onshore before 'Fylingdale's' next Atlantic voyage. In one, addressed to the, "Mr., Mrs., & the Misses Waddell", he describes the difficulty in receiving mail, and also the first mention of his girlfriend Morfydd (known as Monica or 'Moni') Thomas. Monica, the daughter of a local coal factor, lived with her family at 'The Croft' in Bayswater Road, Sketty, Swansea, with her mother, sister Glenna, and brother Vivian:-

"Sailors Home
Victoria Road

Swansea
Glam.
3.12.40
You lucky people,

Received your letter on Monday morning, by collecting it from the agents. Now some say that the pen was sent off on Sat. morning registered post, but I haven't seen it yet. Excuse me for ½ hour while I go up to German's *(shipping agents)* again to speir *(enquire)*.

Half an hour later: Collected the P.G. W. packet. Your fanciful nomenclature 'Herman' had caused the parcel to be pushed around halfa Swansea suburbs. The pencil marks on it say – 'Not known at Swansea', 'Not known at Mumbles' (thrice) & finally some brite person has scrawled 'Jas German' on it. 'Herman's' *(name of ship owners)* indeed! However I got it allrite, thank you very much, and I've nearly finished it.

4.12.40 - The new Skipper and wife & small girl took over from Capt. Pinkney on Saturday. There is very little between them, both are the tops. Armstrong was recently torpedoed on another of Headlams – the 'Goathland', calls everybody 'lad', rolls his own, gets things done & knows his job. Altogether he's a sound guy. *('Goathland', a cargo ship bombed and sunk by the Luftwaffe in the Atlantic Ocean to the south west of Ireland on 25 August, 1940).*

On Friday saw O'C off, later went to Port Talbot to see a dame, stayed the night at digs, found by the expedient of asking a policeman. There I had a cigarette, 4 sausages & tea for supper, a bath, bed, ham 'n egg for breakfast.

Got back to Swansea in time to see Cappy (Pinkney) away on Saturday and went with 2nd Mate to dance. Now this dance was a norrible dance, but there I met a dame. Now this dame is the daughter of a local coal magnate. (I haven't said coal merchant or collier, because these seem to smack of a cart complete with bell). Strangely enough Thomas is the name! The dame kinda reminds me of Bella, Margaret's partner, but is much better of course. Anyway we bussed out of her place. Big house with 16 H.P Chrysler but no petrol, tyrannical Christian Scientist, aged family retainer maid and a sister doing her Higher. This has sumpn to do with Matrix.

My drawing-out conversation elicited that the dame was called Monica, a thing done while she was too young to do much about it, has been to France & Switzerland, eddicated at a convent, ('get thee to a nunnery' was obvious crack here), and 'works' in father's office. Now that I come to think of it, her old man must be dead. Seemingly her duties as secretary start at 10 am, go on until 12. Then from 2 till 4. The whole punctuated with paused for coffee etc. Her pal is shorthand typist in the office so maybe all this accounts for delay in loading *(perhaps referring to the loading of coal from the colliery onto the ships).*

That was Saturday nite. Saw her again on Sunday, went down to Port Talbot on Monday, saw 'The Moral Storm'. Good stayed in same place, this time got 2 cigarettes, poached egg on toast, bath, ham 'n eggs. Nice people. Back next morning. That was yesterday.

I've been worrying Germans for that registered packet for quite some time & I'd better be here today.

All the guys have been sent telegrams to rejoin today, but altho' we're scheduled to check out tomorrow I don't think we will. It'll be Friday or Saturday I guess.

Went to the flics last nite with M *(Monica)*. 'His Favourite Wife' – make you laff, ha ha. Flash – things have moved fast in the last hour. Cap came on board & on seeing me said that he'd got my registered packet but had left it up on the office. 3rd Engineer & spouse, britely hymeneal, have arrived, complete with wedding cake & invitation to come along any time tonite for a spot of the blushful hippocrene (Hippocrene is the fountain of the Muses on Mount Helicon. It was produced by a stroke of the hoof of Pegasus). Also the tobacco is being issued in small quantities. Snatching a ½ tin of St Bruno, I get going with my pipe again. A happy atmosphere reigns. In a short while I shall go ashore & phone Monica.

Do I know anything about Jimmi & the firefightng? I rather think not. But you can tell me all about his visit. Shirt stiffeners duly found.

Air raid warning has sounded. The thought of my rather hasty retreat at Princes Street (marvel of understatement) has been knawing at my vitals for quite some time, but it won't happen again, I hope. All clear has gone.

Remember me telling you about the fires we saw at Bristol on our way down? Well they were still burning a week later & Swansea & Port Talbot fire services had been sent. The city has also had it again I see.

There's nuthin much to report, except that it rained yesterday & it's raining today. I looked at various books here, and them 'Christmas at Cold Comfort Farm and Other Stories' by Stella Gibbons, but it didn't look good as the original one & also it costs 8/- *(£0.40p)*. I didn't buy it.

Are you quite sure it's hirsute and not hirstute (referring to his spelling in previous letters)? And anyway, there are 2 l's in Pullman.

I think you'll just have time to write again par express, but put the ship's name on, in case the letter has to be re-directed back to Whitby. And if we do get held up until the weekend I'll phone you & ship you the latest dope. It was great to get your multi-letters. I'll now go shore.

Skin off your noses, Ian".

Ian's friendship with Monica seemed to be going along nicely with parental approval, and after a night out with her he had a somewhat hazardous return to his ship. In a letter to his family, written on Friday 6 December, 1940, he says:-

"After the flics Mon and me teetered gently homewards. This time we pushed in, to find the Mother. Welcome a' la Prodigal. Offers to bring up any washing or/and darning which the maid could do. Turkish cigarettes pressed on me, as was Xmas cakes, teas'n biscuits. As tempas fuged, Mama phoned numerous taxi people & pressed fare on me, 'as I had probably spent some money taking M out'. Husband died 4 years ago.

Got back to ship to find ladder down & ship 8' from dockside. Pushed ladder to ship's side, rolled 3 barrels on far end to keep it down & crawled out to rope ladder. Feat! Keep all presents. Don't send anything except letters. If I can't write again here's hoping you all have a Merry Xmas. J.H. too *(John Hodge a family friend)*.

P.S. If you write promptly to Headlams, we'll probably get it at St John's. See you next year. 'Bye, Ian".

As it happened things did not go according to plan for 'Fylingdale's departure, and not without some comedy attached to it. Ian described the situation in a letter he wrote to his sister Nancy on 8 December 1940:-

"To you. With very little deduction, you can see that we're still here. The following is the explanation. On Friday O'C and I went up town to do our final shopping. I collected the cake and a Telegraph from German, sent Victor back his loan pen, had haircut and bought sundry requisites.

We met one of our firemen up town who told us we weren't sailing until 2. Rashly accepting this, we knocked off shopping to have lunch. Pushed down to the docks after the eats, in a taxi. It was 1.45. As taxi drew up at quay, ship drew out – too far to jump. Calmly we sped down to the lock gates to wait for her. We could see her fussing about up at the moorings, but making no headway. After about ½ an hour of this we jumped aboard a launch which took us alongside. Once aboard the lugger and the ship was ours, or sumpin.

As we climbed over the side, Cappy hailed us, 'Ah there you are. Do you want any leave, we're here for 8 days'. When all this sunk in, he told us that the ship had cast off, the stern was going to bash the quay, so she was given full-ahead. Only thing was that the mooring-wire was around at the time. Result: Intermarriage of prop and several yards of steel wire! She was moored to the buoys in midstream, where we've been ever since.

The matter Cap reported to the Naval Control who reiterated that we must sail that nite, and sent a diver down to investigate. First he said that he c'd do it in time to let us away on midnite tide. But air raid intervened. I turned in.

Next day passed on board, bored. Cap pow-wows with heid yins *(Scottish slang for senior management or in this case senior naval officers)*. Diver dives during day. But we missed the sailing day and must wait till the 12th. *(This was Convoy OB.256 which lost the 'Euphoria' and the 'Kyleglen', both sunk by 'U-100', with the loss of most of the crews)*. I had the chance to come home, but for only from Sunday until Wednesday. Everybody who did go home had instructions to be back by Thursday morning. I've been trying to get thro' a phone call to you but so far without success.

We stood by on Friday nite & Saturday, going ashore at nite. Went down to Mumbles pier pavilion where dancing held sway. Nite was notable for me dancing with one-legged dame. This emiped I espied on entering the revel, but never contemplated hopping with her. However she appropriated one as I stood harmlessly by, to do 2 Lambeth Walks, 2 Chestnut Trees, 2 Boompa Daisies. She had a crutch which I invariably seemed to knock from her when the boomf came. A septic experience altogether. But tonite I'm slated to step out to the Thomas residence, which should prove a sedative.

This afternoon we rowed alongside a ship which was here, when we were last here. She's American built, French owned, (before capture by British), with a Polish crew on board. There is an English R/O who has spent most of his life in France. She has beautiful American radio gear.

Cappy continues to amuse us vastly with his epigrams and stories. A great lad – not a dull minute with him.

One other thing – I think I'll get an American radio t'other side as well as silk stockings. Will you <u>draw</u> and send, or wire, £5. Going ashore now, mebbe I'll have a chance to phone you. I'll be writing again, Ian."

Today we take communication by telephone for granted, whether it is by land line, or a mobile network. Not so in 1940 wartime Britain. Ian describes his experience of trying to telephone home in a letter to his family written on 14 December, 1940:-

"In the main, the telephonic conversations were successful, only in bits did the dulcet decibels defy detection. For your information, père, I tried at 12 on Monday nite, got thro' quite quickly, heard the phone ringing at 12 Abb., but you must all have taken an extra large dose of morphia that nite, becos there was 'no reply'. On Tuesday, proceedings on advice subscribed by the exchange operator, I phoned at 10.45, heard the call going thro' Liverpool, Cardiff, Newcastle & Glasgow, till finally it reached you. Cost was 1/4d *(£0.07p)*, and office of origin was a common, or garden, phone box".

On 13 December, 'Fylingdale' sailed from Swansea for Liverpool. There on 16 December, 1940, she formed part of Convoy OB.260, with 29 merchant ships and 5 Navy escorts, and sailed towards Canada. Ian resumed writing in his journal:-

"**Friday 13 December 1940** – leave buoys at early hour. Wake when ship is in locks. Peaceful journey round to Milford, which place we find littered with wrecks. Mined & done since we were last here. Settle down for the night.

Sat 14 – Cap goes ashore at din time, taking my 2 letters – to Mrs. Thomas & Mrs. Wad. Returns at teatime with an oath to the effect that we were Commodore. Do I see pleasure under the wrath? To sail at 12 tomorrow, taking charge of the ships until Liverpool, when we'll relinquish captaincy & become Vice-Commodore. This means in the middle of the front line – one of the safest places. As I idly listen to some BBC bosh, phones crackle to the tune that the 'Empire Razorbill', seen by us in Swansea few days ago, is being shelled & followed by sub in 17 west. *(At 21:02 hrs on 14 December, the 'Empire Razorbill', which had dispersed from Convoy OB-257, was attacked and shelled by 'U-96'. Although struck 3 times the U-boat lost contact due to bad weather and the ship docked safely in St. Johns on 24 December)(uboat.net).*

Sun 15 – The kite is successfully inaugurated this morning as one more defensive weapons *(against attack by enemy aircraft)* for us. We repair the Aldis. Weigh anchor at 12, taking up our station in front line.

Pangs for Swansea pit my paunch. To do no watches after Liverpool, but to keep bridge watches, helping Mates with signalling duties. Settle down for testing trip, not reassured by 3rd Mate's vouchsafe that this ship should not be doing a Western Atlantic crossing this time of year – too old. Continuous watches as Commodore.

Mon 16 – On at midnite till 4. 8 till 12. Ether emits information that ship is being bombed 340 miles W by S of Tory Island. Long range. Knock off watches at 8, having picked up Liverpudlian laggards. To start bridge watches tomorrow(?) It'll be cold up thea.

Tues 17 – With no watches, sleep on till 8. The lowering Scots landscape looms up on starboard beam. Pick up Glasgow Section in morning. Do a bit of bridge watch in morning & aft. We have a Yank destroyer as one of the escorts. The Oban Section steam out to us in late afternoon.

Wed 18 – Up at midnite for watch. Stand on bridge in rain & wind, feeling like one of Chas. Grave's drawings in Punch. Have 2nd's sea boots & as much clothing as I can find. Retire to chartroom after a while. Knock off at 4. Up for tripe fritters breakfast! Hear last week's ship total – 23. Hum! Cap says 5 were killed, the engine room lot, when his ship copped it. He never heard any explosion, says only debris was thrown up.

Thurs 19 – Didn't venture on bridge, but as bedclothes kept slipping off, not much sleep was had by all. On bridge in aft. Blow falls. After fog has lifted somewhat, Commodore flickers to us. Decoded, the message orders dispersal & proceed to port of destination. But surely not! If msg had been meant for flying kites at certain time, that would've been better explanation. But after much flashing, flags go up, definitely stating the deed. Of course everyone is dumbfoonered. They can't do that to us. With at least 2 subs' positions reported ahead. With much headshaking, fact is accepted. Heavy jests of being home for Xmas etc.

Before tea, the Greeks push off & just as meal ends, one grazes our bow as she wallows away on her course. Another has a bright light showing. Then 'Ropner' starts a lash-up on starboard. As darkness closes in the ships are spreading out. Continuous watch to Boston (sic) now. Hot dog.

Fri 20 – About 8.30 things break. The 'Carlton', who crossed our bows last nite on dispersal & made a course south, sparks that she's being chased by a sub in a position which we should be in by 9 o'clock *(The 'Carlton' from Convoy OB.260 was sunk by the Italian submarine 'Pietro Calvi').*
Excitement all round and gun is manned. She repeats that she's being chased during the morning, and another ship, a Norwegian, sends that she is being attacked by a sub too, also in a position very near us. 'Carlton' sends her last message about 1. Torpedoed. She lost the race. No further word from the Norwegian, but another message states that a ship is being attacked off the Skerries. This is closest we've heard for a cigar to be. Then a Raider message comes in, to be cancelled later. Fun & games. This won't be the last we hear of our late convoy companions. As we stand on the bridge, Wilf brings us cawfee laced with rum. Good-o. No further alarms, except sighting of ship, thought to be the 'Carlton', this theory being disproved as ship was in ballast *(riding higher in the water than a fully loaded ship).* Quiet afternoon. We zig-zag on. I've a sore throat and a week's growth.

Sat 21 – Still plugging along. Two more days should see us in comparative safety zone. Phones almost dead. As afternoon wears on, rolling becomes more violent. Annoying crackle on phones all afternoon, remedied by tightening a screw. By tea time rolling is heavy. All mobile matter in my cabin is on the deck. In 2nd Eng's room, his water-can has spilled into his slippers. As I go forward for tea, the butt end of a wave neatly spreads itself down my left side as I claw for the door. Not a nice nite at all, at all.

Sun 22 – Sleep on, unawakened, till midnite. As I make my way along the deck, I realise in a flash that there's 6 inches of water underfoot, which as the ship rolls violently, fills my shoes. Staggering along, clinging to rails'n things & with the greater part of the Atlantic cooling my feet, I finally reach the ladder. Prepare for an 8 hour vigil. Get thro' most of Sinister Street, which is just the right reading. A grand book. 8.30 I pitch white-faced down to breakfast. Ham & egg. Stand on bridge a while to grab some oxygen. Ship was going ½ speed all last nite in strong head wind. Today she still rolls with the sea abeam, but we make better westing. Weather deteriorates as aft. progresses. Decks awash. High wind whistles thro' rigging. On the 8-12 many thuds make ship shiver & jump, giving rise to speculation. Ole man who has kept vigil in chart room last & this nite rushes out. Both rafts have been swept off hatches onto rails. Bent the rails. All woodwork on lower bridge is gone on port side. Dirty weather. Uneasy sleep due to rolling.

Mon 23 – Ether *(radio messages)* very quiet on the 8-12, but sea is not. Several times alarming thuds shake the hull, and spray can be heard pelting the bridge work. After breakfus I dawdle round to inspect damage. Rails are bent where rafts smashed against, nearly all woodwork on lower bridge is gone. Steward tells us that ship's biscuits are indicated for some days, becos supply of yeast in ice chest has been rendered sodden. But main thing is we are 30 west. Before tea I remove 10 day's growth, which I'd become rather attached to."

Tuesday 24 December, 1940, Christmas Eve, was uneventful and Christmas Day on 'Fylingdale' is best described in a letter from Ian, written on 2 January 1941:-

"Temperature 34°F
190 miles from Boston
2.1.41
'What shall we do with the drunken sailor?' - OLD SONG
'There aint no Santi clause' - MARX BROTHERS
Illustrious antecedents,

Come off watch at midnite, greeting 2nd & 3rd Mates on my way thro' chartroom to turn in. Roused for toil at 4 am as usual, when I read seasonable 'Strands' in an attempt to instil a Christmassy spirit.

On finishing watch at 8, I issue onto the bridge giving the Old Man to understand that I wished him a Merry X. With a glance at the water, he invites me to furnish him with a sign visible to the human optic of anything merry. I say ha ha ha & go down to brekfus.

Now this meal is by way of being a spread. We have egg, bacon & chips, after which I put an equal strain on all parts for an hour. Once more into the breach at 12. As O'C does not come up for ¾ of an hour. I divine sumpn must be on. Weather has got dirty again, so that ship rolls heavily. When I go down the mess room is littered with engineers surfeited with pud, the pantry, with uniform clad marines, sailors, cooks, mess, cabin & galley boys.

Soon (after an aperitif of rum, smelling strongly of water) dispensed by a stewed steward, we file into the saloon for 2nd table. Butch sits in Cappy's chair while I'm in mine at the opp. end ('You in your small corner and I in mine).

Butch has on a collar & tie, 4th Eng. a blue suit, and I'm in my usual clothes. Mebbe this is something of a fox's paw or quelle bêtise *(stupid)*, but nobody notices. Thousands of shiny-faced apprentices clad in Sunday suits embarrassingly enter (rite centre) to take their places round the groaning table. We were groaning too.

The festive board (board anyway) has gracing it, a plate of broken cheese, ditto of biscuits, a decanter ¼ full of a pale brown liquid. & a water carafe brim full of the demon rum.

The cook resplendent in ducks, flashes in, bearing very professionally five plates of tomato soup which are gifted to sundry fortunate folk. A great deal of skill and physics are needed to retain the soup in their respective plates. Altho' bridge has been asked to steer the ship on a course conducive to a steady keel, the Atlantic has other ideas.

Enter steward with bottle & glass, carolling 'we're all right now, hic'. With a damp and alcoholic imitation of cornucopia *(having a large amount)*, he pours rum in the general direction of diners protesting too much. 'Ha, ha, isn't he a one', and 'he must have his little fun', are the thoughts I seem to observe in the company's minds. Conversation is desultory and strained, we, the officers, relying on throwing each other insults to get the laffs.

Throughout the aft. 2nd Mate spills me the latest developments. Apparently the steward had been having extra special fun'n games in the galley when the Old Man takes a hand, escorting him with a strong hold on the collar to his cabin, to be dumped on his bunk & asked to render up the keys of the bonded locker.

I receive a message from the King to the Merchant Navy in aft. Rolling is so violent that ship is hove-to until seas abate a trifle.

Tea is a cold one – salmon, tongue & cake'n mince pies. Steward nurses what he euphemistically calls a broken arm, caused by falling in the scuppers *(lower areas of the ship)*. Swinging the lead, presumably to divert attention from his erstwhile unedifying exhibition. We eat our salmon & cake in a pensive way. Soon a furious argument about lubber lines & the like springs up, & in this way is passed Christmas nite, while I try to reconstruct scene at 'Glebelands' *(the home of the Hodges, close family friends)*. As I pass the steward's cabin on my way to watch, another 'little party' is starting.

Just after 8, a hideous noise emanating from the lower bridge is heard. It's the carol singers serenading the Old Man. Soon his voice is heard, bribing them with strong wine to cease. All is quiet. Apart from a message from a ship reporting that she's being gunned & chased by a sub, the war seems remote. That then was Xmas Day, not in the workhouse or the harem, but on board our ship, quite the screwiest & most disappointing Xmas ever spent by me."

Ian's journal continues listing events following the 1940 Christmas Day celebrations on 'Fylingdale':-

"Thurs 26 *(December – Boxing Day)* – A few hangovers today. After the feast, the famine. Nothing much happens until about 5 past 3. (18.05 GMT). The submarine message stutters in the phones. '58°12 N 17°25 W *(near Icelandic coast)*, 'Waiotira torpedoed'. I give a horrified gasp and shakily transcribe the distress call. Is it Peter who is sending? *(Ian's friend from Leith Nautical College days).* Is he all right? What's happening on board? A feeling of utter helplessness sweeps over me, and terrible concern. Thing was that I'd decoded a message for her last nite instructing her on a course to avoid subs. It'll also be pitch black at 18.05 over there, with probably a high sea. Will she have troops on board? Valentia Radio acknowledges her distress and immediately radiates it. So some kind of help will be on its way. And he was so near the end of the journey. Probably came from India. Resolve to send wire to 63 on arrival. Old Man on seeing position says it's the one that got him. Well that's 12000 tons of Shaw Savill's gone. What a Christmas this has been." *(At 20.03 hours on 26 December, 1940, Peter's ship, 'Waiotira', on route from Panama to the United Kingdom, was hit in the bow by one torpedo, from 'U-95', about 124 miles west by north of Rockall. The ship was missed by a second torpedo, but hit by a third. 'U-95' was obliged to leave the area due to the arrival of three destroyers, spotted during the attack. 'Waiotira' was again located, this time by 'U-38' during the night, and hit underneath the bridge by a coup de grâce at 01.46 hours on 27 December. The vessel sank a few hours later. One passenger was lost, however the Master, 78 crew members, and ten passengers were rescued by HMS 'Mashona' and landed at Greenock on 28 December)(uboat.net).*

Ian later learned that his friend Peter and his fellow Radio Officer, on the 'Waiotira', had kept sending their distress signal for as long as they could before abandoning the radio room. When they went on deck they found that the Captain and the crew had taken to the boats and had abandoned them. The Captain refused to return to 'Waiotira' to take them off, however the crew insisted he do so and Peter and his colleague survived the trip.

The remainder of the voyage was uneventful, and Ian celebrated the New Year on watch on 'Fylingdale':-

"**Wed 1 Jan (1941)** – Log on at midnite (Ship's Time) to hear broadcast of do in Times Square, New York, 1,000,000 people there to bring in the N. Year. Then from N.Y. it switched to Chicago, then Pike's Peak (mountain top) where they set off fireworks, & finally to Hollywood. Very funny ha ha program. On to San Francisco, then Waikiki, home of the hula & aloa. Dance music until 4 (ship's time). EST *(US Eastern Standard Time)* is 5 hours behind GMT *(Greenwich Mean Time)*. Great fun. Crack from announcer – 'on this day of national headaches'. Do sample grams which O'C drew up for me to practice on. Great struggle with sundry rates & charges.

Drink from Old Man before dinner time. Hear broadcast of Mississippi State College v Georgetown rugby. Shades of H.B. Wakelam! Sponsored by Gillette. (Rather misty here today). Scotsman calendar up in cabin. Quite a cheery day. Snow & very cold."

United States coastline was sighted on 3rd January, and Ian's journal continued:-

"**Frid 3** *(January 1941)* – At about 7 I go out, & there it is the coastline. Craft comes alongside asking our name. Pilot comes aboard, very typically looking American. Go alongside after celebratory drink with Cap on completion safely of ½ of trip. Immigration & dozens of other officials come aboard. Afternoon spent watching, registering & fingerprinting of lucky ones who had Mercantile Marine Identity Card. At nite, as unable to go ashore, write out papers for Consul. Fingerprint the men. Turn in disappointed."

Morfydd ('Moni') Thomas, seated on right of picture with her sister Glenna, dressed in Land Army uniform, her Aunt, Esther May, and Brother Vivian.
(circa 1940)
(Photograph by kind permission of Trevor Williams and Mary Daly)

Chapter 9 – Ashore in Boston – The sinking of S.S. 'Carlton'.

Ian went ashore in Boston on 4 January, 1941, and began a tour. On 6 January, he sent a cablegram to his family saying, "Arrived safely Happy New Year". His adventures ashore were described in a letter to the family:-

"Halifax, Nova Scotia
Monday 20th January
You lucky people,

Get ready for diatribe two. Our life was so crowded that it'll be difficult to recount it fully, but here's a valiant attempt.

When we were at last permitted to go ashore with the requisite passes, a party consisting of the Old Man, 2nd Mate, O'C & me, climbed down the ladder onto the quay. There a Jewish shopkeeper who specialises in swindling ships met us & drove us up to his store. We trooped in, but on seeing that we didn't want anything he showed us the door. We progressed uptown, looked at shops, had tea in a self-service joint, saw the 'Santa Fe Trail', had supper in a rib joint, bearing over the door the sign – 'thro' these portals pass the world's most beautiful show girls'.

Next day, Sunday, O'C & I went to 'Kitty Foyle', a good flick, from Christopher Morley's novel. Then on to see Boston Bruins tie with Chicago Blackhawks, a game notable for its many free fights. Crowd booed the ref as soon as he skated onto the rink. It's a wonderful game to watch is ice hockey.

Next morning we went upriver to Lynn, a smaller town, & correspondingly quieter. We looked up the local YMCA, & were warmly received. Next day, on their invitation we padded up to make good use of a shower-bath and swimming-pool. Ditto the following day, until we were repulsively clean. All this cost us exactly nothing. The Y's over here are on a much bigger scale than ours. But it was not until our last night in Lynn that we really 'went to town'. Early on one evening a gent sporting a pseudo-tartan tie came over and vouchsafed that I was in the MN *(Merchant Navy)*. I was, so he followed up with info. that while in the US Navy last war, he'd been stationed at Invergordon & other Scots bases. I said 'oh yes' & we got to talking. After a few gambits of chat he rounded up his 2 pals & with O'C, I piled into his Chevrolet (new 1941 model note) thereafter driving round all the joints in town. In one, I was prevailed upon to try clams, which I found quite good. With an exchange of addresses & promising to write, telling them of our safe arrival, we parted when we'd exhausted the town's entertainments. Three very hospitable middle aged businessmen.

Next day we were back in Boston again. That night, Saturday, we tried the Sailor's Haven, close to the docks. Here we were warmly welcomed by the boss of the place, introduced to a lady & gent who took charge of us & played whist with us. I, with the rudiments of the game at my fingertips, must've caused my partner some heartburn. However everything was all very jolly, then the dance in the hall below started.

Here I again observed the jitterbug. It isn't so hot, only a matter of matching improvised steps to the music. I discovered the best way for coordination was to grasp the doll firmly & make her follow my steps until she got into the way of it. From this I earned unstinting praise on my terpsichorean prowess & grasp of rhythm. Modestly bowing, I hurried away lest too much praise spoil me."

Socialising with the local populace continued and he and O'C were invited out to supper by another local family. Ian continued:-

"So on Sunday, in our best, we were up at the Haven meeting our saviours (becos it was pork for lunch aboard). In a Chevrolet (again 1941 model, please note) we bowled away. The gent, Andrews was the name, was principal of a blind institute some miles out of Boston. On our way out we passed Harvard University, a fine set of buildings; also the Massachusetts Institute of Technology, renowned. People were skating on the river. Arrived at the house, we were greeted by Mrs & for a while before dinner, chatted. A lovely house, with American long, bright rooms with removable rugs on floor so that dancing is easy. Lunch was a masterpiece". Ian went on to describe the feast they had and the extremely generous manner in which they were treated. As a result Ian's Mother wrote to the Andrews and thanked them for showing so much kindness to her son.

Ian and the others met up with other individuals keen to show them some hospitality, and Ian went on:-

"Met 2 Chief Petty Officers of the Coastguards, & a Lieutenant of the Army. Soon plans were underway for us to come down to the Navy Yard next day & visit their ship. The Lieut. also asked us to meet him the day after, & we'd do a show. Promising the C.P.O.'s to call, we were driven shipwards by the Lieut.

True to our pledge we bearded the sentry in the Yard next day, & after some little trouble located the desired ship, straightway asking for the lads. Found them & were shown round the ship, had tea & then wonders of wonders, went into mess room & saw a flick. Two sound projectors with sound apparatus'n all, screened that nite 'I was An Adventuress', with Forina (the ballet dancer), Erich Von Stroheim, Pete Lore, & Richard Green. It was the full picture, fully appreciated. In port they're shown every nite, at sea, 2 a nite. After another look round at laundry, galley, bridge, wireless room, & hospital, we all went uptown to a joint.

There we found the latest novelty – an automatic gramophone which, when you insert a nickel, enables you to talk to a dame located somewhere in Boston who plays the record you wish. She'll also dedicate it to someone if so desired. Very tricky. Her replies are heard in a speaker atop the machine".

At the end of the letter Ian compares the austerity of war torn Britain with what he found in the U.S.A. "Impressions – tempo of living; hospitality; their wonder that we were here; palatialness of cinemas which are huge & have Old Masters (real) hung in foyers, hugeness of railway stations – towns in themselves; comfort of trains; very cosmopolitan population; pro-Britishness; & in general the large scaleness of everything.

Will soon be homeward-bound".

Mr Andrews later wrote a letter to Ian's mother saying how much they had enjoyed the visit from Ian and O'C. Mr. Andrews expressed a mixed view, probably shared by many US citizens at the time, on how involved the United States should become in the war against Germany:-

"Mr. Francis M. Andrews
Perkins Institution
Watertown, Massachusetts
April 6, 1941
Dear M. Waddell,

Mrs Andrews and I were more than surprised to receive a letter from you and greatly touched by it. We really did so little for your son when he was here; all we did was have him for dinner and the afternoon then tea and invited another couple for tea. We were so pleased to receive his letter for now that we actually know people who are on the ships we feel even more concerned. We certainly hope if your son returns to Boston he will telephone us so we may invite him out again for we thoroughly enjoyed him.

We are having our troubles in this country. There are all too many strikes which are interfering with national defence. I believe drastic action should be taken to prevent them and to punish those who strike. Yet at the same time labor should receive a just amount and capital should not make too much. War is no time for profiteering. America must wake up! The little kindnesses are all very well but we must help even more. I don't believe in sending men (I was in the last or rather first world war) but I do believe in sending supplies, arms, food and if necessary in convoying those materials". He ends the letter, "May the summer bring peace to a victorious England. We shall always be glad to receive word concerning your son and hope to see him again. Sincerely, Francis M. Andrews."

Ian continued in his journal:-

Sun 12 *(January, 1941)* – Very doggy we stroll up to Haven & meet Mr. Q. outside. Chevved out, chat, dinner (superb & sherry), chat all aft, phoned for pals to come for tea (good), leave, driven back to ship. Go uptown to miles Oasis. Draw band.

Mon 13 – Up to the Oasis again. Meet the CPOs & Ryan. Quite a nite. Driven back by Ryan who dates us for Wed. Invited down to the 'Donane' by George.

Tues 14 – Aboard cutter at 4.30. Meet the boys (a trifle embarrassment). Have tea. See movie. Up to the 'Morning Glories'. Discover the possibilities of the Automatic Hostess Gramophone.

Wed 15 – Up at 4 to the Recruiting Office & are shown round by Ryan. After oath ceremony etc we go on to the Old Howard burlesque after supper in the New Yorker. Drive out to Oasis to finish off the friendship.

Thurs 16 – In 'Morning Glories' to see cheerio to the CPOs."

'Fylingdale' left Boston and sailed for Halifax, Nova Scotia, on Friday 17 January, 1941, arriving there the following Sunday. On 21 January, Ian recorded in his journal the harrowing experience of survivors from the 'Carlton', a British steam cargo ship, which was sunk on 20 December 1940, 300 miles west of Ireland. 'Carlton' was sunk after a fight with the Italian submarine 'Pietro Calvi', during which 'Carlton' fired on the submarine, and then tried to ram it. The attempt to ram failed and the 'Carlton' was sunk by a torpedo from the 'Pietro Calvi'. The crew of 35 abandoned ship in two lifeboats. However one lifeboat capsized and the other was found 18 days later with only 4 survivors from the ship. It was another reminder of the dangers faced by all merchant seamen on ships plying the cold Atlantic Ocean, which could be very cruel:-

Tues 21 *(January 1941)* – Old Man & O'C shore for a conference. I've barely time to seal envelopes & thrust them into O'M's hands as he leaves. At nite O'C comes alongside - wrong side for ladder. As bote starts round to other side, rope becomes entangled in prop. He drifts away. Finally another bote takes him off & brings him aboard. We're bound for Barry Roads for orders. Tells of tales of 'sparks' *(Radio Officers)* he met at conference. One, now on the 'Hadleigh', told how on last trip home, about 6 subs surrounded convoy on moonlite nite & potted 19 of them, including this 'sparks' ship.

Also hear of the survivors of the 'Carlton's' crew, landed here on Sunday after 18 days in an open bote. She got it on 20 December – remember? Only 4 finally made Halifax – others went mad, & remainder, just went to sleep. A mate & an apprentice, who were pals, were in opposite ends of the lifebote; they both rose at the same time to go towards each other, but never made the journey – died at the same time. The negro firemen went first, after singing spirituals. Then some drank sea water. Others flung themselves overboard to be rescued by the sane ones. On Xmas Day they wished each other seasonal greetings. We reckon the 'Carlton's' position was wrong, but even then, surely a greater effort should've been made to find survivors. She was only 18°W. It was an Italian sub. It came alongside lifebote with – 'where is ze Captain?' He had gone down with the ship. Not so good. Listen to radio at nite in bed". *(The 'Pietro Calvi' would herself be attacked on 14 July 1942, by HMS 'Lulworth', one of the escorts for Convoy S.4, sailing from Freetown to the United Kingdom. This engagement resulted in the 'Pietro Calvi' being severely damaged, scuttled and sunk) (www.wrecksite.eu).*

On Wednesday 22 January, 1941, 'Fylingdale' formed part of Convoy SC.20, destination Liverpool, with a cargo of 5786 tons of wheat. The convoy contained 48 merchant ships and 7 escorts. Ian's journal continued:-

Wed 22 – After fits & starts we get under way in afternoon. No watches, except in fog. I get the account wages book to go over. If a maths teacher could only see me! Our escort is the P & O Armed Merchant Cruiser 'Ranpura'. Big convoy".

Thurs 23 – Do watch on bridge 8-12. Very cold. Two pairs sox, 2 prs. gloves, vest, shirt, 2 pullovers, jerkin, jacket, scarf, raincoat, & helmet! 'Ranpura' looms up, about 3 times the size of other ships, & takes up her position. Her after funnel has been removed, so as to mount guns.

Fri 24 – Up for Rugby *(the UK's maritime radio transmitting station)* at breakfus. On watch on bridge till 12. Snow & cold. Hear story that the 'Rampura' is there as a decoy to entice a raider, believed to be somewhere around, to attack, then one of our 'big ones' will appear as prearranged and surprise him. Well - ! Spend aft in getting warm. Sea becomes rougher, rolling starts again. At nite do some more of the Accounts & wages. I c'n tot up quite well now! On short wave Britain comes in loud & clear.

Sat 25 – Burns' Day. Quiet day. A ship almost rammed us last nite. Clock forward an hour.

Sun 26 – Weather deteriorates. On watch in aft becos of fog.

Mon 27 - One of the worst seas I have seen. During intervals throughout the day convoy is hove to. Very high winds & mountainous sea. Alarming thumps shake the ship. While up in Cap's room doing sums am shaken about by rolling. In my cabin everything mobile is on deck.

Tues 28 - Still very bad. She ships some alarming seas throughout the day. We've completely lost the others in the convoy. Go on watch as we're by ourselves. At nite I pick up a msg. from escort giving rendezvous for tomorrow which helps to straighten things out a bit.

Wed 29 – Up at 1 am for watch. On till 7. For 1st time for a while, sights are able to be taken showing where we are. But no ships appear. At tea time we sight a ship on port beam. Aldis her, to find she's the 'Baron Ogilvie', also separated from main convoy. But she can't pick up our name. After tea I get another rendezvous from escort, & a bit more certain, we set our course for it. The Atlantic is such a big place. Weather has moderated somewhat today. Sunday damage is repaired.

Thur 30 – On at 1 again. Little doing. Breakfus lousy ham & egg. Dinner just as bad. About 3 we sight ships ahead, outstanding one the 'Rampura', who comes fussing towards us. After chatting a while by Aldis we neatly swing round, take our place among the odd 10 ships, and retrace our steps, metaphorically. Watches are dropped once back in convoy. As nite draws in the weather gets rough again. Report of a sub sighted off Canadian coast – probably one of ours. Seemingly a rationing of clean linen has been decreed by the steward as I only get 1 sheet & pillow case. A gathering assembles to hear the news at 8.

Frid 31 – The days are so much the same that, writing this the day after, I can't remember anything to distinguish this from the other days. Eat, read, eat, read, sleep, eat, listen to radio, sleep. Clock forward an hour.

Sat 1st Feb *(1941)* – About 20 ships now. We can't get Rugby on long wave. Commodore suggests that she's broke down. Luckily we pick up the messages on short wave.

Sun 2 – Spend morning in wireless room. Fix the emergency batts. in aft, vaselining terminals & repairing wires. Before tea I remove nearly all of the 16 day growth, all except an embryonic beard which I shall cultivate until we reach the U.K. at least. It is of the Vandyke type. It is the subject of some comment at tea & the conversation very hirsute as a result – all about how fine clean old men look with white beards etc.

Mon 3 – On medium wave we pick up Home & Forces programs perfectly during the day. In aft learn from GKU that the 'Dionne II' who was with us up till the storm set in had been bombed. She's seemingly forged away ahead by herself, with consequent fate. *(At 17.21 hrs. on 3 Feb, 1941, the 'Dione II', loaded with 2650 tons of iron ore, straggled from convoy SC.20, and was bombed and damaged by a German Condor aircraft. This attack was seen by 'U-93' which had previously tried unsuccessfully to attack her. At 04.40 hrs 'U-93' attacked again. The ship stopped and a fire broke out and the ship sank by the bow. The master, 26 crew members and one gunner were lost. Five crew members were picked up by the British steam merchant 'Flowergate' and landed at Glasgow) (uboat.net).*

Another message shows that a ship's been torpedoed ahead of us a bit. Write up this recoding the Lynn & Boston experiences. Clock + 1 hour.

Tues 4 – During the morning I slave over the washtub getting dish pan hands in the process. Late afternoon the 'Rampura' hoists 'Good Luck' & returns to Halifax on approach of 5 local escorts.

Wed 5 – We know we're approaching Britain becos it's raining.

Thurs 6 – Wake up tired. In afternoon 2nd Mate tries to fly the kite with disastrous results. It falls into the sea & is dragged along behind the ship. I think it was cut adrift finally. At 5 to 4, the 'Maple Court', sister of the Commodore, gets hers 22 miles to the north of us. She was in convoy before the storm, when she, like us, became separated from the main body. Think one of the escorts went to pick up survivors. *(The 'Maplecourt', loaded with 3604 tons of general cargo and 1540 tons of steel, straggled from Convoy SC.20 and was torpedoed by 'U-107' about 120 miles west of Rockall. The ship sank rapidly by the stern, and although the Germans saw survivors abandon ship in* *two lifeboats, they were never seen again. The master, 35 crew members and three gunner were lost) (uboat.net).*

Fri 7 - Tragedy! When I issue on deck at noon I notice tension. A plane is pointed out to me cruising low, parallel with the convoy. I'm told that the corvette has opened up on her with her pom pom, peppering the plane's immediate vicinity. From the shape of the crate I'd have no hesitation in saying that it was friendly. Make my way onto bridge where great excitement reigns. Of course I, a veteran of Narvik, remain calm and blasé. The gun's crew is manned and everything is ready. But the plane cruises round, banking overhead, showing clearly the British cocardes. It's a Vickers Wellington bomber of the Coastal Command. Next report is that a destroyer has let go at him, on the opposite beam. Still crate continues her patrol. She must've failed to give the recognition signal or sumpn. Anyway, the Commodore hoists the signal that attack from enemy aircraft may be expected, and everything is keyed up again. Then the lookout shouts that the bomber has crashed into the sea. We hurry out to see faintly thro' the telescope a tail sticking up. That's all. Story was that she was flying along steadily when her engines cut out and she fell. The destroyer ploughs speedily thro' a heavy sea to the scene, waves breaking over her forepeak & bridgework. She's going all out. The corvette, too closes round the spot. Soon the escorts are left behind as they stand over the tragic 'x marks the spot'

Then comes the unusual – exciting order from the Commodore – 'drop smoke floats overboard'. Gunner strikes the lighter part of the drums & two floats are heaved over the stern. Immediately grey, chlorine-smelling fog envelopes the ship, & as others jettison their own, the convoy grows hazy. Very effective, but whit fur? As wind is following the fogging out is accomplished, but I thought that smoke was used only in the case of a raider cf. 'Jervis Bay' do. Must've been a sub. Later comes rather funny signal – 'cease making smoke screen' – funny becos the floats are overboard & far astern. Continue to billow out clouds of smoke. However things clear up later & everything goes on as usual.

That was a big loss, the bomber, & perhaps the crew. Hope they got them. Hear plays & music at nite on medium. Should be in North Channel tomorrow nite.

Sat 8 – Land. Old Rathlin Island looms up early in the day, to be followed later by the Scottish Coast. It's good to see it again – very good. Clean the wireless room & polish the brass leads in view of our impending departure(?) Commodore sheers off for the Clyde in middle of aft & we take over duties of Commodore for the remainder of the vessels. Go on watch at 3 when this happens. Usual messages of appeals for help from attacked vessels are received. Doing 4 on 4 off. Should be in early Monday morning.

Sun 9 – Ham & egg breakfus. Day proceeds calmly with our making 8 knots down Channel. A few ack-ack gun-manning enlivens the day. In the morning I see corvette aldising – 'to go to Swansea', & dash along with this very unofficial news! It turns out to be the destination of another barge. Too bad!

Watches all thro' day. Should be in early tomorrow. Debate whether to declare *(to Customs)* radio *(bought in Boston)* or not – weaken & declare it. Whisk off the whiskers on chin after their long stay. Make ready for tomorrow.

Mon 10 – Just as predicted in Boston, we arrive at Barry Roads on the 10th – to the minute. Jump about after the breakfast cleaning more brass in the cabin & watching the planes perform overhead. Target practice at an envelope towed by a plane & we can smell cordite after the crates has passed by. The corvette leaves after an interchange of 'courtesy of the sea' signals with us. First she loudspeaks – 'Goodbye & good luck'. We hoist WAY, meaning approx. the same. She hoists - 'well done', & 'thanks', to which we retort 'thanks'. A pretty ceremony. Examination vessel comes alongside & we learn – Sharpness. Just after dinner we're startled by a crash & a hiss. I thot it was a steam pipe gone, but rushing out, see a small parachute floating gently to earth in front of ship. Guns had accidentally set off the parachute & cord rocket, which had entwined itself round the aerial. The wire was over the side & in danger of being drawn in by the screw (see Swansea!). See the castle formerly owned by Randolph Hearst, the American newspaper owner. Big place, on coast edge. But we proceed to Sharpness on account of the ports around here being closed. Hun was over last nite, & approaches have to be swept. We anchor. Spend afternoon lounging on deck in bright sunshine, like a Scots summer. As I issue into my cabin to my surprise & delight a dame singing Braw Braw Lads, nae less! I drag everybody I can in to listen to 'the hometown's song' *(Galashiels).* It turns out to be a program of Scottish songs, compared by Auntie Kathleen. Finish off spool on Beel, Chief, Pete & Butch. Pass nite quietly.

Tues 11 – Very heavy fog in morning preventing our sailing upriver. At dinner the pilot forced to stay aboard last nite very unmusically inhales soup & is banished with hints. Spend day with radio. Get under way after tea, but get only as far as Avonmouth when fog comes down, forcing us to return to our anchorage. Passed Portishead Radio on way up. Good ole GKV. At nite hear a funny sketch about a Glasgow flitting plus Scots songs. Then 'Strike up the Band', & dance cabaret with Cyril Fletcher. Should start up tomorrow early.

It is assumed Ian went home on leave after 'Fylingdale' docked, but there is no record of his journey home or time spent there.

Chapter 10 – Voyage to Canada – rough weather & reports of many ships sunk.

Ian rejoined 'Fylingdale' at Swansea on or about Thursday 6 March, 1941. On Friday 7 March he penned an amusing letter to his family relating several of the difficulties he had to overcome on his bus trip from home in Galashiels to Edinburgh, and then on to Swansea:-

"At sea. Friday 7th March '41
To the House of Waddell:
GREETINGS,

Today finds us at our appointed task of ploughing the deep, so here comes, once again, the last review for a while.

Piled into the bus, to be wheeled to the Market Square; soon after seeing us on the road to Embro *(Edinburgh)*. Things went smoothly until Bowland, when we dived suddenly under the rail bridge. Dumfoonered I watched the vehicle pause, then turn into a cart track, & proceed gravely, but slowly on its way. Satisfying myself that there was a driver I allowed Nature to run its course. We stopped frequently to unlatch 5 barred gates, until after about 10 of these, the road inclined. The wheels turned impotently in the mud, so everybody was instructed to move to the back seats.

This had no appreciable effect so ruddy cheeked land-men leapt out, to tear the dyke down & stow it under the juggernaut's wheels. We gasped & shuddered for about ½ hour, but with no avail. You'll understand the effect all this had on Peter *(Ian's friend Peter who graduated with him from Leith Nautical College)* who hadn't envisaged that such extremities were entailed in returning to Embro.

Regretfully the driver sounded the retreat & we reversed down the road, rubbing shoulders with the wall. At one bad corner a dispatch rider screamed up on bike to tell us that the trail is open, & we revert to the main road, *(It would appear that the main Galashiels to Edinburgh road had been closed for some reason, and the bus driver had been obliged to try a side road which runs parallel to the main road, but runs through several farms on its way north towards Edinburgh.)* arriving at the McB's at 2 pm. A quiet afternoon soothed our travel-jaded nerves.

Around 5 Louis drove Alma, Peter & I to the Calcy, where I safely entrained. After a 10 min. wait at Carstairs my train (& several others I suppose) pulled in. Just before boarding, a gent enquired if I was a Wireless Op. Seeing it futile to deny it, I fearlessly confessed.

From Carlisle to Crew was dull, with a large man, wearing slippers, sneezing at me. He snored. Train left Crew at 2.41*(am)* ostensibly actually about 3.15. Checked in case wandered about looking for a drink of water, met O'C, leaning despondently over a table in the refreshment-(ha ha) room. He'd been there for 7 hours or sumpn. Climbed aboard our train, found an empty compart. Stretched out on seats & put out lights.

Arrived in the beleaguered city at 10 am, saw Marconi & went aboard. Looked round the effects of the blitz. Aboard, nuthin much doing, so at 6 went up town to get the bus to Thomas Towers. Arrived at the gate to find the family turned out for what I thot was a welcome party but in reality was fire-watching, as the siren had gone. Moni & I went in.

Then when all was ready for me to catch the last bus back at 10.45, siren goes again & planes drone about. I don't catch the bus. Am put in Moni's bed – she sleeps with sister.

At 10 next morning I'm awakened for R. Crispies (Snap, Crackle, Pop), ham 'n eggs 'n coffee. Rise & bath at 11.30. Spend day in house. As nite draws in I'm prevailed upon to stay, so performance is repeated. Only diff. is that breakfast was Puffed Wheat (whiz, bang, crash) & Boiled Eggs. Thinking perhaps that I'd like to see the ship again, I ramble down around 3.30. Find O'C has gone off to Cardiff.

3 guesses as to where I went that nite, the nite I phoned you, as I came back to the ship. Next day I settled up with Marconi (£7.2.7) *(£7-12.5p)* & collected a duffle-coat from the Naval Base where Cappy had told me to get it. It's for O'C & me when we do bridge work.

Up to the moated grange *(Monica's house)* for last time at nite where taxis were vainly phoned for. (None go out after 9.30 now). So it was to be the bus again. I left, loaded with soap, matches & books which were pressed on me. Embarrassing, that's what it is! Phoned for 6 mins. about 9 pm. Just as well, as it turned out. The bus had gone.

Started walking, directed by cops. As a car flashed past I thumbed it, & it pulled up. My first venture at hitch hiking proved successful. He was a factory worker going on nite shift & took me (out of his way) down to the docks. Thus he saved me an inch of leather & 2 hours' walk."

Ian finishes the letter with a P.S., "I think ours is a nice family, ours is".

On Sunday 9 March, 1941, 'Fylingdale' began her voyage to Canada. She sailed from Swansea to Liverpool where she joined Convoy OB.296 with 40 other merchant ships and 7 Naval escorts. Ian continued recording in his journal, and his entries continue to highlight the dangers faced by ships' crews crossing the Atlantic, from the weather, as well as German submarines, aircraft and surface raiders:-

"**Sun 9** *(March, 1941)* – off around 3 *(pm)* in aft. With duffle-cote we keep 2 on, 2 off bridge watches. Couple of Spitfires & a Hudson pirouette above us. Cabin & galley boys have succumbed *(to sea-sickness)*. Too bad for them when we hit the North Atlantic.

Mon 10 – Up & on b. watch. A gusty day. Nutin exciting to report. Spend most of aft & evening figgerin out the new code.

Tues 11 – A beautiful day all thro'. Enter code corrections in morning. Cap says we've to learn flags so we can supervise flag sigs. of monkey island *(monkey island - a deck located at the top most accessible height on a ship, directly above the navigating bridge, used to perform solar and stellar observations)*. I paint the flags on a post card for us to refer to. Hear shipping losses – 29. Hear from Haw Haw that survivors of 'Anglo-Persian' were picked up & landed at Boston by 'Nailsea Manor', ship O'C nearly joined in Swansea. Still going up Scots coast.

Wed 12 – With scenery of snow-capped rugged mountains & a glassy sea we cruise along. Our convoy has now swelled to large proportions & we've a reassuringly adequate escort. Strong sun with a cooling breeze – perfect weather. Full moon at night as we head for America. In aft run about hoisting flags for an AB *(Able Seaman)* who knows nutin about flags! He was on this ship 7 years ago & hopped out at Genoa.

Thurs 13 - On at 8 as usual. In morning see patches of grain & a plank float by – mute evidence. We roll a bit in the swell & it starts to pipe. Around 5 when I'm taking GKU, a raft with 3 men on it floats past us, down the convoy. Accounts state that they looked as if they hadn't been there long, & that 2 were sat down, hands in pockets, while the other was standing, waving his hankie. A corvette picked them up. O'C tells me that afterwards, a constant stream of planes droned out to a point ahead of the convoy. Then came the order to hoist kites. Ours was flown without too much difficulty, but when bringing it down - ! Firstly, the rope for pulling the kite back down to the deck broke. 'Tiny', an apprentice climbed up to the mast head & tied the rope again. The rope was hauled on – and broke. Tiny dashed away & brought back some heavier rope, climbing up the mast to fix it again. The rope was hauled on - & broke. They managed to catch the end of it, & with Herculean struggles the kite was brought down. But Tiny perched on the extreme top of the mast as the ship rolled heavily was memorable. He did 3 trips up & was rewarded with a drink from the Old man.

Fri 14 – Nutin of interest to report until aft when a small ship gets alongside & bawls to us to get into our correct station. We retort likewise with much waving of arms. The sailors are painting our rafts in red & white stripes so as to make it easily seen. During the morning a Sunderland cruises along, shooting two coloured flares out as she passed the destroyer – her recognition signal.

Sat 15 – Escort left us early this morning. That usually means dispersal. Get a sub position 40 miles astern of us. Probably one of the stragglers from our convoy. Weather deteriorates a bit, glass falling & fog setting in. And as it gets dark & fog settles down, we disperse & we start our wireless watches for the next 2000 odd miles. Here we go again!

Sun 16 – On at midnite till 4. Raider 40°N & 40W *(mid North Atlantic)*. Usual list of sub positions. We roll & buck heavily. On leaving the convoy last night, we did 12 ½ knots for an hour or so. The day & the ship roll on.

Mon 17 – high wind & unpleasantly rough sea. I feel vaguely unwell. At dinner, soup & two tumblers of water deluge onto my pants as ship rolls violently. I am disgustipated as it would've been good soup too. However steward brings another plateful. Sun reported off the NW coast of Africa. O'C tells me this is St Paddy's Day & he wished he was home for it.

Tues 18 – I hear that an upturned lifebote drifted past close to the ship this morning. Then in aft, O'C receives an SOS from the 'Iris', (a little Dutch coaster we surmise), saying that they'd a fire on board caused by a time-bomb would assistance be sent for the Chief Mate who was seriously injured. She gave her latitude as 42°N & 5°W, which put her in the middle of Spain, but she later amended it to 52°, which position (somewhere round the Skerries) was more likely. So that's something else we've to contend with – time bombs on board! Views have it that it was probably out from Swansea, a hive of 5th columns & sabotage. They instanced the case of a Greek in dry dock which had 3 on board, which blew the stern off. Hear shipping losses – 25 & references to Churchill's speech re 'The Battle of the Atlantic'.

Wed 19 – When I go on at 4, O'C shows me 3 sub sinkings. Two Clans, the 'Macnab' & the 'MacIver', and the 'Mandalika' were all torped. after midnite. The 'Clan MacIver' got hers in her noon position yesterday! The other 2 were sunk off the Cape Verde Islands which has recently become Hell's Corner for torpedoing. Heavy fog envelops the ship most of the day. *(The 'Clan Macnab' collided with the Norwegian tanker SS 'Strix' and later reported that she was taking in water. Shortly afterwards she transmitted an SOS, and sank east of the Cape Verde Islands with the loss of 16 crew members. The 'Mandalika', loaded with 9200 tons of sugar was sunk by 'U-105') (uboat.net).*

Thurs 20 – We continue to wade thro' blanketing fog all day. Nutin much during day – only thing is that I have a wash before tea: the refreshing novelty of it was fine, put on clean clothes, others having been worn since Swansea. Was also going to shave sideburns but hadn't time. Turn in to closing stock prices from Boston. Another 9-10 days should see us in.

Fri 21 – Another clan last nite – the 'Ogilvy', it too going off the Cape Verdes. 3 clans in 3 days. In aft learn of the 2 raiders, 'Scharnhorst' and 'Gneisneau', operating W of 42°W *(somewhere in the mid North Atlantic)*. Gulp! At nite hear Lowell Thomas mutter that the Navy has nutn to look at these 2, except King George V, for speed & firepower. (27 knots & 11" guns). We bowl along in alternate fog & sunshine. Try new watches, 6 on – 6 off as from tonite. I'm 2am-8am, 2pm-8pm. Shave off all but the Vandyke embryo.

Sat 22 – Hear German news that the raiders have sunk 22 ships of a convoy today in the Atlantic. Funny, we didn't hear any SOS's! As I come off at 8 it has developed into as fierce a nite as I've known. Wind of hurricane force, pelting rain & quite black gloom. Pick my way along to cabin. Engines stopped for a while this morning when gauge glass burst. American stations booming in at nite.

Sun 23 – Wind rages & whips sea with resulting roll.

Mon 24 – Some of the wildest rolls I've seen her do she does today. One partikler wave swamps bote-deck, pours thro' my not-quite-firmly-enough-screwed-up port & soaks the bunk. It also cascades down the mushroom vent. Sheets & blankets I hang up to dry. The continuous watch bizness is beginning to pall, and I to pale. However we'll have a 3rd *(Radio Officer)* next trip.

Tues 25 – A dull day with dull food & dull weather. I champ restlessly at the bit & long for land & congeniality.

Wed 26 – When I stagger out at 8.30 I find that the sun shines & a warm breeze plays over my white face. We must be in the Gulf Stream or sumpn. Sea is quite peaceful so that throughout the day we do 9½ knots."

The remainder of the Atlantic crossing was uneventful, and 'Fylingdale' arrived off Halifax, Nova Scotia, on Sunday 30 March, where she anchored in the basin and was ordered to observe a blackout. On Wednesday 2 April, Ian and O'Conner went ashore, where they sent telegrams to their families to let them know of their safe arrival. Most of the time in Halifax was spent building extra accommodation for ten gunners and replacing the ship's furnace and top-mast, work that was to last some days, if not weeks.

While Ian was away, Galashiels buried one of its famous sons. Pilot Officer Tom Dorward, aged 24 years, Royal Air Force Volunteer Reserve, died of wounds sustained while serving with 25 Squadron, RAF, which flew Blenheim night fighters. Before the outbreak of war Tom Dorward had worked as a Director in his father's firm, J & J.C. Dorward, Ltd, Waukrigg Mills, Galashiels. He had been a talented scrum-half, playing for, and being elected as Captain of his home team, Galashiels R.F.C. In 1938, he was included in the Scottish team to play Wales at Murrayfield on 5 February that year. He is buried in Eastlands Cemetery, Galashiels. *(Border Telegraph, 11 March 1941)*.

Whilst in Halifax, Ian wrote to the family:-

"Halifax
Thursday nite 17th April 1941
Dearly beloved,

I am gathered here, pad on knee, the smoke from a fragrant Turkish weed curling round my little curly head which is bowed over this loving task, all ready to shoot you another transocean tittle-tattle. It is 15 days since I sped the last one on its way by air mail.

Well we did get ashore eventually. As I stepped onto the quay, birds twittered in admiration of the uniform (newly pressed), bees drew in their breath sharply as they eyed that impeccable shirt (newly washed), beetles directed one another's attention to the spotless scarf. The gatekeeper stopped a car for us at the gate & directed the driver to take us uptown, which he did. There O'C sought out a shop which said that it changed English money. Inside the owner said that he would give $4 for £1's worth of silver, and $2 for a £1 note. We said thank you & left. In banks were told that only through the agents could money be changed.

Some days we went to the 'Y' *(YMCA)* for a shower or did some shopping. Three dances received our attention, but somehow they didn't seem to go so well. The rhythm of the music was different & one had to press the dames into the English style of hoofing, a style which admittedly they preferred, but I dunno, we didn't seem to have a very great time, you feel more danced against than with.

The hilite of entertainment, however, was the Sunday nite we dropped into a 'holy roller', (negro church). Issuing in, we sat down. The hymn singing began. To a lively music-hall tune the congregation stamped their feet, clapped their hands & beat time on anything available. They certainly swung those hymns. Then the preacher began. As he thundered away, those present shouted words of encouragement or agreement. 'Yas suh', and 'true enuff' figured largely. One old lady in the front row repeated continuously throughout the dissertation, 'Praise de Lawd' in a screechy voice. At one part of the preacher's sermon this cry was kinda inappropriate. He'd just finished saying – 'Ah'se passed a good many milestones, an ah don't expect to pass many more' – when the old dame chimes in!

He referred to us as 'strange faces among the congregation tonite', and hoped that we 'seafarin' folk wouldn't meet up with any hazards on our travels'. More hymns were sung and accompanied till the end of the service when we escaped.

All the time we've been here, the long overdue repairs to the ship have been going on. Now we're at anchor, marooned on board. On Monday Cap brings mail for us – an agreeable surprise. Learn of Tom Dorward's death from a letter from Bill Anderson.

Yesterday the 2nd Mate decided to change the lifeboats round. We lowered one away & rowed it round to the other side. Then we decided we w'd go for a sail in the other one, so we hoisted the sail & bowled along, only we didn't make any headway – it was all leeway. The wind & tide did not let us take much regard of the Mate's instructions that we shouldn't go too far and we drifted past various ships until we had to pull very hard to make a little headway. We crawled up to the Greek's side & held on with a bote hook.

Various members of the crew looked over, grinned & went away. With the 2nd Mate muttering about the tide changing soon (he was really het-up that time, but pretended that he'd command of the situation), we pulled ourselves along the ship's side by the bote hook & tied up on her anchor-chain where we bashed against the side at each wave. After much deliberation we decided to oar up to another ship & shelter in the lee, and from there pull back to our scow. We strained & panted at the oars – 2nd Mate broke one in his efforts – but made little or no progress. But help was in sight! One of the launches that brings the workmen to the ship was speeding in our direction & soon we were tied to it. At about 30 knots we were towed back, drenched by spray in the journey. Greeted by jeers from about the entire ship's company, which we passed off with easy laffs, we retired to change.

At tea the Mate facetiously talked about salvage dues we w'd have to pay as he'd sent the launch out to us, but we just laffed and berated the 2nd Mate's seamanship. I retired at nite kinda sore & still after that strenuous pulling.

I'm becoming a trifle sun-burned what with basking in life botes and painting things on deck. We will soon be on our way home, so some time in early May you'll be hearing from me. The birthday (Ian was born 6th April, 1921) passed off quietly with no celebrations. Hope Margaret and you are all radiating health. Cheerio, Ian."

Ian's journal entries continued as preparations were being made for 'Fylingdale's return voyage to the UK, loaded with wheat, and her eventual destination of Sharpness:-

"Thurs 17 *(April 1941)* – The buzz buzz come on board. All day & nite welding goes on, making it 5th Nov as the sparks fly & make the new mast stand out eerily. Write letter at nite.

Fri 18 – Have wires fixed to bring current up to wireless room. O'C & Old Man have gone to conference. Learn of sinking of 'Georgie', probably with our mails on board. Also learn that 5 ships out of a convoy which left here last week have been popped. O'C comes back around 7 with parcels for last minute shoppers. Then Ole Man returned. We learn it's Liverpool with quite an adequate escort. We're in middle of convoy. So let's away out of this. Learn of sabotaging of 'Silver Prince' at Panama. Sand in bearings & cylinders – completely wrecked the engines.

Sat 19 – Pilot comes aboard & we move out – the first ship! Sea calm, no wind. Engines much more silent now. Convoy forms up in aft & evening. Paint guns in aft. Our old friend takes up her position in middle of convoy. The newcomer is on our starb. beam." *('Fylingdale' was part of Convoy SC.29 with 46 merchant ships and 18 Navy escorts).*

For several days the voyage was fairly uneventful as the convoy sailed towards the UK. The only notable event was Ian celebrating one year at sea on

Wednesday 23 April, 1941. The following Monday 'Fylingdale' was told her destination was Belfast.

Kites were flown from merchant ships during World War II for either carrying antennas for ships' radios, or as an anti-aircraft device. They required a strong wind, and were not always reliable due to the weight of the equipment attached to them. They could also get entangled in the masts and rigging of ships, and be dangerous if a conductor was attached to them, as they could lead a high voltage to the ground if not properly earthed. They could also be a source of embarrassment to the ship if the launch did not go smoothly. Ian wrote about one instance in his journal and describes the difficulties they had:-

"Sun 5 *(May, 1941)* – On at 8 till 12. Nutin much in morn except that an attempt is made to fly kite. Its wire twists itself round everything near it. At last the kite blows onto the aerial where it twists round titely. Frenzied attempts to free it avail nutin. We even swing the ship 2 point to starb. so as wind'll catch kite, but we only fall back out of station. Sloop morses, 'what is the matter?' I reply – 'I'm trying to get the kite up'. Then I watch him reporting this to another escort – 'He's trying to get his kite up.' You could almost see the exclamation marks! Slip down to engine room to tell the engineer to give her every ounce so's we can get back into position. It's not for 3 hours that we regain our place after abandoning attempt to launch the thing.

At a quarter to 8 signal from Commodore – 'Enemy submarines are known to be in the vicinity.' Tell Ole Man & Gunners to close up gun's crew.

While attending to flag hoisting, a bang disturbs us. Look up to see a black pall hanging over outside ship. Deduce it was the blank round which the escort fires as a warning of action. Then astern the depth charges start. First 2 or 3 in quick succession, then as the navy craft stand round a position, 4 or 5 boom out, thudding and making the ship quiver. The escorts buzz round their spot 'like dogs at a rat hole' as Ole man puts it. Must have located sumptn when they're letting go as many as that. Very probably they got him. When they shake our ship about a mile away, imagine what they'll do to a cylinder submerged, especially when they're set at the right depth.

It must shatter the crew's nerves to have these things bursting round their cigar, & when & if they get home, they won't relish another trip. 'The Battle for the Atlantic'. *(The damage that an underwater explosion inflicts on a submarine comes from a primary and a secondary shock wave. The primary shock wave is the initial shock wave from the exploding depth charge, and will cause damage to personnel and equipment inside the submarine if detonated close enough. The secondary shock wave is a result from the cyclical expansion and contraction of a gas bubble caused by the initial explosion, and will bend the submarine back and forth and cause catastrophic hull breach, in a way that can be best described as bending a plastic ruler back and forth until it snaps. The effect of the secondary shock wave can be reinforced if another depth charge detonates on the other side of the hull in close proximity to, and at the same in time as the first detonation, which is why depth charges normally are launched in pairs with different pre-set detonation depths).*

A Hurricane appeared this morn & after circling round on patrol, flashed up our line! He passed us not 100 feet off, at our bridge level. Could see the pilot's leather helmet as he roared past. Others thot he was going fast, but he wasn't really – he must only've been at ½ throttle if he was looking for periscope wakes. Beautiful machine.

Mon 6 - On 8–12. Kite is flown successfully after a few attempts. But in aft when wind drops, our kite drops too – into the sea! So do most of the other ships'. Started gun watches today; to stand by Hotchkiss during hours of daylight.

Around 10, 2 depth charges shake ship. Notice Greek has hoisted flags – calling attention to bearing so 'n so. Destroyer screams across to the other one which dropped the explosives. They circle round. At 11.45, leading ships swing round in alteration of course. No blasts, no signals, they just turn followed by those behind. Very impressive, tho commonplace.

Tues 7 - On around 5 am. At 6 or so, hear a bang from leading destroyer. The lookout points out the plane to us. A bomber far out on the horizon, very low. Corvette lets go with her pom pom. The plane continues its low altitude cruising, far out on the starboard side, curves round behind the convoy & flies up the other side. Sloop then gets in a few shots. I sound the Klaxton for action stations, & don my tin hat. Impudently the Hun had shot out a flare as he passed, trying to deceive the Navy into thinking that he was a British coastal reconnaissance plane! But it wasn't the correct recognition signal & the escorts let go. Shortly after he disappeared far out on the port side, another plane appears on the starb. bow – a flying boat, looking to me very like a Jerry one. But it wasn't & he was given free pratique *(practice)*. We then later intercept a morse signal from a destroyer who said that he'd received a msg from the aircraft reporting that he'd chased the Focke-Wolf but he'd disappeared into a cloud.

Things quieten down for a while. Before 8 the Hun appears again on starb. beam & we see the flying bote bank & dive towards him. The faster bomber beats it, puffs of black smoke coming from him, & the British plane in hot pursuit. Phoned to the gunner to close up the gun's crew before this. No more sign of the Jerry, but I hear that later in the morning the dog-fite was continued, but I was turned in grabbing some well deserved sleep.

Kite is flown after tea but later it drops into the sea & when winch is started to pull it in, wire breaks & kite is lost. This is the 3rd kite we've lost like this – they're not practicable. Should see land tomorrow aft.

Wed 8 – On morning watch. Air alarms & excursions, but no crisis. A glassy sea, little or no wind & 'channel feeling', as the Ole Man puts it, help to keep the ships in perfect station. We change places with the ship astern so as we can drop back into Belfast when we leave the convoy. Sight St Kilda's in aft.

Loch Ewe section continue straight on while we alter course to starb. An impressive sight as all those ships are on port side of Commodore & others on starb. Bright lite which flashes every minute & discover it's Barra Head & we're further ahead than we reckoned. If we keep this good going we'll be in tomorrow nite easily.

Thurs 9 – Well well! Another cloudless day complete with sun. Pass Rathlin Island & enter N. Channel. Opposite Ailsa Craig, Clyde ships sheer off & we continue. We ask Commodore if we can enter Belfast Lough after dark. He says no but may save daylight now, meaning, I suppose, to press forward. Then ship ahead of us pulls out of line, hoisting 'I have engine trouble'. Destroyer dashes round her & blinks 'as'. She then dots 'Aren't you for Clyde?' We deny this, saying our last orders from Comm. were for Belfast. She replies her msg. from England of 2nd May was for us to proceed Ardrossan! We ask him to corroborate this from Comm. & turn up the Firth. She replies that we definitely are for Ardrossan, so we try to make up leeway we've lost to ships already on their way up Firth.

There's been a bad slip up here when not 5 minutes before we'd been asking Comm. about Belfast mentioning the place about ½ a dozen times! Also we'd been put in the column which was bound for Belfast. Soon we're shooting thro' the water at about 10 knots. Ailsa looming up large & we pass it about 10.45.

As soon as Ardrossan was spelled out by destroyer Cap turned & grinned – 'You'll be laughing now!' And O'C realising the convenience of my getting home I should be alrite. That's if we discharge cargo here, & not just the 'accessories'.

Fri 9 – Ugh! Wake up in Rothesay Bay. A very pretty & peaceful sight. Wonder whose mansion it is opposite Rothesaytown. It's much commented upon. This seems to be a ships' graveyard, as about 3 ships are beached, & 1 is gutted, this one at anchor. No definite info about our destination. Special bote comes to us later, the officer concerned with the unloading of the things. He leaves to phone the high ups in Glasgow. We chat with the bote's crew who slip us papers & bomb gossip. Greenock a shambles, H & W's *(Harland & Wolfe)* factory in Belfast got a direct hit etc. Machine gunning of bombed out folk who were making for the woods at Greenock. Two Hun aviators from wrecked place thrown into fire by Greenock populace as raid rages. Still no definite orders.

Around 7 pilot & exam vessel come out & we go to Belfast. So near yet so far! I cd've been home so soon too. Leave at 8 & I go on radio watch till 1. Very disappointed, while Guns & O'C are gleeful. Fate, I suppose, if somebody is pleased another is sad. Hope to get mail tomorrow. Look at map to catch upon Clyde's topography. Pick out Loch Ranges, & all the places Mummy has ever mentioned. Pass Ailsa Craig again around midnite. Just before I come off at 1, comes a blue from Cullercoates Radio – 'South Rosyth' & an SOS from 'City of Winchester' in 8°N, 26°W *(south of the Cape Verde Islands)*.

Sat 10 – 3 weeks from Halifax. Cor lumme! Wake up in Bangor Bay. Naval Control comes aboard but with no orders. Later in morning pilot boards us to take us in. This is better. Get alongside crane which soon gets things underway. But heid guy says we don't discharge here! Coo! Send off wire when we learn that it's now Sharpness! Blimey!

At tea pilot tells us that 4 ships of the convoy which left before us got it. One was the 'Port Hardy' – Big Jim Robertson's!! I'm awfully concerned, but he believed that most or all were saved. Cor chase me round the barrack square! Two tankers got theirs, burst into flames from stem to stern, only 1 soldier picked up.

Subs came up in middle of convoy; there were 3 of the rats, & rumour has it that all 3 were despatched! We certainly are the luckiest ship ever; it's either convoy ahead or astern of us. *(About 19:25 hrs on 28 April, 1941, the tankers 'Oilfield' and 'Caledonia' were attacked by 'U-96' and sunk. 46 people on board 'Oilfield' were lost and 8 were saved. In the 'Caledonia' 9 men died in the engine room of the ship and 5 who jumped overboard died when they drifted into burning oil from the tanker. 25 men survived. The 'Port Hardy', carrying food and general cargo, was struck by a torpedo intended for another target and sank after 3 hours. 1 crew member was lost, but 82 were rescued and landed at Greenock.) (uboat.net).*

Letter from Bill Anderson; 2 sheets, both cut in ½ by censor – 1 sheet has bottom missing, other has top; little or nutin to read.

After tea explosion shakes ship – rush out & see rolling cloud of brown smoke rising from buildings across from our berth. Unexploded mine just exploded. The town, I gather is bad, but Ole Man says later that most of damage caused by fire. Inefficient & insufficient ARP fire services. Town that was immune from raid. Tales of thousands of fountain pens & shaving brushes dropped. Pens explode on picking up. Brushes cause rash – or explode too or sumpn.

Guns given 2 hours to go and see his wife. Comes back – 3 houses in which she's successively gone to have been demolished but she's alrite only he couldn't get to her at present address. Goes ashore later on promise to rejoin in Bangor Bay tomorrow. We quit the berth & go down to the Bay & anchor.

Sun 11 – Still here. Guns comes back from seeing his wife with raid damage tales. Later the idea of swimming was mooted, so one by one, bold spirits climbed over the side. Muttering about 'never let it be said' – I run & borrow O'C's trunks & prepare for H2O. As I shiver Guns gives a belly laff to us by coming out in white duck trousers over his costume, 2 lifebelts, a leather helmet & gloves. Very funny. He's really a very good swimmer with medals etc.

I dive in & swim for about 10 secs then hastily climb up again. Yes – it was cold, but the refreshing value was great. Have shave & don tennis shorts & felt very cool. Sleep uneasily in aft becos of heat.

Naval Control aboard at tea & we're Commodore for the channel convoy – which means continuous W/T watch for <u>us</u>. To have a strong A/A escort. I'm to be called at 2am.

To Sharpness Ho – but will we discharge there? Probably – not – likely! By September they should mebbe've found a berth for us somewhere, mebbe Caithness or sumpn. Bah!

Mon 12 – On at 2. We proceed away alrite & I endeavour to keep awake till 8. Ole Man comes in for hours of watch, so's to divide radio watch between us & Vice Comm. We do 16, he does the other 8. Alrite for us. Off at 8 till 6pm. At dinner destroyer lets go a string of depth charges which we see exploding astern of her. Awful bang. So if destroyer hadn't have been 'ere, we probably wouldn't been here! Did I say lucky! Spend rather delightful aft reading all letters I've received at sea. Some from home dated Sunday 26th May – Der Tag!

Like to think that convoy depends on one when on watch for whole lot, but actually escort is listening too.

Tues 13 - It must've been about 3 or 4 o'clock when I heard a plane. Hun I thought somewhere round. The rise & fall of the unsynchronised engines grew louder, then there was a hellish bang somewhere aft, followed immediately by another. With every nerve screaming for me to get out and see what was going on, I remained, listening to the phones. Suddenly, just after the bangs, a machine gun clattered on the port wing of the bridge. 'The 2nd Mate', I thought. It was quite dark outside and I couldn't imagine he c'd see much of the plane. Cursing him for using the Hotchkiss which has alternate tracer in the strips, the streaks of which would give our position away, I slid out to the bridge. There the dope was babbling sumpn about the destroyer calling him up, when he'd opened up with the gun. 'Of course', I gritted, 'to ask what the hell you were doing'. Plane was still around up there so I go back into the wireless room. Find out that the second bang had been the 12 pounder of the ship astern. Why not leave the shooting to the destroyers, there solely for A/A (anti-aircraft) work. At breakfast Guns tells us that the egg *(bomb from the aircraft)* had dropped somewhere astern of us & privately cursed the 2nd for his machine gun madness.

Grab some sleep in morn. Some Whirlwinds *(RAF heavy fighters)* cavort over & around the ships, coming alongside us as they flash past with a roar. After they'd dived and banked for a while & left, the destroyer called us up – 'For your information these were Whirlwinds'!

Arrive off Barry Roads around 6. Pilot aboard who takes us to Walton Bay, it being too late to get up to Sharpness.

Wed 14 – In Walton Bay. Go up in morn. to Sharp. Go ashore & meet most everybody we know. Charter for loading starts 28th – Swansea or Port Talbot. Dictate NLT at nite after failure to contact home on phone.

Thurs 15 – To Berkley probably."

'Fylingdale' tied up at Berkley on Friday 16 May, 1941. Ian and the others went ashore. Time was spent either going to the pictures or trying to find out where the nearest dances were. On Saturday 17 May, Ian went to a dance in Cambridge, near Bristol, where he reported, "Good fun & dancing. Most of dames we've seen at last dance here. Rushed a bit in L's (ladies') Choices. Woo woo!", which would indicate he was somewhat of a favourite with the opposite sex.

Not all went smoothly, and on Monday 19 May, Ian wrote in his journal, "Yes, you guessed it – to B (Berkeley). Get wind of dance at Wotton-under-Edge, about 9 miles away. Assured of likelihood of lift. Start out. Finally get on to main Glos. *(Gloucester)* road. All vehicles going wrong way. Those that do pass us. Nice people. Arrive at Dursely, where lifts were likely we were told. Getting dark & starting to rain. Everything shut. Chat to a not-very-helpful Special Constable. Motor hirer not in. Start retreat from Dursely at 11 pm. Arrive back on ship at 1.15. We've walked 22 miles with almost no pause! Never altered our pace but kept plugging away, jesting whiles. But what a journey! I never thought I'd walk 22 miles in my life. Left Berkely at 8.45, so you can work out our mph". On Tuesday 2th Ian wrote, "Leave on aft tide. Ashore for last time while she's in basin, for last look round. Kinda stiff after last nite!"

Ships' crews always looked forward to home leave. It was a welcome relief from the dangers which presented themselves from enemy submarines, surface raiders and aircraft, the severe stormy weather of the Atlantic Ocean, and the additional stress of long frequent periods spent on watch. Leave during wartime was not always possible due to the pressure to turn ships round with the minimum of delay so that vital supplies were delivered to Great Britain to further the war effort. However those pressures took their toll.

Ian was no different to other young seagoing men, and the thought of getting home was never far from his mind:-

"Mountstuart Drydock
Newport, Mon
Thursday 22nd
Dear, dear,

I'll try an' clarify the leave posn. in its present lite. We dry docked here yesterday afternoon, and after Superintendents an' people had poked around at the hull for a while things stopped for the day.

O'C & I went ashore in rain (see Welsh summer) to look around. Peered hopefully at train times in the station & in need of entertainment went to the 'Empire', which stank.

This morning, after various authorities had given us the once over, Cappy said – 'no leave from 'ere'. We shall be out on Sat, or something like that.

There was almost a mutiny this morning when the sailors heard that the 2nd Eng. had told 4 firemen to make themselves ready to go home, and the sailors had been told that no leave was to be granted. On whose authority the 2nd spoke I donno, but the posn. still remains – 'Leave is outa the question' I quote.

It'd be allrite if I could come home, rejoining at Swansea, but this unfortunately, is agin regulations & 2 RO's have to be aboard, even for an hour's run. They're apparently not doing much to the engines here, which the engineers tell me, will give up ½ way across the Atlantic unless seen to.

From reports r'cd (most of what we have to go on are rumours & counter rumours) the repairs'll be effected in Swansea where we load, but O'C wants to go home, & still more important – SO DO I, but we're afraid the Ole Man looks none too approvingly on this coup of both going together, becos he thinks that one of us sh'd be around for firefighting, etc. The ideal, of course, w'd be to sign on our long overdue 3rd *(Radio Officer)* & he'd stand by. Nous verrons cc que nous verrons *(we shall see, we shall see)*. But never fear, I'll make a resolute attempt to get home, be it even for 48 hours.

It's all this quick turn round of ships that's upsetting some well earned leave. It's all very well running ships until they drop, but they can't run the men the same way – or can they?

Dunno if this Pool will be a good thing or a bad thing (it won't affect us if we sign on the same ship again). The leave is 2 ½ days for each month on arts *(ships articles or contract)*. Sounds allrite, but at the end of leave you'd get pushed on another ship – good or bad. Anyway, in Marconi, you c'n be shifted about as they like, so again it doesn't make much diff. to us.

I believe they're abolishing 6 months articles – instead we pay off at end of each trip, & this sh'd mean more leave. This is a good thing. But our present 6 mths won't be up till August or Sept."

Ian did manage to get home, although there is no record of when he arrived home. He returned to the ship at Newport, and on Tuesday 27 May wrote to his Mother:-

"I knew it! – Not till Thursday! Resume: Arr. Carlisle, walked round & bought some books. Train at 12.23. Very long & crowded. On seeing crowds I slipped unobtus. to the last carriage which was completely empty. Pleasant run to Crew, reached abt. 3.40. Cuppa tea before entering the barouche at 4.7 *(4.07pm)*. Good seat, (not like the standees) allway to N. in brilliant sunshine. Ate my sandw. on Carlisle – Crew run, & very good they were too! In N. at 8.15 – staggered out into station yard with case in search of taxi. As I app. one, a large red face leaned out & screamed at me. It was 3rd Mate who told me I was going to a dance. I said 'oh', and we rushed down to docks where I dumped the case & rushed next to dance. I had asked when we were going & was told that word had come thro' that afternoon stating Thurs. as the day! Ole Man, I'm told was very wild, and he said that I c'd'v still been home. Otherwise we were already for sea only some dope decided in some office that she'd stay until Thurs. Very sickening. I'll try phoning tonight. Luv, Ian."

Ian's Mother replied to his letter, and her disappointment that he could not be at home longer was apparent:-

"12 Abbotsford Road
Galashiels. 29.5.41
My dear Ian

Glad to know you got safely to Newport. Were you not too tired after four day's travelling while off to a dance?

It was very tough luck that you didn't sail till today – you could easily have been here till Wed. & that would have given you time to look around a bit & not rush all weekend. I can imagine that the Capt. would be very wild. It must be very irksome for him to be so controlled.

As in my previous letter which you should have got today, I am sending you some shortbread – a cake from Browns & some wee cakes I made from some of your Canadian butter. Will be glad to hear again. Hope there may be a chance of seeing you soon again. Cheerio. Love Mum."

Ian also received letters from his older sisters Nancy, and Margaret a primary school teacher, letting him know of the news from home, some written in a light hearted and amusing style:-

"12 Abbotsford Rd.
Galashiels
29.5.41
Dear Kid,

It's a real shame hauling you back like that and all for nothing but that's just life – it's a hard, hard, struggle. This week has been hell, pure and simple just one dammed thing after another.

To begin with on Monday my 'date' didn't materialise so I phoned the billets and learned that he had gone FISHING!! That's a new on me but we live and learn an' how!

That bugger Gordon hasn't written so you write him & challenge him to a duel if you like. Still, Eric phoned up on Tuesday fresh from his Sunday's triumph. We had 3 lots of pips and I'm going to Edinburgh to see him next Sat. Have just heard today that a woman in Scott St. fainted, & the coalman's wife hit her chin on the table ducking.

We now have a garden seat so you'll have to make a big effort to come & sit on it. Last night was 'music' night and I duly hammered Cland's *('Clerklands', home of family friends)* piano for 1 hr. Met the sentry afterwards and 'went for a walk' – pretty stale, in fact boring. Today we write a composition on the school clock which develops into a list of times of entry & exit of pupils e.g. 'The bell rings at 9 o'c. Then it rings again at 10.30. Then it rings at 10.45 etc, etc. Very, very, sad.

Thelma & I are going out on our bikes tonight to drown our sorrows. Saw Barber on Mon. but wasn't speaking to him – silly mug. Nothing ever happens here and I'm going slowly nuts. More news later.

Love, Margaret

P.S. Nice of me to write isn't it?"

Eric Brown, mentioned in Margaret's letter, was a pilot in the Fleet Air Arm. Although born in Edinburgh, his parents were natives of Galashiels. He was acquainted with the Waddell family before the beginning of the war, through Margaret, who was one of a group of teenagers who travelled regularly to Edinburgh by train. Eric and Margaret were part of a social group who attended the cinema and dances etc, in company with each other. Eric Brown met Ian once, before the war, when he was invited to 12 Abbotsford Road for supper.

The incident Margaret mentions in her letter was Eric Brown 'buzzing' Livingston Place, Galashiels where his family home was, in his aeroplane, which caused some consternation in the town. An article in the Border Telegraph on 17 March, 1942, reported that he had been awarded the Distinguished Service Cross, for gallantry and tenacity in combat, after shooting down a German bomber and having a share in the destruction of another both of which were attacking Allied convoys. Eric Brown survived the war and went on to become one of the most celebrated and decorated pilots produced by the United Kingdom.

At that time Britain's fortunes were mixed as the war progressed. An article in the Border Telegraph on 27 May, 1941, reported that the pride of the British Navy, H.M.S. 'Hood', had been seen to blow up after an exchange of gunfire with the German Pocket Battleship 'Bismarck', with the loss of over 1300 lives. It also reported that Britain was almost air raid free, and the R.A.F.

had made a vigorous attack on Cologne, Germany. A later report stated that Allied forces were withdrawn from Crete after 12 days of fighting due to the lack of air cover, despite inflicting heavy losses on the German forces. However 261 enemy planes had been brought down that month during air raids over the United Kingdom. It also reported on the later sinking of the 'Bismarck' by H.M.S. 'King George V' and H.M.S.'Rodney'. *(Border Telegraph, 27 May & 3 June, 1941).*

On 1st June 1941, Ian's Mother expressed her pleasure having him home the previous weekend, as well as her fears for her son's safety:-

"12 Abbotsford Road
Galashiels, 1.6.41
My Dear Ian,

It was grand to have a word with you last night & to know that you were safe in Swansea & had seen Monica. You must let us have her a/d so we can write & thank her for looking after you so well.

I am just listening to our withdrawal from Crete. It is very disappointing that once again we find our air power inferior – or rather that we had no bases near enough to help our forces.

It was a surprise we hear this morning that clothes are to be rationed. Pity you didn't manage to get your sports coat when you were here.

You think you will be leaving on Thurs. I'm glad they got the 'Bismarck'. I would have been rather disturbed if I had known it was rampaging about the Atlantic.

I have finished a pair of gloves for you. Let me know if they fit & I will knit some more. I enclose them herewith, also a tie which I found in the dining room.

It was a blessing you snatched that weekend seeing you are going away so soon. Hope to hear again from you soon. Cheerio & best love, Mum."

It appears that Ian's Mother approved of his continuing relationship with Monica, revealed in a letter to him written on 5th June, which said:-

"We will look out some photos for Monica. We will send her those of you from your earliest days up to the present. What a grand display that will make & will show what rapid development you have made 'for better or for worse'? Wasn't it a good thing that you snatched that weekend's leave. Perhaps the next time you will get longer." She ends, "Cheerio & very best of luck. The trip should be pleasanter this time – Hope so at any rate. Best love, Mum."

Ian also received letters from his Father, who like his wife, looked forward to Ian's periods of home leave, and worried for his safety:-

"Gala: 5.6.41
Dear Ian.

This is in the hope of your getting this before you leave. Just three months since your last departure which I see was Sunday 9th March. I am hoping the Atlantic is getting a little more safer. I was listening to a north country skipper yesterday saying he had sailed the Atlantic for I think he said 13 times since war broke out & he had never seen any enemy. He must be a rare species.

Glad to hear last night you had got all the 'comforts of the Saut Market'. I have put a Navy Roll collar jersey on order for you which perhaps will have been delivered by the time you get back.

We will expect a cable from you by 30 June/ 1 July, & will again ask for Agent's address to send you a cheap one. You should be back by the beginning of August. The Gala holidays are the week commencing Monday 4th August. Should we come & see you if you are not to be home on leave?

This coupon rationing of clothes is another blow at the old firm. I don't see why retailers should be called upon to bear the brunt.

It is a good thing the 'Bismarck' was accounted for as I'm afraid it would have done untold damage among the convoys. I'm disappointed about Crete, & am just afraid we won't act quickly enough to forestall the Germans in Syria.

I expect we shall be getting a letter from you telling us in more detail what you have been doing. The weather should be finer this trip.

Well cheerio & the best of luck. Off we go now, down the hill to post

Yours Dad."

The comments made by Ian's mother and father were echoed in newspapers at the time, and the competence of those directing the Allied campaign was questioned. On 5 May, 1941, the following article appeared in the Southern Reporter:-

"CRETE AND US – After what has been called the most terrible and fantastic battle of the war, we have had to withdraw from Crete. Our fighting men displayed wonderful valour and fortitude. But once again it has been proved that the courage of men is not enough to defeat the machine. It is not surprising that questions are being asked whether after six months in that Island the fullest preparation had been made to cope with air-borne attack. Was the anti-aircraft defence as strong as it might have been? Was it not possible to mine the aerodrome? We are told that Crete has taught valuable lessons for the future; and it is to be hoped these are salutary and do not require to be re-learned. Crete has a lesson for us at home. Let us be inspired by the courage and devotion of our fighting men to provide them with material necessary for victory. They depend on us to do our duty to them and the Cause."

Ian wrote one more letter home on 7 June, 1941, before his next voyage. The letter revealed that his relationship with Monica was still strong, and that he was more than welcomed by her family. He wrote:-

"I think it was Friday 30th the drift south to 'The Croft' began. Arrived up there in the evening where lipstick was received with glad cries. Met the 2 sisters, (aunts) both teachers, one looks like Madame Tabouis, & chatted away. Later everybody discretely disappeared, leaving Moni & me and the fire. At 9.30, as usual, food was brought in, and at 10.45 I just snatched the last bus. That was the first nite.

Well Saturday came round (it always does) so I pick my way up with a suitcase of dirty linen and a tooth brush. Went to a dance that night which stank out loud. Turned in at a late hour in a pair of small boy's pyjamas.

Breakfast at 10 or so. Shirley Temple's favourite cereal, 2 s. eggs, coffee & marm. A beautiful day it was to stroll in the garden, peering closely at peas 'n things. Then we examined the car and its upholstery, pulled to sleep with the usual siren accompaniment. Returned to ship in time for lunch next day".

Later that day Ian returned, "…to desirable r's'd'nce *(desirable residence – a reference to Monica's home at 'The Croft')*. To flick that nite – 'Comrade X'. Clark Gable & H. Lamar; very good too. All about Russia. Ben Hecht was paid $20,000 for the script. Tomato, egg & lettuce salad figured largely when time came for me to take aboard some vitamins. This was almost a standing dish each nite."

In the same letter, after detailing a meeting with a Marconi Inspector, he wrote, "You're quite rite – I went up that nite, next nite, nite after, and nite after that. You can send the fotos of me paddling when you wish, to No. 16, and of course thank them, especially Mrs. H. W., very much", which would indicate that he was always made most welcome on his visits to Monica and her family.

Ian was having difficulties with his income tax assessment, but he wrote, "Also on Saturday I had completed 12 months continuous sea service, & my pay is correspondingly jacked up, making it now £19-15/- *(£19.75p)*, £11-10/- *(£11.50p)* increased to £12-15/- *(£11.75p)*, plus £7 War Bonus. Radio overtime for last trip was £2-5/- *(£2.25p)*. I also have some overtime for gun watches coming to me, I think. He finishes the letter, "Until next month's, cheerio.

LUV FROM IAN".

Ian's Mother, it appears, sent the photographs of Ian to Monica as requested. In a letter of thanks written on June 11, 1941, Monica enclosed two photographs of Ian:-

"Dear Mrs Waddell.

Thank you for your letter and your kindness in sending the snapshots so promptly. Here are two snaps taken on Whit Sunday. From these I think you can say his development is all to the good in comparison with the youthful ones.

Ian & I spent a very happy week together. We are all looking forward to the time when he will come again, as I daresay you are too.

Wishing you all the best.

Yours very sincerely, Monica."

Chapter 11 – Ian's dream of being bombed, and sunk by U-boat – 3rd Radio Officer goes mad.

Ian's next journal begins on Wednesday 4 June, 1941, as he prepared for another Atlantic crossing, leaving Swansea for Quebec:-

"**Wed 4th June** - Parcels & mail arrive. Marconi & Bote Inspector aboard. New wiring & receiver next trip. Weeds *(cigarettes)* released from bond. Buy boots from Martucci for 2/6. Up to No. 16 *(Monica's home)*. Steak & chips & mandarins. Bus back. Phone home. Up to Glamtax for car. Wait.

Sordid cameo enacted in office. 2 dames caught pinching 2 lambs & vegs from Market. Caught by taxi supervisor. One weeping, other cheekily pseudo defiant. Cross examined by polis. Matron & van arrives for them & they are hauled off still protesting their innocence. They'd been up in court last week for different charge.

Taxi finally materialises. Share it with Dutch seaman going to Prince of Wales Dock. Drop him at turnbridge. Taximan says he can't go any further – lack of gas. Lie as he filled bag at garage. Bridge opens as he drives off. Siren goes immed. Walk along docks. Meet cook (?) from 'Big Island'. He chats long to me. As all clear goes, terrific flash overhead. Lightning. Then big glow flares sky. Look out & see sumpin burning. It's a barrage balloon! Then another catches, & another. Terrific sight as they spiral down flaming. Clear as day. More litening & others go up. One overhead falls in pieces on cook's ship. Derrick catches afire. Soon put out. Glow further up dock. Bits still burn on ground. Walk back in rain at 1.45. Another siren at 2. Hear planes at 2.15. Get ready for bed."

'Fylingdale' put to sea on Saturday 7 June, 1941. On 10 June she joined Convoy OB.333 at Liverpool with 38 other merchant ships and a Navy escort of 7, The first few days of the voyage were uneventful, and Ian's journal continued:-

"**Wed 11** – On at 4 as usual. Cold wind whips around. Bovril at 5, tea at 6. No one can make anything of the 3rd *(Radio Officer)*. Never says a word at meals. Clyde & Oban join us.

When signal to test guns is given, find that starb. Hotchkiss won't cock & fire. Succession of gunners – 1st the soldier, who knows little or nutn about it, then Mr McDermott, who tries to put cartridge strip in with bullets pointing towards him! Cor blimey. Quite hopeless. My day draws to a close. Nothing untoward happening.

Thurs 12 – Vaguely unwell in belly in morning. A quiet day altogether. Take wheel for minute or two in aft.

Fri 13(!) - When I wake up I find that I've dreamt we were torped. I was on the bridge when torp came at us on starb. beam, not very fast. With lightning actions I rang the engines to 'Stop' & spun the wheel. But of no use – we were hit. Next thing I noticed was the U-bote Commander on the bridge beside us. I enquired of him how long we would take to sink to which he replied – Five minutes. So I went to collect a few belongings. Next, rather hazy, picture was us aboard another ship. We were all saved except the 3rd (no wonder)! It must have been the cucumber sandwiches at supper.

Trevor John *(3rd Radio Officer)* doesn't improve much. Discover from his ticket that he'll be 21 in August. We'd put him at 16 or 17. His meal time manners are a bit rocky. On being asked by Ali to pass bread, he picks up one slice & passes that. He'd also get a certain amount of noise response from mashed potatoes. He also hasn't said a word at meals. Various people have found it impossible to carry on a conversation with him. However I try to do the best I can with him. Weather pretty lousy. Misty, rainy, blowy & unshining. Quite heavy seas.

Sat 14 – 3rd comes in at 3.40, moons around & leaves door swinging & banging. Th' a brite lad! A dirty morning, rain & squalls. Amused over solemn conclave which Ole Man & Mate have when deciding who shall use which lavatory. Rules set out after are: cabin & galley boys AS WELL AS THE COOK shall use one aft in sailors' quarters. 3rd shall use Engineers' one as he's on that side. Our own shall be locked & key kept in mess room until people get into the way of the new order. Funny how important they regard these seemingly petty things.

Dreamt we were bombed, last nite. 2 nites running calamity has hit us in dreamland.

Rather a lotta flags today, & I'm not helped by cretins of AB's *(Able Seamen)* who still don't know the flags. Our last kite breaks away this morning. In aft the 'Cressdene' tries to signal us a msg. from Comm. But her lamp is lousy & I give up. After tea she semaphores us, still lousily. Finally we ask Comm. directly & get orders for a pleasure (?) cruise. We pass on, only the Greeks astern of us have no Aldis lamp & we don't know whether they got msg. or not. It's late before I get away from the bridge.

Sun 15 – Foggy all day. Miserable weather. However it's ham & eggs for breakfus. First shave & wash since leaving – which I find good.

Mon 16 – More dirty weather, wetting rain & fog. Learn of lamentable accident suffered by Wilf Smith, the dopey AB. Thinking he was stepping along the flying bridge aft, he pranced forward. Only he was on top of ladder leading down to the well deck. He suffers a bruised arm & a most perfect peeper. Unique, I hear it called. First he swore blind that sumbuddy'd thrown him down. Later he says he thot he'd been thrown out of 'The Red Cow'. But he's quoted as having chuckled later – 'This'll be good for some weeks' a most peculiar person. About 5'1", asthmatic, wearing slouch hat & wind breaker. Dubbed Gene Autry thereby.

3rd eats his breakfus grape fruit with knife & fork! A horrible sight."

The convoy eventually received the instruction to disperse and the ships to sail independently to their destinations:-

"**Sat 21** *(June, 1941)* – Hose down the bridge at 6 & become dampened in the process. Flags to the effect that station keeping by the convoy has been good, indicate that we're gonna break *(dispersal of convoy)*. Iron in the morning.

At 2, while O'C & I are sunbathing, the convoy gets the "DT's" & the break up begins. Ships morse to us "Good luck & good voyage" etc. We reply in kind. Ringing full ahead on the engines we leap ahead, leading the field. Slowly the ships, now stood out in widely different directions, fade away. Life bote drill at 4. On watch at 6.

At tea I personally witness the 3rd's knife wielding of food. Horrible sight. When he wants something, he jabs his knife at it & mutters the wanted thing's name. We push ahead at 9 knots.

Sun 22 – On at 4, radio watch. O'C had stayed on with 3rd till 4, showing him what to do. Not that he takes much notice. He relieved me 25 mins late at breakfus. Hear news about Russia & Germany *(On Sunday, 22 June 1941 Hitler launched Operation 'Barbarossa', Germany's invasion of Russia).*

Mon 23 – Inspect gun's crew while they're at practice. In aft go up to monkey island, strip to the waist & absorb large quantities of ultra-violet. Very pleasant, cloudless sky & enough breeze to make things rite.

Off watch at 8 while on bridge, I ask Cap about Cancer thinking it is a star. But a sign of the Zodiac he explains & dashes away, presently hauling out volumes about stars. Shows me chief areas, Orien, Alpaca, Vega etc. etc., then we go out & he points out the various orbs. & constellations. I'm very pink at night.

Tues 24 – Sunbathe very extensively in aft clad only in bathing trunks. Olive oiled most exposed parts. Message in early morning – convoy attacked by submarines 55°N, 37°W *(mid North Atlantic about 950 miles south of the tip of Greenland).* At tea Cap, evidently noticing my increasing plumpness, enquires how much weight I've put on since coming to sea.

Wed 25 – A busy day. Aft breakf. gun practice, consisting of firing off all small arms on ship. I fire Hotchkiss on bridge, then go aft where soldiers & sailors are firing savage Lewis's at barrels etc. Try one, but I'm deafened by clatter, gun jams or requires cocking. Next try the Ross rifle, which is nice'n restful. Fire off a pair of Lewis's. They get very hot.

Very windy & rough today. At nite engines slow & finally stop. Engine room full of smoke. Packing burning I believe. We roll with engines out.

Thurs 26 – make enquiries about last nite's stoppage. Chief says it was all the 2nd's fault, who allowed the HP piston rod to become hot. 'I told him it's only 1st trippers and old men who get hot rods', says Chief (age 60). Extensive repairs had to be carried out at nite.

Inspect the target which had been constructed. Burlap *(hessian sack cloth)* with bracers on floats. At 10 it's slung over & it falls astern. Up on bridge Cap puts her over 10 points then calls up gun – 'sub in sight, bearing 110, range so in so, deflection 010 .' Soon reply comes back – 'sights set'. Then 'Fire' from Cap. dead in line but short. 'Up 400 again'. Very near. By now target difficult to see & last shot is to the right. Bob is brought up & congratulated. The guns crew collect a tot.

Fri 27 – First thing I see going on at 4, is reports of 5 sinkings in 60°N, 30°W *(North Atlantic, midway between Iceland & tip of Greenland)* since I turned in. All in exactly the same positions. A horrible day with rain and cold."

Apart from foul weather the remainder of 'Fylingdale's' voyage passed without incident, although the 3rd Radio Officer's strange behaviour continued. The coast of Canada was sighted on 30 June, and 'Fylingdale' arrived at Quebec on Tuesday 1 July. On 3 July Ian's family received a telegram from him saying, "All well and safe greetings good luck".

Ian spent a fairly eventful time in Quebec, and wrote a wonderfully descriptive letter home on 20 July, two days before 'Fylingdale' set off on the voyage back to the UK. The following are extracts from that letter:-

"Sydney N S
Sunday 20th July'41
My Good Woman,

Our finding an elevator which hurls one to the Heights *(of Abraham)* took much of the toil out of Quebec, an important factor, as the heat was terrific. First things done on our arrival were – large feed and a gentle stroll on the promenade.

Next morning, the 3rd (Trevor John) *(Radio Officer)* behaved even more queerly than before. At breakfast he kept closing his eyes and grimacing, so that Cap asked him if he was tired. His answer was that he thot he had been having too much sleep. Then he dashed away mid-way thro' the meal. His next act was to rush up to a workman on deck, snatch off his cap, stand on it & make faces at the astonished artisan. Throwing pieces of coal at people became his next diversion. After this Cap told O'C & I that we'd better find sumpn for the guy to do or he'd go screwy on us. I'd tried conversation with him before, with no notable success. This time it was quite obvious that he was mad. To've seen me in his cabin pseudo-nonchalantly muttering about 'soonbegettingback' and 'yououghttofindsomethingtodo' while he was sitting beside me, a fatuous leer on his face & his eyes glaring – well! We finally had him fitted into my (that is cook's) boiler suit & given a pot of paint.

He danced about with the brush, flicking a stroke on, and then standing back to admire his work, so that he was just in people's way.

When the Ole Man came back that nite I said to him that he'd better have a doctor to examine the guy as he was definitely nuts. Cap said he'd keep him under observation over the weekend.

But next evening we came back – to find him gone. The Mate told us the story. In the afternoon Trevor had been prowling about deck, then, as a workman was climbing out of the hold he let fly with a wooden wedge & missed the gent by a few inches. The fact that the labourer was perched precariously on a steel ladder & an empty hold beneath him made the affair quite unamusing. With gentle words the 3rd Mate disarmed him of the other wedge and reproved him for doing such a thing in colourful language. Muttering – I'll get you – Trevor retired to his cabin. Seeing that things had taken a turn for the worse, the Mate phoned for a doc. An ambulance, 2 cops & a medic soon sped down.

They found the 3rd turned in, fully clothed, even into his (mine, cook's) boiler suit. I believe the doc questioned him first, then he stood up, one hand behind his back. 'Look out, he's got sumpn there', one of the cops yelled, and made a dive for him. It was an orange & he'd squeezed it quite flat, only the pips being whole. With the cop clinging on he struggled ferociously until finally the combined weight of 2 flatfeet and a doctor bore him down. They held him on the deck until his strength ebbed away and quickly strapped him on a stretcher. The ambulance whirled the party to a hospital, but not before the 3rd *(Radio Officer)* had kicked a cop under the chin. The 3rd Mate had been detailed off to accompany the loony, only at the bug house he was mistaken for the patient! For a minute or two anyway. And there the 3rd *(Radio Officer)* was left. The only news we heard was the doctor's report just before we left – dementia praecox *(A premature dementia or precocious madness usually beginning in the late teens or early adulthood).* He's to be kept under observation for 6 weeks to see if he responds to treatment. His diary showed definite aberration, even before he came to sea, Cap says. And that was our first 3rd!

All other things that happened during our stay seem to pale in comparison but I'll try'n remember the main things."

Much of Ian's, and his shipmates', time seems to have been spent socialising when not engaged on duties aboard the 'Fylingdale'. He mentioned going to several dances and meeting local girls and their families. Even in the 1940's it was considered a 'small world' and one of the families Ian meets up with originally came from Selkirk in the Scottish Borders, only a few miles from his home in Galashiels. A new 3rd Radio Officer, from Manchester, was also assigned to the ship. His ship had been torpedoed and he picked up and landed at Quebec after 23 hours spent in an open boat. In that same letter Ian told of another amusing, and embarrassing incident involving Ian and his shipmates:-

"To try out one of the lifebotes we (2nd & 3rd Mates, O'C, Steward & me) lowered the craft & rowed lustily for a while. Seeing verdant *(healthy green)* shores we pulled inshore & secured the bote to a tree. Uttering glad cries at being ashore we plunged into the woods, bird nesting & wild strawberry picking. For 4 hours we capered happily in the fine scented country until we finally arrived back at the beach. The bote was high & dry and the tide was going out! Our futile efforts to push the bote were desperate to watch. Where all this happened was in front of some log cabins, summer abodes of city dwellers and one of the occupants cheerily told us the tide didn't come in until 9. This at 3pm!

The steward & 2nd Mate volunteered to row a skiff out to the ship so's to bring us some tea. Shortly afterwards we fed picnic-wise on the shore. Topped the meal by plying rummy. It was very pleasant.

Another long walk was indicated, only this time we were back in loads of time to observe the tide's movement. It was still going out. Played some more rummy & finished the last piece of cake, and played soccer. By now it was dark and the husband of one of the cabin's occupants invited us in. Mrs. had made us salmon sandwiches & cake, the next door person sent round another plate of sandwiches so we ate rite heartily as we were almost starving. Listened to 'Patience' on the radio. Most appropriate! Also we heard Winston's speech in which he referred to the 'rising tide' *(Churchill's speech paying tribute to the civil defence forces, the 'Rescuers of London', in the House of Commons on 14 July, 1941).* At 9 the water had advanced 6 feet, at 10 it had fallen back again. Only at 10.45 was there enough water for us to push the bote off. With farewells we sprang aboard & pushed hard till we sailed free. The people had given us their address, 'for any time you're in Sydney' & had enjoined us to come across again. Back to the ship, at 11 we heaved up the lifebote & retired. Breakfast next morning was a quiet meal."

Other ships arrived in port and Ian and the rest of the crew spent much of their time visiting their friends and colleagues on those ships. In a poke at Fascism Ian wrote in that letter of, "...an amusing account of a meeting held by Mosley *(Oswald Mosley, leader of the British Fascist Movement).* He marched up to the platform surrounded by his bodyguard of Black Shirts and followed by a spotlite. Reaching the platform, he turned with infinite solemnity and raised his rite hand in the fascist salute. In the silence came a clear voice from the balcony: 'Yes Oswald, you may leave the room'."

Ian finished the letter on a slightly disappointed note, "And that's all the news up to date. No letters had arrived at Quebec while we were there so I told them to send them home if they did finally get there. A letter from Moni, one from Aunty Belle, & one from Jim Walker have been the total received in Sydney. Hope you're all as tanned as I am. So long for now, Ian".

'Fylingdale', with a load of grain, began her return journey to the UK on Tuesday 22 July, 1941, bound for Sharpness in the Bristol Channel as part of Convoy SC.38, with 30 merchant ships and 18 Navy escorts. Ian wrote in his journal, "We up anchor at 1. Many old friends in convoy. Sunbathe in aft. It's good to be at sea again." On 25 July a different hazard presented itself to the convoy of ships:-

Fri 25 *(July, 1941)* - Cor! On at 4, when slight fog is hanging round. At 5 it blankets down so I go on radio watch. Shortly after, there's terrific activity on bridge. First "hard aport', engines rung to stop, then hard astarboard. An icy chill seems to permeate the atmosphere. Ole Man comes in saying "We've just missed a huge berg. It went past so closely that you c'd've stepped onto it". Cor! We go on dead slow. All round, fog horns are asking melancholy questions. Occasionally, we hear the prearranged siren signal – 'I've encountered ice'. Then the ether crackles.

A Greek, who was behind us before the fog sends – 'Struck large berg. Making water fast'. Another msg. soon after reporting a collision between 2 ships. Commodore sends 'I've encountered ice'. More reports from collided ships. They're the Greek & Butch's ship. 'Foc'sul peak flooded, unable to pump', comes from Greek, and 'fifteen feet of water in No. 5 tank', from Butch's.

The messages continue to pour in – 'Have struck ice' being the most common one. Later msg. from Butch's says 'Afraid will have to take to boats'. Then another berg comes on us from port side. I go out to see it – a ghostly greyish-white shape, very big, slowly drifts past, quite near. The chill from it makes us shiver. Gallant msgs. – 'Sinking, but will attempt to reach Sydney', come in next.

All morning we hear the morse messages come thro'. In all, when we reach light, six ships have been damaged. Ships stand by their battered comrades. We grope along, siren booing continuously. Others come thro' the binding blanket of fog eerily.

Early in aft. I hear a putt-putting of a motor boat alongside. Look out to see a small whaler, towing a dingy beside us. The men in it are shouting to the bridge. Evidently, just before they came out, the lookout *(on Ian's ship)* had shouted, "land close in on starboard beam!' We were almost aground. A sounding showed 30 feet of water – we draw 23 or so *(lower part of the ship which is below the water line)*! Another few minutes & we sh'd've been ashore. The motor boat crew tell us that we're at Belle Isle.

Shortly after, the fog lifts, sometime in late aft. Before this happens we get a bearing from a coast station. Also we call Commodore, but there's no answer to the msg. Kinda depressed with this ghastly weather we thud onwards.

Sat 26 – Again we call Comm. this time getting thro' to him. Have to repeat some of the groups several times over before he finally acknowledges receipt. A hopeless sender & receiver he is. Fog lifts to show a cold grey world. Still we plug on with our little band trailing behind us. At last in the evening, the sight of the AMC *(Armed Merchant Cruiser)* cheers us, & he morses to us full instructions as to where to go & when to be there, & countless other courses & bearings. With a final blink he eases away & we continue reassured.

Sun 27 – Still on wireless watch with unerring Pinkney judgement, we as Commodore of remnants left, bring our little gaggle up to the main convoy. Funny incident when corvette on starb side telling us to join big convoy, and AMC on port side telling us to rejoin our original bunch. Seeing the AMC is the bigger, & more likely to be the Senior Officer of the escort, we comply with him and soon we're steaming along as tho' nutin had happened, only we're very depleted.

Mon 28 – At about 5 a burst of steam issues from the engine room skylites. We slow perceptively. Steam continues to belch out. Shouts are heard from below. Ole Man is called & Chief soon bustles up to bridge, looking funny in flannel shirt, girt with braces, baggy trousers & untidy curly hair. He explodes to Cap that a gauge valve cock has blown completely off, so we'll have to slow down for some hours. I get onto the Commodore with Aldis & report our plight. We fall back slowly *(this was a dangerous position to be in as U-boats, wary of the warship escorts, would try and pick off ships that had straggled from the relative safety of the convoy)*. The steam slowly stops & we go ahead again. Chief reported that repairs had been affected. We tell our 'Moon' this & he's relieved. First a broom handle'd been stuck onto valve & a temporary cock made.

Tues 29 – After too little sleep, up to the bridge where it's raining & blowing. Retire to chart room, there to drowse. All morning it rains & howls. Roof leaks a bit. In evening while morsing my cap-helmet blows into sea, but Teddy slips me another, as well as mitts & socks, from Whitby Sewing Circle or sumpn.

A dirty nite, with seas. Not July weather. Hear on radio German claim of sinking 19 ships & corvette & destroyer in convoy today. Ah well."

The poor weather continued as 'Fylingdale' ploughed on:-

"**Mon 4** *(August, 1941)* – Catastrophe! Retiring las'nite at 11, I found it difficult to woo Morpheus. After restless tossing sleep I awake & look at watch. 6am. Curtain rod has fallen down & while replacing it fail to notice that the aerial lead wound round the rod has drawn taught. It tips the radio, atop of which is a full cuppa cocoa. It spews all over mattress & sheets &

pillow slip. Curse & throw the soaked linen into a pail. While all this is going on, 3rd Mate comes in and laffs. I'm annoyed, doubly becos it's not 6 am at all but 12.30! Picking dry bit of bunk retire again.

Up at 4. A Sunderland appears today. A gale springs up during the day. We part in aft & our section pursues a course which makes us roll very heavily thro' mountainous seas.

I sit calmly throughout the aft darning socks. Then at 4 face the tempest on the bridge. Patches of blue sky gleam deceptively while a gale whips the sea into steep rollers & white caps. The ship rolls over to her rails. Seas batter down on her & sometimes, with a twist & a shudder, she frees herself. We curse the Commodore for so rigidly pursuing his course when the ships could turn a little so's not to have the seas full abeam, & then head thro' it on another tack.

I notice the 'Dunsley' on our starb. side. She has one of her lifebotes hanging over the sides, the davit smashed. Also her 'D' flag is up, showing – 'I'm manoeuvring with difficulty. Keep clear of me'.

Other ships turn away from the constant battering for respite, including us. Cap reports, that of 2 doz tumblers he bought in Sydney, 6 are now whole. Later the Comm. puts up – 'You have been keeping station badly. Endeavour to do better!' 'He's alrite in his built up passenger ship', & Ole Man dryly bites – 'He'll be up there on the bridge enjoying it, saying it was like the time he went round the Horn in some sailing ship or other'. And he's a Scot too.

Our flags part in the shrieking tempest, & whip about at the end of their line. Tiny climbs masts to secure them. Still rolling badly when I turn in."

The weather improved and the rest of 'Fylingdale's' journey progressed without incident. She anchored in Belfast Loch on Thursday 7 August. On 8 August Ian sent a telegram to his parents, "All right so far more news anon. Ian".

On 12 August he sent another, "Arrived address care Hodder Sharpness. Greetings. Ian". Although not documented Ian went home on leave from Sharpness minus some of his luggage. On 20 August, his friend O'C wrote to tell him that enquiries he had made at Cardiff and Crew had not produced any positive result. On 29 August, Ian purchased a sports jacket at Adam Black, 20 High Street & Sime Place, Galashiels, for the sum of £4.17/- (£4.85p).

.

Chapter 12 – Ian's posting to 'Treminnard' – Cardiff to Argentina, Halifax, Nova Scotia & Boston. Chief Radio Officer goes mad.

Ian's leave finished on or about Monday 8 September 1941, and on his way to Swansea he wrote to his parents:-

"En route to Swansea
3.45 Tuesday aft
My dear public,
Cor ----!

I haven't much time to tell you about things, but 'ere goes. Had tea in Carlisle, went to 'The Philadelphia Story' till train time, when I boarded for Crew. First person I saw in the refreshment room was Jock Weaver, our ex 3rd. He was reporting back from Manchester. We travelled down together, having no trouble with luggage.

Arrived Cardiff around 7, checked in luggage & had breakfast in the Queen's Hotel. Strolled round the town & reported about 9.30. Jock was soon seized and bundled of to a ship, one 'Treminnard'. While he wuz away I heard that O'C had been back & was now on the 'Empire Sunbeam' in Newport. A letter card was waiting for me from him dated Monday & saying he'd like to see me on Wed.

But before all this we'd met the 3rd Mate of the 'Fylingdale' going back to Barry at Cardiff Station. So during the morning at the Marconi Office the fone rang & it wuz for me. It was Bob Bell the Gunner asking me down to Barry tonite.

Then Jock came back with his new 3rd. From the office came confused roars & after a while the gent came out and told me & another sitter to get down to the shipping office & sign on the 'Treminnard'. I barged in to find Jock & the 3rd busy writing out their resignation from Marconi. From the snatches of conversation I gathered that they'd been down to the ship, inspected it, seen that the 2nd & 3rd shared a cabin, refused to sign on & had come back up to Marconi's.

By resigning they enter the Pool & aren't able to rejoin Marconi. & that is rather a drastic step but I was hurried away to collect my wireless certificate & directed to the shipping office.

Down there I was met by an Old Man who guided me joyfully to the counter. One has no choice in the matter – either join the ship allotted to one or one resigns from M's.

The Union man had left the office, the 1st R.O. *(1st Radio Officer, named Cahill, commonly referred to as 'C')* was on board, the ship was sailing either tonite or tomorrow morning, the 3rd *(Radio Officer)* was a small sickly child of 17 3/4, very new, Marconi had pushed down to the shipping office muttering that 'they'd had no complaints before of this ship', the captain & the shipping master had their pens poised ready – so I signed on."

Ian boarded 'Treminnard' and continued, "I prowled around. The cabin was small with 2 bunks, & it had a fan & a wash basin. From sundry individuals I learned that she was for the 'Plate' *(River Plate estuary in Uruguay, South America)* & 'not a bad ship'. The latter I accepted with reserve. Also the Captain who signed me on wasn't the real one, but only a relieving one". Ian also learned that the voyage will last for at least 3 months.

Ian finished the letter lamenting, "I wish I was on the Fyl! But I've wanted to see S. America & at the worst I can only do 6 months on the barge. I'm not especially cheery rite now, but we'll see what a shave, face massage & haircut in Swansea can do. I feel incredibly filthy & never want to see another train in my life. I haven't seen my chief yet, but the persons I've met don't seem to be too bad. It's a mixed crew, Maltese, Norwegian, Welsh & Scots. Laskars too I think. I'll phone you tonight. Here's Swansea, Cheerio, Ian".

Ian paid one more visit to Monica's home before he sailed, and wrote home in his usual light hearted manner:-

"At sea.
Wed. nite, 10.30
10th Sept. '41
Dear, (yes, isn't it),

Here's summore songs dance & genteel patter. I left you just as I got off the train at Swansea. Losing no time, I warned the Thomas turnpike of my imminent arrival & dived into a barbers there, to have administered a shave, face massage, & a haircut.

Soon in pristine glory I was up in the Croft, giving tongue. Moni was bronzed from the Llangranog holiday, Glenna had passed her sumpn & sumpn (Oxford & Cambridge, is it) Metric, with distinction in Maths, & Vivian the small boy had gained a scholarship to the Grammar School. I think all above is correct.

The disappointing part of all this was that I had to make the 9.40 train back to Cardiff. They of course started phoning taxi people, but no go – the 54 miles seemed to put the drivers off. We w'd have taken the T's (Thomas') car but it wasn't properly dimmed or sumpn.

After a discrete interval, supper was wheeled in. Lobster, egg & tomato salad & logan berries in cream. But I just pecked. The remains were borne away & until 9.10 there was almost perfect peace for us. At that time preparations for departure were began, a large bag of apples were laid in homage before me as well as fags & Penguins.

I sped away with M. *(Monica)* to a bus which brought me to the station with about 3 secs. to spare."

Ian made it back to 'Treminnard' on time, and the next morning he met the Chief Radio Officer. He also met the Mate, and the Captain, who gave him a friendly welcome. Ian also reported that the food aboard was good and plentiful, and the radio equipment was more up to date than that on the previous ships he had been on. Ian finished the letter, "You should hear from me in about 24 days, then after that there might be a long pause. Only info here is that we'll be back around Christmas time".

On Wednesday 10 September, 1941, Ian began a new journal:-

"Cardiff to Bahis Blanca (Argentina). Return via Trinidad, U.S.A. & Nova Scotia.

Thurs 11 *(September 1941)* – Can't enter at 6 owing to mines. Scull around till 9 when we go in. Get ready for conference & write lotsa letters, but no go. Give mail to Marines on launch. Proceed out.

Fri 12 – Up St George's Channel *(stretch of the Irish Sea between the south east coast of Ireland and Wales)*. No watch in convoy. In evening write more letters & hand them on arrival in B. to sailor on RAF launch. *('Treminnard' left Liverpool as part of Convoy OS.6 with 31 other merchant ships and an escort of 9 Navy vessels. The destination of the convoy was Freetown on the west coast of Africa. 'Treminnard's' ultimate destination was Bahis Blanca in Argentina. Although it is unclear from Ian's journal entries, at some point on the voyage 'Treminnard' left Convoy OS.6 to continue her journey to Argentina as part of one of the 'FB' series of convoys from Freetown to South America).*

Sat 13 – Start gun watches. See from ship's library list that Haines have 33 ships (possibly more?). Get 100 Woodbines *(cigarettes)* in round 50's from Steward. Impressed by general ship-shapeness of everything on board, the QM *(Quartermaster)* being a stickler for it apparently. Sloop spends most of morning shooting at a floating mine.

Sun 14 – Issued with life jacket, complete with red clip-on lite; also whistle for calling attention to one's plight no doubt. We slip along very quietly, running into occasional patches of fog. Gun watches prove irksome as standing in a box behind a Hotchkiss doesn't take much initiative, but continues to amuse.

Mon 15 – Doing 4 hour watches puts me on from 10-2. The aircraft attack flags flutter all morning & practice firing can be heard from most ships.

Watch the stowing of the new improved & increased lifebote & raft rations. Tins of Carr's biscuits & chocolate, Bovril's pemmican *(concentrated mixture of fat & protein)*, & Horlick's concentrated milk tablets, replacing the old condensed milk & water ration. The water supply too is increased to nearly 3 quarts per person. We have a portable receiver as well as xmitter for the lifeboat; pumps which can be used to wash down the botes when on the open sea are also now standard equipment.

Collected valves from owners of radios on board yesterday & fix up my radio in wireless room for all to hear. Connected to the main aerial she fairly booms in.

Chas grows rather grubby about the hands, face & neck. He mutters away about his Marcella (girlfriend). Touching y'know!

Go on radio watch from 9-11 becos of fog. Some sub warnings & positions. A sub alarm took place this morning – 2 depth charges & alterations, but nothing came of it. Lotta fog today."

'Treminnard's' progress across the Atlantic was slow and the mental state of the Chief Radio Officer or 'C' was giving cause of concern:-

"Tues 16 – weather deteriorating, as is C's stomach. Daily he moans of his constipated condition and his former ulcerated belly. He stays in bed most mornings, refusing all but a cuppa tea. His internal organs & marriage, plus Chas' Marcella provide a limitless source of chatter.

Wed 17 – At O.M.'s *('Old Man' or Captain)* instruction I rig up the radio in the saloon so's everybody can hear it. The set works OK.

She's shipping a lotta water over the bow & aft – wind quite fierce. Gun watches are rather boring. She rolls somewhat at nite, displacing a fire extinguisher which fizzes merrily.

Fri 19 - This morning we receive – by flags – rather important news. We've to continue in our present format. The 3rd Mate curses audibly, becos he figers this'll add days onto our time, but the consensus seems to be that it'll be safer anyway. Chief is visibly cheered & mutters about long stretches of raider ridden ocean. So on we plow. It's become warmer today & the sun can be seen higher in the sky. The food continues to be varied & plentiful – pancakes today & very good ones. I had two. Coffee after it all is imperative now".

Despite the rough weather 'Treminnard' made progress. Her Captain appears to have been a stickler for discipline and procedure, and Ian wrote:-

"Sun 21 – In morning watch while I stand on bridge, the 3rd Mate chatting to me, OM comes up bumbling – "Come along there – one officer on each side of the bridge. I don't want any chattering up here!" I seethe, becos whatever other failings, I don't chatter. My regard for him increases. Believe he's a Scilly Islander by birth, now lives in Glasgow."

Later in the voyage Ian wrote:-

"Mon 29 – Chief is pulled up for bringing a fag onto the bridge by OM (altho' he & the Mates all worship at the shrine of the Goddess Nicotine when up there). Bah!

Tonite I have my first quinine tablet which tastes, I shouldn't wonder, like gall & wormwood. Starting Thursday all hands, (as laid down in the articles) are to partake of 1 tablet a day for 20 days.

It gets dark very quickly here – 6.30 & dusk sets in. Pyjamaless & coverless, fan whirring, I court sleep. I swelter.

Tues 30 – A busy day. Since the sun glares unmercifully, the awnings over the bridge are dragged out and fitted on the spars. With them overhead it is quite pleasant in the shade.

The slower ship leaves us today, so now we c'n slip along at a rate of knots. I hunt distractedly for a pair of shorts. Ironically I've carried my pants across the western for months, unneeded, & now on this run I haven't them."

'Treminnard's' progress is steady and without incident, with Ian's time spent either on routine ship's work or sunbathing in his off duty hours. The tropical heat continues to be quite oppressive:-

"Sat 4 October *(1941)* – Strike on happy idea of wearing pyjama trousers on 4-8 for coolth. Prowl about in morn. having nutn to do. Shave myself as some kinda recognition to crossing the line. Evidently it's only on liners that they perform the Neptune ritual. 3rd Mate tells me on his first crossing he was chucked into a barrel of oil!

C. *(1st Radio Officer)* silent & morose at meals. The food becomes more standardised as stores diminish. Corned beef comes into its own. Tasted corn on the cob for the first time & liked it.

C. unburdens himself to me about his fears of "getting the hammer" if not down here then certainly when we return. He bases his morbid outlook on some quarrel with 2nd & 3rd Mates & O.M of last ship; his missing birth cert.; his Irish nationality; his marriage & the certainty that Marconi have it in for him. He's all so mixed up & vague, naïve & morbid. Let's hope he doesn't go the way of Trevor John! *(Trevor John, 3rd Radio Officer, was removed from 'Fylingdale' to hospital after he became mentally ill in Canada).*

Sun 5 – Still windy. From 4 am when I relieve him, throughout the morning & aft, C. drops in on me to say with a gloomy sorta satisfaction, 'I'll get the hammer alrite'. At this fantastic assertion I pooh pooh as convincingly as I can, considering the disjointed & vague self-condemnation which he drools.

In a perfect frenzy of unburdening he seizes on people on deck, then up to the OM on the bridge. Down in C's room I hear snatches of pooh-hooing similar to mine. This evidently goes on for a while then OM comes into cabin & advises to take over 12-4 watch, 'as he isn't feeling very well!' This means going on watch again in about 2 hours.

Chattering outside of 'sedatives' & insomnia, (C's statement being that he hasn't slept since he came on board). OM & C go into Mates' room where cheering up & "don't worry boy" talks go on & on till I fall asleep.

Fantastic statements – "I was forced into marrying; all Mates & Engineers are Masons; I must've done something wrong; they want to get rid of me", etc. etc. Another Trevor John?"

The Chief Radio Officer's mental state became worse with Ian and Chas, the 3rd Radio Officer, having to cover C's watches:-

"**Tues 7** *(October)* – Wakened by C who greets me with, 'yes I'll be shot alright'. Next incident is around 9 when, from the W. room shouts from OM to C ring out, exhorting him in no uncertain terms to quit worrying & 'for God's sake forget about the last ship!' At this I shut off lite & simulate sleep. Sure enuff, in a wee while, the OM comes bogling round our cabin enquiring if either of us were awake. I snuggle down & keep quiet. Chas, below, intimates that he is & is told that we 2 were to keep watch & watch until Chief is completely better. I curse softly & go to sleep."

The Chief Radio Officer became even more depressed and threatened suicide. Ian and Chas, the 3rd Radio Officer became quite fatigued and the Captain tried to relieve them by making the Chief Radio Officer do his turn. On 10 October, Ian wrote in his journal, "He *(Chief Radio Officer)* says he'll do the 12-4, but OM comes down & sees Chas on watch, who sensibly explains that this'll be his 3rd 4 hour watch today, so OM gets C in from somewhere on deck (tailed by a squaddy) & he goes on watch. Soldier keeps him company in W/T room."

For the rest of the voyage the radio watches were maintained by Ian and Chas because of the Chief Radio Officer's mental condition. The heavy schedule began to wear both of them down:-

"**Sat 11** – As watch finishes at 8, I'm told by cabin boy that 'Chief is bad – you've to do watch & watch'. I say ho.

The soldier whose turn it is to chaperone him goes away to see him & evidently cajoles him to get up for brekf. But by the time I'm at table he's away back to bed. After chow I go back to see him, glean that he's 'bad' (you're telling me) & to keep cont. watch.

While relieving Chas. I'm set upon by OM who berates me for not informing him of C's condition. I point out that I knew only at breakf. Later in morn OM calls me out on deck. Where we have a heart to heart talk about C. decide to give him 24 hrs clear rest, Chas & I to do watch & watch. I've to note the time & date, so that if there's any overtime to come, we'll get it.

Chas & I keep watch & watch, but the sod doesn't take advantage of his day's rest to take it easy, but prowls around making everyone depressed and/or fed-up.

As I was on in aft & had to take Rugby *(radio watch for messages from Rugby Radio Station in Britain)* at nite I was seldom out in God's fresh air & as the 8-12 watch finishes I was helluva tired (after 13½ hours watch) & eyes were gummed with lack of sleep. Took Rugby for more'n hour at 12 – the longest transmissions I've known. I take down code until my hand aches. Never mind, they'll come a day or sumpn.

Sun 12 - Drag myself out for 4-8 & prop my eyelids up. C not up for breakfast so on OM's instruction we let him lie. Some warm remarks passed, sotte voce, by Mates at brek. & I bask as I realise that 3rd (Chas.) & I are objects of kindly concern since we have to sweat & strain overtime."

While Ian was coping with his extended working hours, the Border Telegraph reported on the courage shown by another son of Galashiels serving with the Merchant Navy. Details are sketchy, probably due to the secrecy surrounding ships and their movements, but the report stated:-

"BRAVERY AT SEA – BRAW LAD'S HEROISM GAINS AWARD

A thrilling story of the sea lies behind the information that Mr. W. M. College, elder son of Mr. and Mrs. D. Kemp College, Buckholmburn, Galashiels, has received an award for his part in the saving of his vessel.

We understand that Mr. College played an important part after it had been attacked by the enemy and badly damaged. He received a special letter from his employers congratulating him on his exemplary conduct and devotion to duty in the emergency, and stating that his conduct at such an early age and after completing his first voyage at sea was most praiseworthy.

As a mark of their appreciation the Company have presented Mr. College with a suitably inscribed memento and a money bonus. It might be added that the presentation took place on Friday. We hasten to congratulate Mr. College on the part he played in such an emergency, and to wish him good health and safe voyaging." *(Border Telegraph, 14 October, 1941).*

A further entry in the Telegraph the following week gave additional information. "As a mark of their appreciation his employers sent him a congratulatory letter and presented him with a memento, which took the form of a silver cigarette case bearing the inscription – 'Awarded to Cadet W.M. College for meritorious service at sea, M.V.' Donovania'."

Meanwhile on 'Treminnard' the condition of the Chief Radio Officer became worse, and he lost rapidly any sympathy the crew might have had for him as some suspected he was 'swinging the lead'. Ian's journal entry continued:-

"Fri 17 *(October)* - At brek. C. starts in, with vigorous hand rubbing, 'Well gentlemen they'll be disposing of my body' – when the 2nd Mate cuts in, 'Shut up with that rot.' Not a bit shaken C goes on with 'Ah yes I'll be taken ashore & shot' – only to be met with the 2nd's more vehement 'Shut up, we're having our breakfast'. And this silences the morbid moron. This obviously is the only course to adopt as his gruesome gabble gets in one's gullet. I try to avoid him becos altho' I haven't adopted the 2nd's forthriteness as yet, I feel very tempted to do so, when on our every meeting he hands you that jittery jive.

The soldier escort still emulates Mary's little lamb, one Tommy at least keeping watch & ward in the saloon allnite. Even in daytime one can usually be seen lurking."

Several days in Ian's journal are blank. However he recorded, in his journal that on Sunday 19 October, 'Treminnard' was at anchor off Puerto Belgrano, near to Punta Alto on the east coast of Argentina, and on "Wed 22 *(October, 1941)* - C ashore to doc. Returns with medicine bott. 2 once every 7 hrs. Take Chas up to P Alta in aft. Pause at gate while sentry reads pass upside down & new stamp applied."

There was not much to entertain the crew in Punta Alta. In a letter home Ian said, "The town (Punta Alta) is a small place, 10 mins in the bus from the dock. Percentage of English speaking is infinitesimal, which makes things kinda difficult. Tomorrow night a bus is coming from the mission at Bahia Blanca to take us to a 'social evening'. We drifted into some kinda show last nite. It consisted of a fat gent (heavy comedian?) who would've done well to've put himself in the hands of a good tonsil specialist, & a dame who might have been beautiful three chins ago. The bloke did some ventriloquism & the dame did a half hearted sort of dance with a child in spurred boots, but it was all too overpowering a S. American dialect, so we came out soon".

Another complaint was the high cost of sending air mail letters and telegrams home. A short air mail letter could cost 7/- *(£0.35p)*, and a brief cablegram 12/6d *(£0.67p)*.

In a letter home, dated 22 October 1941, Ian tells of another incident involving Cahill the 1st Radio Officer:-

"Soon after we started in & picked up pilot & 2 Navy gents. One of them had a large revolver slung on hip, & C sees this & makes a dash aft down to soldiers' quarters. When later this Navy guy comes round the ship some bystander shouts to C, "He's just outside" & he tries to climb onto racks above hammocks to hide! I didn't see all this as I was engaged in supervising the sealing up of W. *(Wireless)* room, & also going round with the manifest, but I believe from then on he was just a quivering mass. Goes round asking when the execution will take place.

Thurs 23 – roused by OM at 8 am, gist of whose talk is could I take over for homeward run? C evidently being sent home from BA *(Buenos Aires).* Say he will see if any Sparx in BA, but doubtful & satisfied anyway that I'd officiate. Overtime etc.

Usual quiet morning in saloon (ship's!). C packs his grips. To my query of 'anything I can do?' – he negatives. Also burbles about 'if I get killed it'll be an innocent man', etc. & 'probably this'll be the last time you'll see me - except heaven'. He writes a screwy note to 'Managing Director' of Marconi in Chelmsford to the effect that he's turned the gear over to me today 'in perfect working order'. He disappears for hours on end – wasn't on board at all last night.

Sun 26 – Tales of C running away – out of taxi. Round 2 blocks. Behaviour in agent's house, inspec. of food. Reluct. to enter Consulate, growls."

'Treminnard' left Punta Alta on 30 October, bound upriver for Bahia Blanca. At Bahia Blanca, most of the time was spent going ashore to see films, or sight-seeing when not engaged on ship's maintenance or practice with the ship's guns and small arms. On 'Treminnard', the Chief Radio Officer was eventually removed from the ship, and in a letter to home, Ian relates the tale:-

"**4 November 1941** - From OM we hear tales of C's behaviour when being taken to Consulate in BA. Ran away from his 'guides' who chased him round 2 blocks. Reluctant to enter Consulate grounds & in the end 2 keepers were sent for who whisked him uncompromisingly to an 'institution'. We've heard no more of him except today that 'he's quieter'. Day he was taken away OM asked if I could take charge if no No. 1 *(Chief Radio Officer)* could be found in BA, & yesterday when none had materialised he asked if I was confident that I could take over. He'd expressed his confidence to Marconi in BA so on my OK, he appointed me officially Chief. So – responsibility continuous watches & overtime are my lot now. Chas is OK on receiving, but tho' 18 he's 'very young'."

Later in the same letter he gives an opinion of his time in Argentina:-

"Now we're in Ing. White *(Ingeniero White nr Bahis Blanca)*, upriver. It has one main street & a few dust roads with a sprinkling of wooden shacks, exactly what the ole western towns must've looked like. But I don't think I like S. America much; probably the language difficulty accounts for part of this, but I shouldn't like to live out here. I now have C's room & it's a relief having a separate cabin again esp. when everyone admires Chas' gloves until he takes them off with Lifebuoy & other times when someone asks, 'Is that a new perfume or are you just laying a drain?', whereupon Chas departs to dip his socks in Sen-Sen.

But these are stirring times – this will go down in legend & song. Children in ages to come will cluster around their Grandfather's knees, saying 'Tell us how the great Wad. stood the strain of having two colleagues led away to institutions, Grandpa!' And he will tell them & they will rise from the recital better, deeper, broader children."

On 5 November, 1941, 'Treminnard', loaded with 7800 tons of wheat, left Bahia Blanca on the homeward voyage. On Thursday 13 November, Ian logged, "Altho' currents are against us we maintain quite a good speed".

The voyage appears to have been uneventful, filled with ship's maintenance and routine. There are several gaps in Ian's journal, which he puts down to fatigue caused by the extra radio watches he and Chas had to do in the near tropical heat, and extra maintenance on the radio equipment. 'Treminnard' crossed the Equator on its journey north on Wednesday 19 November, and on 20 November, Ian noted in his journal, "The 4-8 watch & morn is a killer. Sticky heat & difficulty in keeping one's eyes open. Discover that float of hydrometer is leaking – small wonder the S.G. readings were low. Replace & keep on charging batts. The heat, I learn, slows charging rate". On Monday 1December, 1941, he noted, "Dredful lethargy where recording this is concerned."

'Treminnard' anchored in the area of Chesapeake Bay on Wednesday 3 December, to take on coal. The ship was only allowed to stay alongside the jetty during daylight hours as US Health Officials found 15 rats below decks. The crew were also unable to get ashore. 'Treminnard' also lost her anchor and another had to be brought by railroad to be fitted. She sailed again on Saturday 6 December for Sydney, Nova Scotia.

On Sunday 7 December, 1941, Ian noted in his journal:-

"Heavy seas shipping a lot. W/X reports. Hear Japan's war entry. Programmes int. every cuppla mins. to bring new bulletins." On Thursday 11 December 'Treminnard' arrived at Sydney and Ian noted, "Arr. Around dinner time. Snowing las' nite & v. cold today. Thankfully knock off watches & huddle round coal fire in saloon. Mags. put aboard but crew got there first. Also large box of 'cookies & candy' for ship having had longest run – from Mothers of Syd. B. Crosby at nite & on the program they play G. Save the K. – cornily.

"Frid 12 – Open the parcels – choc cake, sponge c., ginger cake etc. Stew. cuts it all up into equitable pieces for all hands."

On Wednesday 17 December, Ian sent a cablegram from Sydney to home saying, "All well and safe. Best wishes for a speedy return. Best wishes for Christmas and New Year. Ian Waddell." A cablegram sent to Ian from his family was returned with the message, "Your cable to Waddell SS 'Treminnard', Sydney N Scotia is undelivered. Addressee left", presumably on 'Treminnard's' homeward voyage, loaded with wheat, as part of Convoy SC.60 with 23 merchant ships and 14 Navy escorts.

A ship is a community made up of different people, and occasionally domestic disputes would occur between individuals who were fairly closely confined with each other for long periods during a voyage. Ian was also clearly fatigued by the weather and the extra radio watches he and Chas were obliged to carry out. Ian noted:-

"Fri 19 *(December)* - Lousy 4-8 watch. Ship rolling heavily, stove emitting nauseous fumes, things falling about with the rolling. Quite fed up with the grinding monotony of 4 on 4 off, the eternal buzz of the dynamo in the fones, the snail's pace at which we're proceeding & Vasco Da Gama *(reference to the ocean)*.

Bit of activity in aft. Hear OM in pantry muttering to someone, Everything'll be alrite', or words to that effect. Chief ushers a fireman – 'General' Jackson into saloon & sits him down. The 'General' has a nasty bash on his dusky brow, but seems to be bearing up. 2nd M *(Mate)* comes down to administer 1st Aid – looks at the cut, pronounces clean & sticks a piece of lint & antiseptic over the wound, securing it with sticking plaster. When the stoker leaves we get the story. Word had come to the bridge that a cuppla firemen were fighting with pokers.

Sat 20 – Heavy rolling takes place. Enter room to find a stiff white paste on floor – ¼ full bucket has been overturned & talc powder has fallen down - the two make a good cement on the rug. Haircut, remarkably good one, from Steward at nite.

Sun 21 – On and on it goes. I've never had a lengthy look at convoy yet, but it's not one of the best I've been in. Start and finish.

Wed 24 – Spend large part of a.m. watch singing Scots songs for my own & Chas' edification. Meals have degenerated and now almost always include cabbage. We go into our regular grumble-fest & agree that it's small wonder the sailors indulge too well when reaching shore, having consideration of their slum quarters in the foc'sul & lengthy sojourns away from home, & the way the food is served to them. It's a dreary grey day with sea. Remark on the lack of Xmas spirit.

Thurs 25 Dec *(Christmas Day)* – Heard Winston at White House on American Program. As Xmas Day has fallen on a Thurs, there's no question of our ham & egg for breakf. In a.m. listen to BBC. Very little splicing of the mainbrace in morning but dinner is a masterpiece. To a not quite groaning table we sit down 7 strong & are served with smooth chicken soup. When the plates have been removed from the pristine cloth, the turkey is ushered in (in portions), with sage & onion stuffing, cabbage, (oh ubiquitous vegetable!), roast & boiled potatoes. Very toothsome it is, & a goodly portion is served to all. (Chas reported having seen 4 large turkeys being placed in the ovens yesterday). The Chief retired to the Mates' Room to loosen his trousers ½ way thru' the gustatory epic.

Plum pud without money in it follows – also very good. Apples & oranges & nuts provide the …."

'Treminnard' arrived at Belfast Lough on Wednesday 31 December, 1941, and anchored there. There is no record of Ian going home on leave on his return to the UK, but he did, and probably in the knowledge that he would be transferred to another ship.

The Steam Ship Treminnard.

Chapter 13 – Ian signs on to 'Narragansett' – Cardiff to Galveston, Texas

On Wednesday 28 January, 1942, following his return from leave at home, Ian sent a telegram to his family from Swansea saying, "stand by for delirious diatribe on dandy show tonite". This was followed up by a letter written on 29 January, telling of his somewhat trying journey back to Swansea, a common occurrence at the time, but one which has parallels today, and his posting to 'Narragansett', a 10,000 ton motor tanker owned by the British Mexican Petroleum Company. He was also reunited with Monica. The letter is written in Ian's usual descriptive and humorous manner:-

"Swansea – Cardiff
Avonmouth. Thursday
29.1.42
Dear People,

Here it comes; journey to Carlisle was comfy & uneventful. Arrived at 1.15 *(a.m.)*, connecting train was 47 mins late. Obeying instructions we shuttle back & forth over bridge till finally our train settled into its allotted platform. Left at 2 am. I think I must've slept rather more than somewhat, becos I recall wakening suddenly with the horrid thot that we'd gone past Crew. I enquired shakily of my 2 fellow travellers who were inclined to think that we hadn't, but that we'd been standing out in the moors for a long time. This was about 7.20 & going by time this seemed to indicate our having passed C *(Crew)*.

But at 8 the conveyance rolled into the desired station & all was well. Bags were deposited and tracks made for Crew Arms Hotel. Brekfus was cereal, 2 split sossiges, marmalade, toast & coffee – 4/6d *(£0.22p)*. Thes's weren't very toothsome, but hunger wasn't too rampant anyway.

Left Crew at 10.32 on the nose, our companions being a fat, rouged lady with her son who was evidently going to public school. They played cards. From Hereford on, we had a county lady complete with blind dog & conversation. She ran a café in Tenby for troops, her husband was Navy & she knew a man who'd died from over-smoking. A sprinkling of Army Officers provided her with gabble-fodder altho' she was no empty barrel, but just obviously liked talking.

Cardiff was reached at 3 pm. First person in office to be seen was Chas, a clean collar prominently displayed. After a while things quietened down in the depot & everybody went away inc. me with instructions 'don't be too late tomorrow, we may have sumpn for you.' So we foned & hopped a train to Swa. *(Swansea)* Moni was there & soon we were ensconced in fronta fire lapping up scrambled eggs. Passage of time.

Next morning we had time only to stab at b. and egg before springing smartly up washing hurriedly & running for the 8.30 bus. Train left at 8.55 & we just made it.

Ole Marconi saw us again at 10.15 when, after a short wait, the name rang out. All was prepared. Beaton hands me my go-and-sign-on-form & indicates the 3rd R.O. who, he says, wants to sign on again. We rub noses.

'She's a 10,000 ton tanker Mr W., a lovely ship', avers B *(Beaton)*. 'Oh, ah', I riposte, 'tanker eh? M'mm'. You've got a good ship at last', B continues. I smirk & fill out sundry forms."

Ian's contemplation of the posting was probably due to the fact that he had already served on a tanker, the 'Oleander', and tankers were considered prized targets for enemy submarines and bomber aircraft. His friend Chas was posted to another ship.

Ian's new colleague and 3rd Radio Officer was W.T. Lewis, who was the same age as Ian. Ian wrote, "W.T. Lewis & I set out, sealing the new partnership with cups of R.T Jones' best coffee." Ian and W.T. arrived at 'Narragansett' around 3 pm, signed on and had a brief introduction to the Captain, who welcomed then both.

The 'Narragansett' was built in Kiel, Germany, and completed in 1936. In his letter of 29 January, 1942, Ian described his accommodation:-

"Amid carpeted elegance & soft lites & warmth I was ushered in. The Chief Steward, a twisty faced, W.W. Jacob type, apologises for the presence of bonded stores in my room, pending arrival of Customs.

Adopting my cosmopolitan air I looked over the cabin (or rather, state room). In one corner there was a bed with snowy linen, the other side of the room held a settee, well-cushioned, a wash basin with tap for running c. & drainage pipe (not the usual can under the sink), numerous tables, with drawers, wardrobe, bookcase, clothes drawers, elec. fan, steam heater, wall to wall pile carpets (not usual coco matting) in a green pastel shade, clean smooth whitewalls and beautiful wood doors. Indicating that this would do at a pinch I unpacked the Emerson & plugged it into a handy wall plug & music came forth. The lite fittings are the American screw in type. I unpack in a kinda daze.

W.T. has more books than I have. His passion is Aldus Huxley, & from a quick glance at his shelves I noticed Albert Sitwell's & others. He's a quietish intelligent lad, same age as me. He was in a ship in a convoy which was shelled by the Scharnhorst about June '41. He got away, but his Chief & others didn't. But we don't talk about that."

Ian paid one more visit to Monica's before he sailed. In Swansea he bought a couple of Van Heusen shirts for 14/11d *(£0.75p)* then, "Rushed up to The Croft, burst in on a startled band (Moni was about to go to a dance) & started in on some more eggs (poached this time). Passage of time. Brekfas this morning (2 boiled eggs). Cor! With trailing adieu Moni & I caught the 10.30 bus & I went on to get 11 train." This would be the last time he and Monica would be together.

Ian finished the letter, "Nuthin definite evidently; some say N.Y. for 3 weeks drydock. You'll probably hear from me again. Cheerio the now, Ian." On 30 January, Ian sent a telegram, "Everything under control Best wishes Cheerio = Ian".

About that time another Galashiels family received the sad news that their seagoing son had been reported missing. The following notice appeared in the Border Telegraph on 27 January:-

"GALASHIELS – REPORTED MISSING – Able Seaman David Gill, H.M.S. 'Prince of Wales' has been reported missing since 10th December, 1941. He is the son of Mr. and Mrs. John K. Gill (late of Manchester), 163 Magdala Terrace, and a grandson of Mrs. Gill, St Andrew Street." The 'Prince of Wales' and the battle cruiser H.M.S. 'Repulse' were both sunk on 10 December, 1941, off the east coast of Malaya by land based aircraft of the Imperial Japanese Navy. 'Prince of Wales' was struck by several torpedoes causing it to roll over and sink with the loss of over 300 lives. *(Border Telegraph 27 January 1942).*

On Sunday 1 February, 1942, 'Narragansett' sailed from Milford Haven as part of Convoy ON.63 with 34 merchant ships and 11 Navy escorts. On Monday 2 February, as 'Narragansett' left for the USA, Ian wrote another wonderfully detailed letter, which described the routine in his new ship:-

"At sea
Monday 2nd Feb '42
Good People,

Here's just a brief note to last until the cable arrives. Things have been turning over very smoothly since we left, the food esp. being first rate. Fr' instance Sunday's meals consisted of: breakfus – 2 eggs bacon & chips. Din. – soup, chicken sweet apples etc. Tea – lobster, cold chicken and all the rest. I seem to remember that there's been ham & eggs since I joined. The food's better & more plentiful than even the last ship could boast. Napkins & efficient service remind me of the old 'Oleander' days.

The OM's *(Captain)* as good as gold, the Chief the same, & Watertight *(W.T. Lewis, the 3rd Radio Officer)* provides the intellectual relief. Only we're not going where we originally intended but still…

I dispatched a note to Swansea, but remember only now that I forgot to enclose the mailing address. Would you ---- thank you! I see that O'Conner's latest ship is in this company too, so it might be as well for O'C to know ---. When you return the stick to Henderson (if you haven't already done so) you can give him all the guff. Tell him I'm keeping the modern humour book until we return.

The latest idea of the Ministry of War Transport is to put on board a receiver & 3 loudspeakers which are mounted in different parts of the ship for the entertainment & edification of those on board. The receiver is in the W/T room & it's our job to select the programs. It'll be kind difficult sometimes when you want a program like the Brains Trust & others want the Hippodrome!

I gave Holder Bros. (the agents) my home address, so if Marconi send the patrol-jacket down, it sh'd eventually come home again. Marcs. might of course keep it in Cardiff, but I'll get it as soon as I return. Anyway this is the kind of ship where uniform jackets are worn at table.

The Mate was skipper last voyage, the OM having the trip off; the 3rd used to be in Headlams so we can talk lengthily about their demerits.

I should've mentioned this sooner, the packing was excellently done, everything lying perfectly. 'nk you. There's plenty of clothes space, and Chas' tattle-tale gray undies don't overflow into my drawers now.

The shortbread is voraciously eaten - very good too. I often take a hot spray *(shower)* to taste the novelty of it, & occasionally I just sit & let my eyes wander around the cabin, revelling in the spaciousness & luxury. She's Jerry built *(built in Germany)*, as late as 1936. You lucky people!

Well I think that's everything of import up to the present. Perhaps I should mention the coffee-maker in the chart room – an affair similar to those seen in ice-cream joints, which supplies coffee, on tap, all day long. Good eh?

Keep the Nottingham letter till my return & also hold the patrol jacket.

It might be a good idea if you wrote asking the Company to air-mail one of your letters, so that when we arrive I'll know the nearly current events. Do as you think best. Now I'll give this to the Pilot.

All the best. Cheers, Ian.

Spread address around as usual please."

This crossing was not to be without incident. At 22:36 hours on Thursday 5 February, HMS 'Arbutus', a Corvette on escort duty with ON.63 was torpedoed and sunk by 'U-106', about 295 miles west of Erris Head, Ireland. The ship broke in two and sank with the loss of the Captain and the crew. On Friday 13 February, the convoy dispersed on the approaches to the coast of Nova Scotia and the ships made their way independently to their final destinations. At 03:37 hours on Saturday 14 February, following dispersal of Convoy ON.63, the Catapult Armed Merchant ship 'Empire Spring' was torpedoed and sunk by 'U-576' south east of Sable Island off the coast of Canada. The Captain, the Commodore of ON.63 and 51 others were lost. *(uboat.net).*

On 24 February, 1942, 'Narragansett' arrived at Galveston, Texas, and on 25 February, Ian sent a cablegram to his family from Galveston, saying, "Arrived safely Ian Waddell". 'Narragansett' then moved on to Port Arthur in Texas.

On 27 February, Ian's father penned a poignant response to Ian, written over the course of several days, with news of how the war was affecting Britain at home and abroad:-

"12 Abbotsford Road,
Galashiels.
27 Feb. 1942
Dear Ian,

Here goes. I am just wondering if you have got my Air Mail letter, altho I've had acknowledgement of it from the Anglo-American Oil Co., and I asked them to let me know how much it would cost, not knowing its destination.

My sainted aunt! But you do get around. We got your cable yesterday, & located you alright. We sent you one in reply which I expect would duly reach you. ('Begin the Beguine' not being played by Sandy MacPhearson in his request programme). Glad to learn you arrived safely at your destination, altho the U-boats apparently have broken out in your path. Did you see Miami & Palm Beach?

Sunday, 1st March - I told Dr L today that we had heard from you. 'For those in peril' was one of the hymns today.

The war drags on its weary length, but our latest evacuation hasn't been as 'successful' as previous ones. Singapore is a bad blow *(referring to the British surrender of Singapore to the Japanese on 15 February 1942)*, and as Eastern peoples put such a high value on 'face', I don't think that in their eyes we can have very much left. It is all very disappointing. Ken P's father said today that they had not heard from him since St John. I see the U-boats are putting down US ships like nine-pins. I suppose they've been caught napping like everybody else – not equipped for defence. I very seldom see British ships among those attacked, but I'd better touch wood & hope you will get through safely if you are coming back here.

Nancy *(Ian's sister)* had a nice holiday. Her address is now Nurse N. W. Royal Infirmary, Glasgow, C 4. She isn't 'Pupil' any longer. She seems to be liking her work all right.

We heard the siren a fortnight since, but only for a short while, altho' Bowden had to be evacuated. However the danger has been removed & the inhabitants are at home sweet home again.

Thursday 5th March - I'll have to write to the Andrews (your Boston host) in reply to his last letter. It's a pity you are not likely to be there as you could have been sure of a pleasant week-end. I got a book at the library last night 'Texan Ranch Life', the only one I could find about Texas. It's pretty ancient however & not much in it. Some pages missing so I took it back & got another – 'The American Illusion', an account of a trip around the U.S.A. The writer went (by train) across to San Francisco, down to Los Angeles &

H'wood, then south through Texas via Houston, but didn't go to Galveston, which was some 50 miles distant. Some friends did who reported they had had a wonderful meal of 'sea-food' – oysters, crab & what-not, and they admired the great sea wall there.

Thursday 12th March - Well it's a fortnight since we heard from you today. Waiting on a letter now which surely should not be too long now. Still cold & wintry. More snow last week, & altho' the sun has shifted it fairly well, temperature is still round freezing point. The top half of the garden is still covered in snow.

I am afraid motoring is doomed for the duration. The business ration is to stop after June. For the 3 months April-June I would get only 7 galls for the 13 weeks. After June it's to be supplementary ration only. So I don't think I'll bother taking out license at all – hardly worthwhile. It is high time some people got to know there's a war on.

(On Tuesday 17 March 'Narragansett' began the journey home from Port Arthur, Texas, with a load of petroleum product).

Thursday, 19th March - This morning when shaving, I heard the glad shout from Mummy, following the postman's ring, 'letter from Ian'. So Thursday seems to be lucky day. Exactly 3 weeks since receiving your cable. Posted 2nd Mch it has taken 17 days. Not opened by censor. So you should be well on your way by now, & I fully expect you will make port in time for your coming of age *(Ian's 21st birthday which would fall on 6 April, 1942)*. Must see if a special party cannot be arranged.

Glad to get all your chin-wag. It's marvellous what you can say without saying much. It sounds like a pleasure cruise, but you do appear to have all the comforts of the Saut Mercat. (Have you read Rob Roy?) Yes I thought you'd be having tropical climate conditions. Texas is I find 'the leader of the world's petroleum industry'. 25% of all the world's petroleum is produced in Texas alone.

Why shouldn't you be back by 30th Mch. if somebody's not taking a pot shot at you. It w'd be a pity to damage such a fine ship.

Saturday, 28th Mch. - I think I should now put the finishing touches to this running commentary. Nancy got home last night, and is looking well happy. She goes off again tomorrow morning. We've got rid of all the snow now & had one or two nice days with sunshine, but it still keeps somewhat chilly o'night.

I'm expecting to hear of you next week sometime, but one never knows unless you've gone away to some other part of the globe. Jimmy's people had a cable from him, wishing them a Merry Xmas & a happy New Year *(James Barbour, a school friend of Ian's, and like him, a Radio Officer in the Merchant Navy)*. That within the last week. A bit late perhaps, but in good time for next.

I am enclosing the words of the grand old song 'The Old Superb', which you can bring back. It seems to me a bit more of the old spirit would help matters now so as to stifle the activities of these U-boats in the Western Atlantic & Caribbean Sea. Why we (or the U.S.) don't nose out their bases beats me, because they must be getting replenished, & I'm certain it's their French possessions – Martinique, Guadeloupe, French Guiana probably *(these territories supported the Vichy French Government, and did not join the Free French cause until 1943)*. The same as the de Gaulle ships did to these islands near the St Lawrence. Went in first, & explained afterwards. The Far East is a tragedy. What little 'face' we had left must be pretty well wiped out now *(referring to the surrender of Singapore to the Japanese)*.

STOP PRESS Monday, 30th March - At church last night learned that Assistant (who is leaving this week for Montrose) has secured a fiancé here, to wit, an acquaintance of yours I believe, Bunty Allan – He is 30, so she must be a bit younger. Poaching on your preserves – what! Nancy had an enjoyable visit. Pity she has to leave at 9.30 on a Sunday morning, but she got here at 5.30 on Friday. Margaret is having a quiet time as Jeff is away.

Thinking of splitting this house if a purchase comes up for a half. Snowdrops & crocuses making a brave show just now. I expect we may hear from you before you receive this. So cheerio in the meantime.

Yours Dad

Dr L greatly taken up with your letter which I got back last night & am now sending it to Nancy."

On 25 March, 1942, Ian's Mother wrote a letter to him, also in response to his cablegram from Galveston. It expressed her pleasure and relief that he had arrived safely, and she looked forward to his return home:-

"12 Abbotsford Road
Galashiels, 25.3.42
My Good Lad,

What a thrill we got when your cable arrived & we knew that once again you had got safely across. Then we were all terribly bucked when your cheery letter came in last week. You have landed lucky this time but, as Mr Ballantyne said, 'you deserve it.' It was a good idea to have that swimming pool. What grand exercise it would be. You are lucky to have been sunbathing. Until this week it has been cold & wintry. But this week the sun has shone & all the snowdrops & crocuses are out. It's good to see them.

I do hope you will manage home for your birthday. It will be a great occasion. Mrs Langlands phoned on Sat to say the Canteen wasn't to be open this week. She was asking about you, & asked if she could see your letter, so Daddy duly took it to her on Sat.

We had Walter Mole on Saturday. He is now fitted with his new molars – very chic, like Douglas Fairbanks' smile. We were in the drawing room & he was on the settee for supper – do you know what he did – he took my Jacobean cushion, & was going to sit on it!! – my good cushion, which took me a year to sew.

I wonder if you got our Air Mail letters. I sent one just after you left & then Daddy & I sent one each after. We are hoping to have another letter & cable from you Ian very soon. Maggie *(Ian's second sister)* is looking forward to her Easter holidays. She gets them on Friday week.

J H's hens are laying quite well & we get 2 eggs every week. I give him all my scraps, so perhaps I will get a few more eggs later on.

Well cheerio, lad, & haste ye back.

Best love from Mummy

Wouldn't it be a good idea for me to come down & see your fine ship."

Little did Ian's mother know that on 25 March, 1942, as she penned her letter to her son his ship had been attacked and sunk by a German U-boat.

Chapter 14 – 'Narragansett' attacked and sunk by 'U-105'

'U-105', a Type IXB U-boat designed for ocean going operations, was commissioned in September 1940, under the command of Korvettenkapitan Georg Schewe. 'U-105's design was an improvement on IXA boat designs such as 'U-37', being larger and capable of lengthier periods of ocean going operation.

In January, 1942, command of 'U-105' passed to Fregattenkapitän Heinrich Schuch. Schuch was another experienced U-boat commander, having joined the Kriegsmarine in 1925. He had been 'U-37's commander following her commissioning in May 1938, before handing over to Victor Oehrn, who commanded the boat when it sank HMS 'Penzance' in August, 1941.

On 24 March, 1942, 'U-105' was on patrol in the Western Atlantic, about 400 miles east of Hampton Roads, Virginia. At 02:28 hrs a ship identified as the 'Uruguay' from Argentina was lined up for attack. The ship displayed the correct identification of a neutral country and the attack was aborted.

U-105's batteries began to malfunction, which limited its ability to dive and caused the vessel to use more fuel. Schuch's requests for additional fuel were denied and he was instructed to operate in a stationary position and keep 'U-105' submerged during the day. About 04:00 hrs on 25 March, 'Narragansett' was on course from Port Arthur, Texas, to the UK, loaded with 14,000 tons of clean petroleum product. The ship was unescorted, but making a heading to join a convoy bound for the UK when it was sighted by 'U-105'.

Although U-boats were deadly weapons, not all went smoothly during their attacks and Heinrich Schuch recorded the following in the log book of the 'U-105':-

"24/03/42 – Surfaced. Come upon and follow tanker. Tanker steering general course 60 degrees. I approach. Intention: surface night attack.

01:20 – Begin to approach. Turn to attack.

25/03/42

04.01 – Because of bright moonlight and good vision I decide on a spread attack. 3 torpedo spread. Tubes I, III, IV, estimated distance 1300m. Spread failed, estimated distance too great. We turn.

04.08 – 2 torpedo spread. Tubes V and VI, estimated distance 1000m. Spread fails, why not totally clear. A torpedo ought to have hit. Considering all the reasons for failed hit, the possibility is that one torpedo went in front of, and one behind the ship. Ready for renewed attack. Approach for attack.

06.09 – Single shot from tube I. Estimated distance 600 m. Hit after 34 seconds in engine room. Ship seriously damaged, but does not sink. I decide on a coup de grace shot.

06.18 – Coup de grace shot. Depth 2m. Hit on prow. Tanker and full load go up in flames and sinks stern first. After first hit tanker sent out SOS call, its call sign and radio call sign. It is the British tanker 'Narragansett', 10389 tons fully laden. Weapons: afterdeck, medium calibre cannon, Bridge: light machine gun".

'Narragansett's distress call was intercepted and a report from Pan American Airways, whose aircraft were used for military operations, states, "Pan Air reports Tanker 34-44N67-38W 1245Z 25/Mar proceeding 8 kts C-320, on fire." 'Narragansett's distress call was also intercepted by the United States Naval Operating Base in Bermuda at 0410 and an aeroplane was ordered to get underway to assist. The aeroplane, piloted by Lieutenant W. A. Thorne found the 'Narragensett', but there was no sign of any survivors. The Navy report read "SS 'Narragansett' torpedoed 0410Z/25 34-46 N., 67-40 W. COMINCH C 250531. VP took off at dawn March 25th to search vicinity SSS from 'Narragensett'. Found ship 34-30 N., 67-36 W., bottom up at 1200Z. Ship sank at 1350Z. VP continued to search during day with no sign of survivors. NOB BERMUDA C 252351."

On 27 March, 1942, Henrich Schuch and 'U-105's crew sank another tanker, the 'Svenor', about 300 miles west of Cape Hatteras, North Carolina. On 30 March, 'U-105' began to run low on fuel because of the malfunctioning batteries. The drinking water supply was being used to cool the batteries which made placing a water restriction on the crew necessary. In the circumstances Schuch decided to abandon the rest of the mission and 'U-105' docked at Lorient on the French coast on 15 April, 1941.

An entry in the 'Narragansett's movement card by the owners following its loss reads, "Torpedoed in 34.46N, 67.40W. (C.L. 558.25/3)(OV 6353/41). U.S. plane repts. sighting 'a ship' floating bottom up & burning 25/3 in position of torpedoing. 'Ship' sank at 1350, 25/3. (C.L. 561, 28/3). Deemed total loss by stats. Return M – 29/3/42".

There is no record of how Ian's family were told of his loss, whether by telegram or letter from Ian's employer. On 21 April, 1942, the following notice appeared in the Border Telegraph:-

"Radio Officer Ian R. H. Waddell – On Friday *(17 April)* Mr. and Mrs. Robert H. Waddell, 12 Abbotsford Road, Galashiels, were officially informed that their only son, Radio Officer Ian H. R. Waddell, is missing at sea while serving on a tanker. He is in his 21st year, and was making his fourteenth crossing of the Atlantic. Radio Officer Waddell, a very promising young man, left Galashiels Academy in 1939, having made arrangements to enter on a two-years' course of training at an Edinburgh wireless college. After he had been there six months he gained a special certificate, and as there was a demand for wireless students he had to go to sea for the duration of the war. At the Academy he was an exceptionally fine English scholar, and was also a very successful art student."

Lord William Scott, the local Member of Parliament, wrote to the Ministry of War Transport, enclosing a letter from Ian's Mother, asking for more information. On 16 June Lord Scott forwarded a letter of reply to Ian's father:-

"16.6.42
Cavalry Club,
127 Piccadilly, W.1
Dear Mr Waddell,

I received the enclosed letter after considerable delay, as it had been wrongly forwarded. I hate having to send it on to you as I know it will give great pain to both you and your wife, but I have no right to withhold it.

I realise that there is nothing that could be of any comfort to you on this sad occasion.

Yours in deepest sympathy, William Scott"

The letter from the Ministry of War Transport to Lord Scott shed little light on the sinking of the 'Narragansett':-

"Ministry of War Transport,
Berkley Square House, W.1.
2nd June, 1942
Dear Lord Scott,

Thankyou very much for your letter of 7th May, enclosing one from your constituent Mrs. Waddell, about her son Ian.

I regret to say that we have heard no further news about him. The only news we had about the vessel was that she sent up a distress signal at 0410/25th March, saying that she was being attacked by a submarine. Nothing more was heard of the ship, but a patrolling aeroplane reported that a vessel was observed floating bottom upwards and burning at 1200/25th March, but there was no sign of any survivors.

I have been in touch with the Admiralty also about the case, but they know nothing more, and they also tell me there was no organised convoy in operation, and therefore no more details are available. I am exceedingly sorry about this case and I should be glad if you would express my deep sympathy with the relatives.

If anything else does come to light, I shall, of course, let you know.

I am yours sincerely, Hector Chief."

There are no words which can describe the shock or desolation felt by any family who lose a much loved son, and the Waddell family were no different. Their feeling of loss made worse by the return of the letter written by Ian's mother on the day 'Narragensett' was attacked and sunk, and that posted by his father on 30 March, which were both returned on or about the 15 May 1942, endorsed, "RETURN TO SENDER OWNER'S INSTRUCTION UNABLE TO DELIVER".

Whilst all the family felt his loss deeply, Ian's mother Peggy and his sister Margaret were the worst affected by Ian's death. In the letter written many years later to her son Ian Briggs, Margaret says, "In March 1942 he *(Ian Waddell)* was on board an oil tanker in the Gulf of Texas when they were sunk by German submarines. We had been hoping for his return in April to celebrate his 21st birthday. The blow was shattering – an only son of aging parents, and for me the first piece of tragedy in a fairly sheltered life. For a long time we kept hoping that he might have been picked up, but it was a vain hope."

The family also received letters from friends expressing much sympathy at their loss, and these also provide some indication of how deeply that loss was felt:-

"Johannesburg
2 June 1942
My Dear Peg,

I suppose in those days we are getting used to shocks, but it was indeed a terrible shock to us to learn the news that your dear son Ian was reported missing, & Meg & I would ask you all to accept our deepest sympathy in this your time of sorrow & anxiety.

Let us hope that the grainy ray of hope may still shine & that he may still turn up. It is so hard to think that just on his 21st birthday that one you loved so well & was about to become a help & joy to you should be taken away.

It is too awful to think of all the misery & unhappiness that has been caused in the world by those murderous Huns & I cannot understand people of standing in England should ask for mercy for German people, as they are all guilty, & when people commit a crime they must be punished.

We have word from Bennie from Cairo & he is well. He is Lieut. in the Engineering Corps, & like most of the Springboks is very keen on getting on with the job. We are all proud of our boys who are doing well & have no mercy. Margaret is still at East London her husband being in the Standard Bank. We are both getting on in years but still keep fairly well but I am afraid I could never stand the cold weather of Scotland.

I don't think that one could wish for a better climate than we have in J'burg. I should esteem a letter from you giving me all your home news as I am rather out of touch. I can only again hope for good news, & pray that you may be granted health & strength to bear up in your time of sorrow.

With best love, Glen. 3 Finsbury, Smith Street, Johannesburg".

"The Manse,
Dalry,
Castle Douglas
28th August, 1942
Dear Mr. Waddell,

Thanks very much for your kind letter. I thought a great deal about you after we parted last Sunday and felt that the brave spirit in which you are facing your bereavement must be a source of inspiration to others, as it was uplifting to me. I often feel how hard it is that one can do so little to help those who like your wife and you must bear your weary burden for the most part alone, though there is comfort in the gospel & burden-bearing – Galatians 65; Galatians 62 & Psalms 55:22.

I always think that those who have passed on are like loved ones in some distant part of the world from whom we are separated. We do not see them, or even hear from them, but we know that all is well with them, and that we shall be with them again, - in God's appointed time. I pray that as the days go by your wife and you may both find ever increasing strength, comfort and assurance.

With kind feelings and regards

Yours Sincerely, Harold G. Nullo Weir"

Ian's name and the names of his shipmates are commemorated on Panel 72 of the Tower Hill Memorial in London, which lists the names of all those merchant sailors lost during World War II.

From the middle of 1942 more escort vessels were available for deployment from the Navies of the UK, Canada and the United States, and convoys were normally accompanied by at least six naval escorts. Submarine detection equipment also improved greatly and new weapons such as the 'Hedgehog' and 'Squid' mortars, which launched their ordnance forward added greatly to their firepower.

In late April and early May, 1943, the U-boat fleet suffered its greatest loss at the hands of Allied ships and aircraft. An attack by 40 U-boats on a convoy was beaten off and a total of 27 U-boats were sunk and many damaged over a short period of time. This made the cost of attacking convoys too high, even for the largest U-boat packs. The capture of the German 'Enigma' machine and the cracking of the German codes also provided much valuable intelligence as to the movements and intentions of the U-boats.

Heinrich Schuch went on to successfully command three more U-boats before serving in various naval staff positions until the end of the war. He died 21 January, 1968, aged 61 years. 'U-105' was herself sunk on 2 June, 1943, near Dakar off the west coast of Africa, by depth charges from a flying boat from the French Naval Air Force. None of her crew survived the attack.

And what of Monica? How did she learn of Ian's death, who told her, and how did she cope with the news? Monica and Ian's relationship lasted for well over a year. At every chance, whether returning from a voyage or journeying from home to re-join his ship, Ian made a point of spending as much time as he could with Monica. It is clear from Ian's letters that he and Monica enjoyed a close relationship despite his long absences at sea. Enquiries to trace Monica have revealed little. Monica later married a wealthy Welsh industrialist, David Joseph, whose son, Sir Herbert Leslie Joseph, became famous in Wales for building the Coney Beach amusement complex in Porthcawl, and was eventually knighted for services to the entertainment industry. David Joseph died in 1959, after which Monica moved to Ireland with another gentleman. It is not known if they married, but he pre-deceased her and she moved to the Gower area near Swansea to live with her sister Glenna. Monica died circa 1997/98 and Glenna shortly afterwards.

Morfydd (Monica), seated left of picture, on holiday in Madeira with her husband David Joseph, his grandson Clive Graham, and his daughter Ruby Graham from his first marriage *(picture circa 1947/48)*.
(Picture by kind permission of Trevor Williams and Mary Daley)

Crew of Narragansett Lost on 25th March 1942 *(U-boat.net)*

Alderton, Terence Norman, 16, Mess Room Boy
Amiss, Charles Leslie, 28, Second Engineer Officer
Bland, Ronald Joseph, 19, Deck Boy
Bray, Arthur Ernest, 20, Cook
Coburn, Frank, 25 Boatswain (Bosun)
Cross, James Henry, 29, Carpenter
Daniel, Joseph Elved, 26, Junior Engineer Officer
Douglas, William John Henry, 20, Able Seaman
Ebanks, Ewald Aldon, 27, Sailor
Fowler, Charles Thomas, RN, 23, Able Seaman (DEMS gunner)
Fuller, Cyril Bernard, 18, Cadet
Green, Fred, 46, Storekeeper
Gregory, Stanley Dennis, RN, 20, Able Seaman (DEMS gunner)
Grey, Lawrence Edward, Chief Steward
Hanaway, William, RM, 34, Corporal (DEMS gunner)
Hancock, William John, 35, Cook
Hardy, Leslie, RN, 23, Able Seaman (DEMS gunner)
Hawke, Maurice Goldsworthy, 18, Mess Room Boy
Heslop, John, 33, Chief Engineer Officer
Hogg, Thomas Herbert, 27, Greaser
Hunt, James Edward, 18, Fireman
Judge, Charles Alfred, 54, Fireman
Keene, William Derrick, 26, Able Seaman
Kelly, Mark Patrick, 22, Sailor
Kenyon, Robert, 17, Mess Room Boy
Lewis, William Thomas, 20, Third Radio Officer
Lincoln, K.B., 18, Ordinary Seaman
McCormick, William, 30, Junior Engineer Officer
Mitchell, Arthur Lewis, 25, Junior Engineer Officer
Morris, John Joseph, 50, Greaser
Murphy, James Cornelius, 19, Fireman
Newman, Arthur Frederick, 32, Third Officer
Piper, Harvey, 32, Able Seaman
Poole, Reginald Edward, 38, First Radio Officer
Richardson, Denis, 35, Chief Officer
Roberts, Michael Blackburn, 41, Master
Robinson, George, 39, Able Seaman
Smythe, Alexander Stanley, 32, Third Engineer Officer
Swan, Peter, 23, Greaser
Tattersall, Frank, 33, Able Seaman
Thompson, Cyril Cecil, 38, Steward
Thomson, Alexander, 20, Deck Boy
Waddell, Ian Robert Hendry, 20, Second Radio Officer
Walker, John Milne, 25, Senior Third Engineer Officer

Wallace, Arthur Edward, 28, Second Officer
Ware, Max Thomas, 24, Sailor
Wilsher, Peter, 40, Greaser

Merchant Marine Memorial at Tower Hill, London.

Panel 72 of the Tower Hill Memorial commemorating the names of Ian Robert Hendry Waddell and the crew of 'Narragansett'.

Right hand panel of the War Memorial in Galashiels.
William Ormiston's name is 15th from the top of the panel; Ian
Waddell's name is 9th from the bottom.

German U-boat – 'U-105'.

German U-boat – 'U-105'.

Radio Officer Ian Robert Hendry Waddell
Born 6 April 1921. Killed in action whilst serving on the
Motor Tanker 'Narragensett' on 25 March 1942.

Epilogue

12 Abbotsford Road was sold some years ago by Ian Waddell's sister Nancy, who moved to a smaller house. The house looks very much the same as it was in Ian's day, although now split into two separate dwellings, and is the family home of Jennifer Borthwick and Alan Baird.

On 23 February, 2015, Jennifer and Alan invited Ian Briggs, Ian Waddell's nephew, to plant a ceramic poppy in the garden of 12 Abbotsford Road. Jennifer and Alan had purchased the poppy which had been part of the World War 1 commemoration display at the Tower of London, with the intention of having it planted in their garden in memory of Ian Waddell.

Ian Briggs, plants the ceramic poppy from the Tower of London in memory of his Uncle, Ian Robert Hendry Waddell.

References

1. uboat.net (http://www.uboat.net)
2. Naval-History.net 1998-2013 (www.naval-history.net)
3. Border Telegraph (1939-42)
4. Arnold Hague Convoy Database (www.convoyweb.org.uk)
5. Merseyside Maritime Museum Battle of the Atlantic Gallery (www.liverpoolmuseums.org.uk/maritime/index.aspx)
6. The Times (27 July, 1940)
7. Wrecksite (www.wrecksite.eu)

Printed in Great Britain
by Amazon.co.uk, Ltd.,
Marston Gate.

PRAY AS YOU GO ALONG YOUR DAILY ROUTINES:100 SAMPLES

By Dr. Elizabeth Enoh

Pray As You Go Along Your Daily Routines: 100 Samples
Copyright by Dr. Elizabeth Enoh
2023

IMPRIMI POTEST:
His Grace Andrew Fuanya Nkea
Archbishop of Bamenda, Cameroon
August 2023

All rights reserved. No part of this book may be reproduced in any form without permission in writing from the author.